Table of Contents

Teaching Games for Understanding in Physical Education and Sport: An International Perspective

Joy Butler, Ed.D., Plymouth State College

Linda Griffin, Ph.D., University of Massachusetts

Ben Lombardo, Ed.D., Rhode Island College

Richard Nastasi, Ed.D., Endicott College

Editors

National Association for Sport and Physical Education

An Association of the
**American Alliance for Health, Physical Education,
Recreation and Dance**

Address orders to: AAHPERD Publications, P.O. Box 385, Oxon Hill, MD 20750-0385, call 1-800-321-0789, or order on line at www.aahperd.org/naspe.
Order Stock No. 304-10266.

Printed in the United States of America.

ISBN 0-88314-749-1

Preface

Teaching Games for Understanding (TGfU) is not a brand new approach, rather it originated over twenty years ago in the United Kingdom. The publishing of this book represents the growth of interest in and commitment to teaching "through rather than about" games. The conference in 2001 which stimulated development of these chapters brought together nearly 200 people from 18 different countries to discuss and debate about the ideas and application of TGfU.

Teachers of K-12 and PETE faculty and scholars will benefit from this clear overview of this student-centered, conceptual approach. Often teachers are concerned about helping students move from performing isolated sport-related skills to actual game situations where skills must be used strategically. The TGfU or tactical games approach facilitates student learning of both skills and tactics of games and focuses on problem-solving and adaptations of classic game play in various sport forms. This model aligns with NASPE standards, especially:

◆ **Standard 2.** Applies movement concepts and principles to the learning and development of motor skills.

◆ **Standard 5.** Demonstrates responsible personal and social behavior in physical activity settings.

◆ **Standard 6.** Demonstrates understanding and respect for differences among people in physical activity settings.

◆ **Standard 7.** Understands that physical activity provides opportunities for enjoyment, challenge, self-expression, and social interaction.

The editors, Linda Griffin, Joy Butler, Ben Lombardo, and Richard Nastasi, have selected quality representative papers from the conference that will help professionals in schools and higher education understand and explore this approach in their own work. Both proponents and opponents of constructivist perspectives will find their thinking stimulated. In our common quest to prepare students to lead physically active lifestyles, this approach has potential to engage students, accommodate and celebrate diversity, and facilitate student learning about sport and skill games in context. NASPE was a co-sponsor of the Conference in New Hampshire in the summer of 2001. We appreciate especially the work of Joy Butler of Plymouth State University and Linda Griffin of the University of Massachusetts who organized and directed the conference and initiated the development of this book. We hope that the book will expand thinking and support those dedicated to student learning through and about physical activities and sport.

Judith C. Young, Ph.D.
Executive Director
National Association for Sport and Physical Education

An Introduction to Teaching Games for Understanding

Chapter 1

Linda L. Griffin, University of Massachusetts, United States

Joy Butler, Plymouth State College, United States

Ben Lombardo, Rhode Island College, United States

Richard Nastasi, Endicott College, United States

Introduction

Currently there is significant and growing international interest in TGfU. This groundswell led to the first TGfU world seminar conference in August 2001. Leading academics responded strongly to the call for papers and the conference provided a forum for quality debate, including four provocative and insightful keynote speeches, as well as a lively, well-attended town meeting. Eighteen countries and 22 U.S. states were represented. Once TGfU was the focus of the conference rather than a sideline, as it was at previous conferences, there was a palpable rush of enthusiasm and energy as its proponents aired their ideas.

This edited book has a dual purpose. First, we want to offer teachers insight into a range of authors' views regarding Teaching Games for Understanding, which is an innovative approach to teaching and learning sport-related games also known by the terms "tactical games," "games sense," "play practice," and "concept-based games." We believe that as a teaching and learning model, Teaching Games for Understanding has the potential to promote more interest and excitement in your students. That is, learning *through* games, not *about* games, motivates students. The aim of a TGfU model is to combine tactical awareness and skill execution to help your students become better games players. We believe that a TGfU model can be sufficiently simplified for the elementary student, beginning at approximately the second grade level.

Second, we wish to celebrate the first International Teaching Games for Understanding Conference, which is the basis for this book. The success of the conference has led to an International Teaching Games for Understanding band of proponents that is committed to spreading TGfU as a highly motivating approach for teaching and learning sport-related games in school physical education and sport programs.

The conference goals were threefold. First, we wanted to acknowledge the importance of the work of Bunker, Thorpe, and Almond (1982) and the willing teachers from Leicestershire, UK who began the TGfU journey approximately 20 years ago. Second, we wanted to put TGfU in action so that participants would have the opportunity to have a TGfU experience through various practical sessions. Finally, we wanted to provide a forum for an international group of scholars, teacher educators, teachers, and coaches to share, discuss, and debate ideas in order to move TGfU (and thus sport-related teaching and learning) forward.

Overview of the Book

The four-section TGfU book provides us with an opportunity to share with you as teachers, teacher educators, and coaches, the flavor of the papers and ideas shared at this conference. Our hope is that it provides each reader with some food for thought about the ways we teach sport-related games.

The first section, "Putting TGfU Into Action Across the Classification System," provides a representation of games across the games classifications of territory/invasion, net/wall, field/run score and target categories. Each chapter provides teachers, teacher educators, and coaches with instructional materials to implement in their learning settings.

The second section, "Teachers' Experiences Using TGfU: Near and Far" describes the process of learning to teach using the model. Each chapter explores the problems and possibilities teachers (i.e., preservice and inservice) and coaches may encounter when initially attempting to implement a TGfU model.

The third section, "Exploring the Construction of Knowledge for Student Learning" examines the learning-process orientation to sport-related games teaching and learning. Two chapters in this section report research, which examines students' ability to construct tactical understanding, while the third chapter outlines the use of authentic assessment to promote tactical understanding when implementing a TGfU model.

The final section, "Evolution of the Model: Extending Our Debate" attempts to extend our theoretical thinking about the TGfU model by exploring dynamic systems, presenting a play-practice approach to sport-related games teaching and learning and pushing scholars beyond the technical-tactical debate.

This first chapter provides an overview of a Teaching Games for Understanding model. First, we will introduce a TGfU model. Second, we will highlight assumptions about TGfU as an instructional model for games teaching and learning. Third, we will explore the benefits of using a TGfU model. Finally, we will provide an historical overview of TGfU.

Overview of the TGfU Model

The TGfU model was developed from the work of Thorpe and Bunker at Loughborough University during the 1970s and early 1980s (Thorpe, 1989; Bunker & Thorpe, 1982). Bunker and Thorpe (1982) proposed Teaching Games for Understanding (TGfU) as a shift from the development of techniques or content-based approach with highly structured lessons to a more student-based approach which links tactics and skills in game context.

The TGfU model is a student-centered model in which the teacher facilitates the learning process. All parts of the process are important and teachers must take care to plan for understanding. First, games are modified appropriately to encourage students to think about the tactical problem on which instruction is focused. Second, questions are designed to develop tactical awareness (understanding of what to do to solve a problem) and are well thought out. Third, skill practices teach essential skills to solve problems in a game-like manner. Finally, the final game provides students with the opportunity to apply their practice in an authentic setting.

Asking questions is an essential component of a TGfU model. These questions link the performance with the need to understand. Literature on tactical-games teaching—whether it be the original work of Bunker and Thorpe (1982), the Australian conception of *Game Sense* (Australian Sports Commission, 1997), or *Teaching Sport Concepts and Skills: A Tactical Games Approach* (Griffin, Mitchell & Oslin, 1997; Mitchell, Oslin & Griffin, in press)—has been consistent in emphasizing the importance of high-quality questions. These questions fall into five categories, which include questions regarding:

- ◆ Skill and movement execution   "How do you . . ."
- ◆ Tactical awareness   "What did you . . ."
- ◆ Time   "When is the best time to . . ."
- ◆ Space   "Where is/can . . ."
- ◆ Risk   "Which choice . . ."

What follows is an example of a TGfU lesson from a soccer unit. Initially, students will focus on the tactical problem of maintaining possession of the ball and attacking the goal, but they will also progress to defending the goal and defending space. The focus of maintaining possession in this unit shifts from solutions applied to players, when they have the ball, to their roles as teammates without the ball. The example is from a possible Lesson 1 in this soccer unit, which focuses on (a) maintaining possession of the ball, (b) supporting the ball carrier, and (c) getting students in position to receive a pass. The lesson begins the students engaged in a 3-vs-3 game in a 30-by-20 playing grid with a narrow goal and no goalkeeper. Game conditions include three touches (each player has two touches to receive the ball and one to pass or shoot). The game goals are for players to (a) pass accurately, with inside and outside of feet, (b) move into position to receive a pass, and (c) look for support from teammates.

After a period of time the teacher would stop the game and ask the students the following questions:

Teacher: How can players without the ball help players who have the ball?

Student: Be in position to receive the ball.

Teacher: Where should supporting players go?

Student: Away from defenders into an open space.

Teacher: Any open space?

Student: Where you can receive a pass-a passing lane.

Teacher: OK, let's practice the idea of receiving a pass in a passing lane.

At this stage, the teacher would arrange students into a situated practice in which they would be in a 2-vs-1 (2 attackers and 1 defender) position in a 20-by-10 grid (See Figure 1). On a signal, the defender picks up the attacker with the ball which

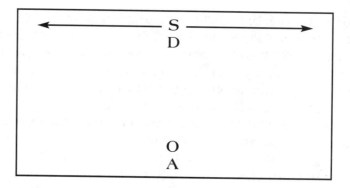

Key: S = Supporter
       D = Defender
       A = Attacker
       0 = Soccer ball

Figure 1. 2-vs-1 Situated Practice in a Teaching Games for Understanding Soccer Lesson

leaves the supporting attacker open to move to either side, the attacker with the ball draws defender and passes. Three repetitions and rotate roles. The goal of the situated practice is for (a) supporting player to move to a good position and (b) attacking player to wait for defender to be close before passing. The teaching-learning cues focus on getting (a) the supporter to move quickly to side on whistle, (b) the defender to attack the ball on whistle, and (c) the attacker to pass as the defender advances. The students would then move into the final game, which would be a repeat of the initial 3-vs-3 game with the same conditions and goals. The lesson would end with a question-answer type closure focusing on questions that highlight tactical awareness (i.e., decision-,making process in games). Each lesson involves a game, question-and-answer segment, situated practice and game-closure progression.

Assumptions of the TGfU Instructional Model

TGfU is not value-free and before making a judgment about any teaching model, it is important to be aware of the underlying assumptions of the model (Mitchell, et. al, in press). The following are the assumptions of a TGfU model:

1. Proponents of the model believe that games are an important part of the physical education curriculum because games are potentially enjoyable and lifetime physical activities, and are based on sport, which itself is a prominent social institution throughout the world. Teachers and coaches, who seek to implement games instruction in physical education at all levels, value games playing as activities in their own right.

2. Games can be modified to represent the advanced game form, and conditioned (i.e., exaggerated by rule changes) to emphasize tactical problems encountered within the game. The use of small-sided games helps to slow down the pace and momentum of the game so that there is a better chance for students to develop game appreciation, tactical awareness, and decision-making abilities. Teachers and coaches must view small-sided games as building blocks to the advanced form, not as ends in themselves.

3. Games have common tactical elements, or problems that form the b[___]
   games-classification system and serve as the organizing structure of [_]
   model. Central to the model are the tactical problems presented by va[___]
   games, referring to those problems that must be overcome in order to [____]
   prevent scoring, and to restart play. Advocates of the model argue that [_____],
   games within each category have similar tactical problems and understanding
   these similar tactical problems can help students transfer performance from one
   game to another.

Benefits of a TGfU Model

The TGfU model is fun (i.e., interesting and challenging), even for students with
less ability, who can be easily turned off and made to feel less competent by a
technique-oriented approach. It empowers all students and engages them in
"hands-on, meaningful learning that places the learner at the center" (Rink, 1996).
Those of us who have become TGfU advocates know intuitively that this is the
case. From our own teaching and coaching experiences, we believe that TGfU
allowed us to turn more students and athletes on to games and gave them a
greater sense of success and feeling of competence.

The TGfU model embraces differential development and allows learners to work
at their own rates. The model employs constructivist theory about learning and
knowledge, and within this context, students are encouraged to construct their
own cognitive maps, as they create relationships amongst classifications and
games. Researchers have found that people learn by "linking new information with
existing knowledge in meaningful ways" (APA, 1997). The role of the teacher is to
facilitate situated learning experiences that allow students to understand games
principles and concepts more deeply. As Brandt (1998, p.4) suggests, this includes
the creation of a "positive climate for learners." This is very different from the
mastery of skills that has dominated the traditional model introduced in many
preservice programs.

Although the excitement at the TGfU conference was generated by this instinct
that we were "onto something good," there is much current debate about how far
our gut response is validated by the research. Rink (1996, p.401) argues that, "The
research support for more constructivist approaches to content has not been able
to show a clear learning advantage for more inquiry-approaches." Some studies,
however, do support the strong anecdotal evidence that TGfU motivates more
students and keeps them on-task and emotionally engaged (Butler, 1993). Other
studies have shown that when this model is employed, students are more curious
and positive, and have greater self-esteem (Gage, 1985; Peterson, 1979). If the
researchers on the Scottish Consultative Council on the Curriculum (1996) are
correct in suggesting that "our ability to think and learn effectively is closely linked
to our physical and emotional well being," then we need to pay attention to social
settings and social interactions if we want to promote learning.

A Historical Overview of TGfU

According to Thorpe and Bunker (1986), the emergence of the technique-oriented approach to teaching games can be attributed to physical educators in the 60s who sought to make the subject more credible when it was elevated to degree status. At this time, there was a move to quantify, evaluate, and measure skill acquisition; courses in these areas flourished. Since researchers wished to control the research environment, the skills being studied were rarely examined in the context of the game itself. As Thorpe and Bunker (1986, p.27) point out, "isolated techniques are so much easier to quantify than other aspects of games."

Lesson plans were easier to produce, document and assess if they delineated distinct phases, such as introductory activity, skill development, culmination, and closure in a technique-oriented approach. When student teachers are encouraged to identify teaching points, then it is easier for them to adopt a command or task teaching style.

In fact, when colleagues, parents, and administrators observed students actively engaged in disciplined drills, they naturally believed that learning was taking place. For their part, physical education teachers demonstrated their effectiveness as well-drilled technical teachers and disproved the notion that 'anyone can teach games' (attractive to cost-cutting administrators). At the same time, physical education teachers did not need to develop games that they knew little about, since those games fall outside their one- or two-game specialties.

Overall, this became a self-perpetuating cycle. Teachers went through coaching technique-oriented programs and remained comfortable emphasizing skill acquisition, thus institutionalizing a technique-oriented approach to the teaching of games.

It is against this backdrop that we can best view the emergence of TGfU in the 60s, 70s and early 80s. At that time, there was a core group of researchers at Loughborough University in England that articulated their dissatisfaction with the traditional approach and its impact on student learning. Thorpe (2001) puts it thus:

> ...we could not understand how we could expect children to learn if they were not involved in the learning process and did not understand what they were trying to do; and moreover, as sport psychologists, Dave Bunker and I could not continue to accept an approach in which children lost the motivation to play and improve.

Several such educators—including Maulden, Redfern, Ellis, and Wade—developed a framework for teaching games that put children at the center of the learning process. Thorpe, Bunker, and Almond (1986) built on the thinking of this group and eventually developed the Teaching Games for Understanding model and a classification framework.

The original TGfU model presented by Bunker and Thorpe (1986) described a six-stage model for developing decision-making and improved performance in game situations (see Figure 2). Stage 1 introduces the game, which in most cases is modified to meet the developmental level of the learner. Stage 2 encourages students to begin learning the need for rules, even if modified, to shape the game. Stage 3 presents students with tactical problems to help them increase their tactical awareness. Stage 4 presents students with questions and challenges to encourage students to explore their ability to solve the tactical problem (i.e., decision-making process) present in the modified game. Students are asked what to do (i.e., tactical awareness) and how to do it (i.e., appropriate response selection and skill execution). Stage 5 begins to link tactical knowledge with skill and movement practice. Stage 6 measures performance leading toward the development of competent and proficient games players.

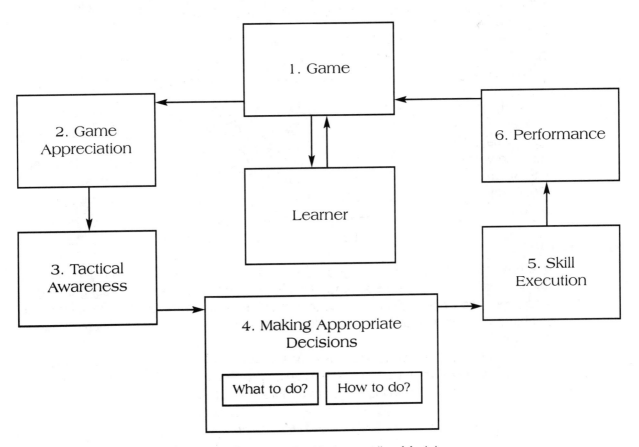

Figure 2. Original Teaching Games for Understanding Model
(Bunker & Thorpe, 1982)

Recently scholars have proposed variations, extensions, or reconsiderations to the original model (Griffin et al., 1997; Kirk & MacPhail, 2002; Holt, Strean & Bengoechea, 2002). Griffin et al. (1997) proposed a simplified three-stage model that focuses on the essential lesson components of the model, namely (a) modified game play, (b) development of tactical awareness, and decision-making through questioning and (c) skill development.

Kirk and MacPhail (2002) modify and extend the original TGfU model that draws on a situated learning perspective. A situated learning theory investigates the relationships among the various physical, social, and cultural dimensions of the context of learning (Lave & Wenger, 1991). The situated learning TGfU model advocates a need for explicit attention to the learner's perspective, game concept, strategic thinking, cue recognition, technique selection, and skill development as the coming together of tactics and techniques, and situated performance as legitimate peripheral participation in games (Kirk & MacPhail, 2002).

Holt, Strean, and Bengoechea (2002) reexamine the four pedagogical principles Thorpe and Bunker (1986) introduced that were to be used in conjunction with the curriculum model for developing a physical education program. Holt et al. present the pedagogical principles (sampling, modification-representation, modification-exaggeration, and tactical complexity) and then explain how these principles may be integrated with the original model. They also call for a need to explore the learner-centered feature of the model by suggesting future research that would consider the implications of games pedagogy for the cognitive, affective, and behavioral domains.

Recently Metzler (2000) called for a move toward model-based instruction (i.e., cooperative learning, sport education, teaching for social responsibility, TGfU) from activity-based instruction (i.e., teaching volleyball, tennis, basketball, soccer, etc). A move toward model-based instruction extends the earlier work of Thorpe and Bunker (1986) who introduced TGfU as a model for teaching sport-related games. Metzler (2000) describes teaching models as having their own set of decisions, plans, and actions by the teachers and students or, simply put, a blueprint for teaching.

Conclusion

We hope you enjoy the following chapters. We wish to keep the spirit of TGfU (i.e., Tactical Games, Game Sense, Play Practice, and Concept-Based Games) growing and thus encourage professional discourse about sport-related games teaching and learning. Our ultimate goal is to develop better, and lifelong, games players around the world.

References

American Psychological Association. (1997). *Learner-centered psychological principles: A framework for school reform and redesign.* Prepared by the learner-centered principles work group of the American Psychological Association's Board of Educational Affairs. Washington, DC: Author. Also at http://www.apa.org/ed/lcp/.html/

Australian Sports Commission. (1997). *Game sense: Developing thinking players.* Belconnen, Australia: Author.

Brandt, R. (1998). *Powerful learning.* Alexandria, VA, ASCD.

Bunker, D. & Thorpe, R. (1982). A model for the teaching of games in the secondary schools. *Bulletin of Physical Education, 10,* 9-16.

Butler, J. (1993). Teacher change in sport education. *Dissertation Abstracts International. 54, 02A* (UMI No. 9318198).

Gage, N. (1985). *Hard gains in the soft sciences: The case of pedagogy.* Bloomington, IN: Phi Delta Kappa.

Griffin, L. L., Mitchell, S. A., & Oslin, J. L. (1997). *Teaching sport concepts and skills: A tactical games approach.* Champaign, IL: Human Kinetics.

Holt, N. L., Strean, W. B., & Bengoechea, E. G. (2002). Expanding the teaching games for understanding model: New avenues for future research and practice. *Journal of Teaching in Physical Education, 21,* 162-176.

Kirk, D. & MacPhail, A. (2002). Teaching games for understanding and situated learning: Rethinking the Bunker-Thorpe model. *Journal of Teaching in Physical Education, 21,* 117-192.

Lave, J. & Wenger, E. (1991). *Situated learning: Legitimate peripheral participation.* New York: Cambridge University Press.

Metzler, M. (2000). *Instructional models for physical education.* Boston: Allyn and Bacon.

Mitchell, S. A., Oslin, J. L., & Griffin, L. L. (in press). *Sport foundations for elementary physical education: A tactical games approach.* Champaign, IL: Human Kinetics.

Peterson, P. (1979). Direct instruction reconsidered. In P. Peterson & H. Walberg (Eds.), *Research on teaching: Concepts findings and implications* (pp. 57-69). Berkeley, CA: McCutchen.

Rink, J. E. (1996). Foundations for the learning and instruction of sport and games. *Journal of Teaching in Physical Education, 15,* 399-417.

Scottish Consultative Council on the Curriculum. (1996). *Teaching for effective learning: A paper for discussion and development.* Dundee, Scotland: Author.

Thorpe, R. (1989). A changing focus in games teaching. In L. Almond (Ed.) *The place of physical education in schools.* London: Kogan Page.

Thorpe, R. (2001). Rod Thorpe on teaching games for understanding. In L. Kidman (Ed.) *Developing decision makers. An empowerment approach to coaching* (pp. 22-36). New Zealand: Innovative Print Communication.

Thorpe, R. and Bunker, D. (1986). Is there a need to reflect on our games teaching? (pp. 25-34). In R. Thorpe, D. Bunker, & L. Almond (Eds.). *Rethinking games teaching.* England, University of Technology, Loughborough, Department of Physical Education and Sports Science.

Putting TGfU Into Action Across the Classification System

The games classification system is a framework that organizes games based on the primary rules (main intention), which identify how the game is to be played and how winning can be achieved (Almond, 1986; Thorpe & Bunker, 1982). The classification system has four categories: (a) target games, (b) striking/running games, (c) net/wall games, and (d) invasion/territorial games.

Once these classifications are adopted, teachers can help students discover the commonalities the games share in terms of concepts and skills, offensive, defensive, and transpositional strategies, player roles, rules and regulations, and playing areas. Students learn to make sense of their experiences and, with the guidance of their teacher, to make connections among games. In this way, learning becomes structured around "big ideas" or "overarching concepts" such as a tactical problem to be solved. Since this is the case, games are no longer delivered in random units, but in units that are conceptually cohesive. Teachers who use a TGfU approach in a classification system have the ability to more effectively teach a game curriculum.

Decisions about developmental appropriateness can be made more easily when the TGfU model's pedagogical principles are employed. These include sampling, modification, exaggeration, and tactical complexity. Sampling allows the curriculum designer to introduce learners to a number of games within the classification and to help them understand the similarities between them. Modification allows all students access to playing games by simplifying rules, skills, and playing areas to accommodate different learning processes. Exaggeration allows teachers to manipulate certain aspects of the game environment in order to pose particular tactical problems to students. One example cited by Rod Thorpe, is to narrow the tennis court to force players to attack the space at the front or back of the court. Tactical complexity is a common-sense pedagogical principle that suggests that teachers should start simply and work in an organized manner toward more complexity in terms of game type, concepts and strategies.

TARGET	STRIKING/ RUNNING	NET/WALL	TERRITORIAL/ INVASION
Main Intention of Games			
To send away an object and make contact with a specific, stationary target in fewer attempts than opponent.	To place the ball away from fielders in order to run the bases and score more runs than the opponent.	To send ball back to opponent so that they are unable to return it or are forced to make an error. Serving is the only time the object is held.	To invade the opponent's defending area to score a goal while simultaneously protecting own goal.
Examples of Games			
Archery Billiards Bowling Croquet Curling Golf Pool Snooker	Baseball Cricket Danish Longball Kickball Rounders Softball	**NET** Badminton Pickleball Table Tennis Tennis Volleyball **WALL** Handball (court) Paddleball Racquetball Squash	Basketball Football Handball (team) Hockey: field, floor, ice Lacrosse Netball Rugby Soccer Speedball Ultimate Frisbee Water Polo

Each of the next four chapters represents one of the classifications described in the table above and demonstrates the commonalities of the games that fall within that classification. The authors of these chapters also provide tactical problem scenarios and their solutions, address some of the pedagogical principles used in the TGfU model and give examples of games and activities.

James Mandigo begins with target games-the easiest of the four classifications in terms of tactics and concepts. He illustrates the fundamental nature of this classification with three games: floor curling, shuffleboard, and Paralympic Boccia. Mandigo offers strategies that prove helpful in solving common tactical problems: how to score and how to stop the opposition from scoring. He suggests four activities that exaggerate the tactical solutions. Connie Collier and Judy Oslin present striking games, the second classification. Their chapter includes six useful lesson plans for generic fielding games, diagrams to illustrate class set up, and examples of assessment materials for use by both teachers and students during peer assessment. Theresa Maxwell uses the game of volleyball to illustrate the tactical progressions that can be used in the classification of net/wall games. The territorial games classification is presented by Louisa Webb, who explores some important issues raised at the TGfU conference. Using the game of field hockey as an example, she explores such questions as when it is best for teachers to introduce specific skills and how they can differentiate between drills and games.

Table III. *Tactical Structure of Target Games Category*

Tactical Problems	Tactical Solutions	
	With Equipment	**Without Equipment**
Scoring Using sufficient force to achieve proximity to target	◆ Aim accurately at target ◆ Place (e.g., proximity to intended target) ◆ Raise (i.e., bump own object closer to target)	
Avoiding obstacles	◆ Spin/turn (e.g., to get around obstacles or to control amount of force such as a back-spin in golf and pool) ◆ Use other objects to deflect object in order to get around obstacles	◆ Communicate with team members (e.g., the skip in floor curling can stand in the house and tell his/her team-mates where to place their shot)
Creating a dynamic reaction with playing objects	◆ Contact at appropriate place (e.g., hit another object in center to move it straight back or hit off center to move it off at an angle)	
Preventing Scoring Defending space/getting rid of objects in scoring position	◆ Guard (i.e., protect shot/ area) ◆ Take-out (i.e., remove opponent's shot from playing area or away from target)	
Getting last shot	◆ Blank an end (i.e., inning of play) or give up point in order to get last shot on next turn (e.g., in curling, team that scores a point in an end shoots first the next end, which gives the other team an advantage with last shot for that end)	◆ Bound by etiquette and rules and therefore, not allowed to interfere with opponent

The following four activities exaggerate the tactical solutions generated by the students' responses and are intended to enhance student understanding of ways to improve performance across various target games.

Activity #1: Aim and accuracy

Fundamental to all target games is the ability to accurately project an object toward a target. This activity is intended to simulate a game situation while focusing on skill development across a variety of target games.

Equipment: Beanbags, golf clubs, indoor golf balls, various sizes and types of balls, frisbees, hoops, pylons

Organization: Two players per team (2 vs 2)

Setup: See Figure 2

Figure 2. Setup for Activity #1: Aim and accuracy.

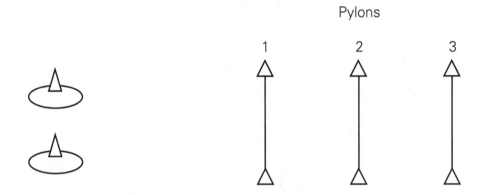

Pylons

How to play:

- ◆ The object of the game is to have one team of two players acquire 20 points before the other team.
- ◆ Players earn points by projecting an object so that it lands inside a hoop.
- ◆ Points are determined by the distance from which the object is projected. Line 1 is worth one point if the projected object lands in the hoop, line 2 is worth two points, and line 3 is worth three points.
- ◆ Players can double their scores if they hit a pin/ pylon that is placed in the middle of the hoop.
- ◆ For example, if a person hit a golf ball from line 2 and it landed inside the hoop and then hit the pylon, the team would receive a score of 4 (line 2 times two for hitting the pylon).
- ◆ Teams of two decide what object they wish to project.
- ◆ The winning team is the first team to earn 20 or more points.

finally team invasion games, which should be introduced last. Werner's argument reinforces the theory that target games are an effective way to introduce learners to the TGfU approach. Demonstrating how game understanding and performance can be improved in target games can help motivate learners to "buy-into" the TGfU approach to help them improve game performance in other categories.

The process outlined in this paper is also consistent with key elements that foster intrinsic motivation. If we consider Deci and Ryan's (1985) self-determination theory, it would seem that individuals are motivated when they feel autonomous, competent, and related to the activities they are doing. When a problem-solving approach is used, individuals achieve a sense of autonomy through a guided discovery approach that encourages them to generate tactical solutions. Individuals also develop a sense of competence throughout the activities by focusing on progressive game improvement and understanding across a number of different target games. Finally, when participants start off by playing the formal or modified game, they develop a sense of relatedness to the game itself and thus appreciate the importance of the tactical solution activities. As a result, participants are more likely to be motivated by this type of approach than by traditional approaches where they do not always understand "why" they are doing certain drills. Further research is therefore warranted to uncover the affective outcomes of using the TGfU approach (Holt, Strean, & Garcia, 2002).

Conclusion

The activities outlined in this paper are intended to provide a framework to help introduce the TGfU approach to students and to improve game performance across a number of different target games. Many of the rules, skills, and tactical problems and solutions introduced through these activities are very similar to other types of target games and to other more complex game categories. Teachers, coaches and instructors are encouraged to modify the activities and to implement the pedagogical principles with the specific needs and abilities of learners firmly in mind. Instructors are also encouraged to build on these activities to develop a repertoire of activities that will help learners improve their game understanding and performance.

References

Alberta Learning (2000). *Physical education program of studies.* Edmonton, AB: Alberta Learning.

Bunker, D. & Thorpe, R. (1986). *Rethinking games teaching.* Loughborough: University of Technology.

Butler, J. (1997). How would Socrates teach games? A constructivist approach. *Journal of Physical Education, Recreation, and Dance, 68*(9), 42-47.

Chepko, S. & Arnold, R. K. (2000). *Guidelines for physical education programs, Grades K-12.* Boston: Allyn and Bacon.

Cragg, S., Cameron, C., Craig, C. L., & Russell, S. (1999, November). *A physical activity profile.* Ottawa, ON: Canadian Fitness and Lifestyle Research Institute Publication.

Crain, W. (1992). *Theories of development. Concepts and applications.* (3rd ed.). Englewood Cliffs, NJ: Prentice Hall.

Deci, E. L. & Ryan, R. M. (1985). *Intrinsic motivation and self-determination in human behavior.* New York: Plenum.

Gallahue, D. L. & Ozmun, J. C. (1997). *Understanding motor development* (4th ed.). Boston: WCB McGraw-Hill.

Griffin, L. L., Mitchell, S. A., & Oslin, J. L. (1997). *Teaching sport concepts and skills: A tactical games approach.* Champaign, IL: Human Kinetics.

Haywood, K. M. & Getchell, N. (2001). *Life span motor development* (3rd ed.). Champaign, IL: Human Kinetics.

Holt, N. L., Strean, W. B., & Garcia, E. B. (2002). Expanding the teaching games for understanding model: New avenues for future research and practice. *Journal of Teaching in Physical Education, 21,* 162-176.

Morris, G. S. D. & Stiehl, J. (1999). *Changing kids' games* (2nd ed). Champaign, IL: Human Kinetics.

Thorpe, R. & Bunker, D. (1989). A changing focus in games teaching. In L. Almond (Ed). *The place of physical education in schools.* London, GB. Kogan Page.

Werner, P., Thorpe, R., & Bunker, D. (1996). Teaching games for understanding. Evolution of a model. *Journal of Physical Education, Recreation, and Dance, 67*(1), 28-33.

Teaching and Assessing Striking/Fielding Games

Chapter 3

Connie Collier, Kent State University, United States

Judy Oslin, Kent State University, United States

Introduction To Striking And Fielding Games

(margin handwritten notes: What it encompasses! What the aim of S and Fis. Nature of the area of curriculum Fundamentals involved)

The striking/fielding category encompasses baseball, softball, rounders, cricket, kickball, and teeball in accordance with the games classification system (Almond, 1986). The intent of striking/fielding games is "to strike an object, usually a ball, so it eludes defenders" (Griffin, Mitchell, & Oslin, 1997, p. 9). Striking/fielding games provide an excellent context for teaching fundamental skills, such as catching, throwing, striking, and running. However, modifications are needed to create an educational context that maximizes learning opportunities, particularly for primary-aged children. The nature of striking/fielding games, with half the team on the field playing defense and half the team off the field waiting to play offense, provides an opportunity to engage children in various learning activities such as playing the role of coach, umpire, or statistician (Siedentop, 1994). Children who are waiting for a turn to bat or kick can also participate in peer and/or self-assessment.

By manipulating game conditions, teachers can easily modify the game form to meet the developmental needs of game players and elicit numerous tactical solutions. The common tactical problems occur regardless of the conditions—one team attempts to score runs and the other team hopes to prevent scoring. These two primary tactical problems require children to develop a range of tactical solutions to the following problems: getting on base, moving the runners, positioning, fielding, and communicating.

In this chapter, we present a progression of tactical lessons. Developmentally appropriate roles and responsibilities associated with sport education (Siedentop, 1994) are integrated into many of the lessons, as are strategies for assessing children's game performance using the Game Performance Assessment Instrument (GPAI) (Griffin, Mitchell, & Oslin 1997; Mitchell & Oslin, 1999; Oslin, Mitchell, & Griffin, 1998). Tactical lesson progressions are offered to illustrate how to "grow" the game by modifying rules, equipment, and/or number of players to accommodate the skill level and tactical ability of the children.

Preseason Organization

(margin handwritten note: Organisation for S and F)

Prior to teaching, consider the number of students in each class and how best to organize teams for striking/fielding season. The amount of available space and equipment will help determine how to safely configure the playing space. We recommend using a cloverleaf or circular formation, with a safety zone in the center (See Figure 1). Be sure the safety zone is large enough to safely accommodate children and equipment. This will depend largely on whether children are throwing, kicking, or striking. If possible, provide alternative equipment such as balls of different size and composition (rubber, foam, leather, etc.) and a range of striking implements.

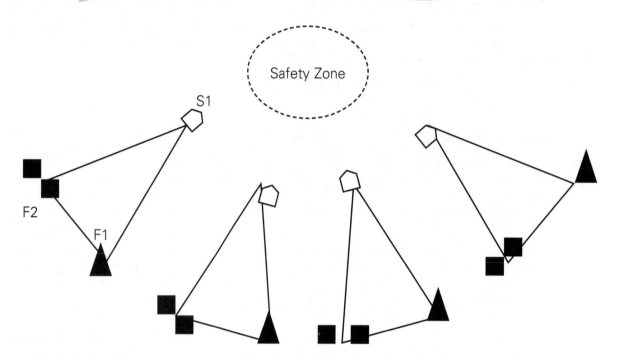

Note: Eight fields (triangles) positioned around the safety zone, with home plate at center and two bases (one inside the line for the first base player and one outside the line for the runner). We've only illustrated one half of the playing area/gym. S1 is the "sender" (roller, kicker, batter), F1 is the fielder and F2 is the fielder/ first base player. The sender rolls/kicks/hits the ball to F1 and runs to first base (located outside the baseline, to avoid collisions). If needed, we can submit and/or fax a hand drawing, as the publisher has people who do these types of diagrams.

Figure 1. Cloverleaf with Safety Zone

We recommend forming teams of four and assigning them to a "home" field—a field or space where they will routinely gather at the start of every class. Teams of four can initially play a 2-vs-2 game and then combine to play against another team in a 4-vs-4 game. We also recommend assigning students to mixed-ability groups to avoid creating dominating teams that could defeat the educational value of games teaching.

Critical to the success of integrating the sport education roles is the preparation of instructional materials. Consider what roles and responsibilities would be most valuable for children to perform, such as coach, statistician, umpire, and/or equipment manager. Prepare a handout describing the responsibilities associated with these roles, which will help the children understand what is expected and also how to perform these sport specific roles, such as the umpire making a call at first

and a peer coach providing feedback to help teammate
(See Siedentop, 1994, for designing a contract and oth

Tactical Lesson Progression

The following progression of lessons is intended to pro
appropriate striking/fielding games. Teachers may sub
equipment and sport specific rules depending upon
begins with a small-sided game, which is designe
(Griffin, Mitchell, & Oslin, 1997). The game is followed by
segment, in which the children are guided to the solution to the tac
Once the solution is identified, a practice situation is initiated to highlight
development of a particular skill or movement as it relates to game play. Following
practice, the children return to game play. This game-practice-game format provides
the structure for each lesson (Griffin, Mitchell, & Oslin 1997) and allows for
frequent game play, which children enjoy.

Day one (See Table I Block Plan for Striking/Fielding at end of chapter) should focus
on management and organization. Introduce rules and routines that are specific
to the unit or season. Organize teams and assign them to their home fields. Introduce
the safety zone and pertinent safety rules as well as consequences for not adhering to
these rules. Teachers may want to assign the roles, or at the very least carefully
guide the students as they select roles matching their personal attributes.

social / personal development

Introduce the initial game, playing field, and etiquette, and then let the children play
it. This will help them become familiar with the roles, rules, routines, and playing
areas. It will also allow the teacher to reinforce the roles, rules, and routines and
make any necessary adjustments to the playing space or player/team assignments.
To reinforce appropriate behavior, consider awarding a "free out" or an additional
half or full inning of game play. It is important that children play the games as they
are designed, not only for safety, but to increase the potential for learning. Active
supervision is critical.

Organize the initial game so that it matches children's skills and tactical understanding.
Lesson examples here begin with the fielding game of Roll and Run, where offensive
players roll the ball out into the field and then run to first base. Players can then
switch to kicking, which requires less complexity than most striking games
(Mauldon & Redfern, 1969), and eventually move on to striking the ball with a bat
from a tee. Initially the playing field is comprised of first base and home plate and a
cone marking foul territory (See Figure 1).

The striking/fielding tactics assimilate those found in baseball and softball and are
organized according to tactical problems related to offense (batting/kicking and
base running) and defense (on-the-ball skills and off-the-ball movements) as well as
tactical problems that evolve from a particular situation. For example, when the
situation involves no outs and a runner on first base, the batter must solve the
tactical problem of how to advance the runner and, if possible, get him/herself on
base, and the runner must solve the tactical problem of how to advance to the next
base. The sample lessons below relate to the tactical problems associated with the
situation of no outs, no runners on, and a ground ball to the infield. More lessons

be added to this progression by "growing" the game to focus on more complex situations, such as 0 outs and a runner on first base, which will create the need for second base as well as additional players (i.e., 4 vs 4). The more complex the situation, the greater the need for more complex skills and tactical understanding.

The initial game situation is no outs and no runners on base. The offense kicks a grounder to a place in the field that will give them the best chance to arrive at first base safely. The tactical problem is throwing out the lead runner. The focus of the lesson is on executing the skill of fielding, which emphasizes the transition from catch to throw and its appropriate use in the context of the game. Students should receive the rolling ball with two hands and immediately bring (transition) the ball into the throwing position, then step and throw to fielder covering the base. Efficiently combining skills (i.e., catch to throw or roll and run) is an important aspect of game play performance and should be intentionally taught.

The game is played on half of the infield (See Figure 1)—half-infield game. Conditions require the offensive player to roll/throw/kick/bat a ground ball away from the defensive players then run to first base, attempting to beat the throw. The ball must remain on the ground, or at least touch the ground, before it passes the base or fielders. The defense fields the ball and attempts to get the ball to first base ahead of the runner to get the runner out. Teams switch from offense to defense after three runs or three outs, whichever comes first.

The goal of the defensive team is to get three outs before the offense scores three runs. Questions that help the defense focus on the tactical solution include:

1) How many of you were able to get three outs before the other pair scored three runs?

2) Why were you not able to get the runner out? A: Throw too late, throw not caught or off target, misplay at first.

3) What can you do to get the throw to the base more quickly? A: Make a good, quick throw to the player at first and a good catch at first.

A practice task follows the question-and-answer session. Extensions and/or progressions can easily be added to this or any of the practice tasks provided in these sample lessons. Cues are also provided, to emphasize the goal of the task and emphasize the lesson objective. The teacher and peer coaches can provide performance feedback using the cues: 1) Two-hands, 2) Scoop it up, and 3) Step to the target and throw.

Assessing Fielding and Striking

The practice segment and final game frequently provide opportunities for teachers and students to assess game play. Responsibilities for assessing self and peer performance can be integrated as part of student roles. For example, in the second lesson, the teacher can informally assess skill execution by making judgments about what aspect of fielding needs correction and providing instructional cues to improve performance. Within the second lesson, the teacher may also ask the umpire to make judgments on close calls at first base. Both of these types of informal assessments prepare students for observing and recording via the Game Performance Assessment Instrument (GPAI) (Mitchell & Oslin, 1999) as a formal peer assessment.

Using peer assessment in the primary and intermediate grades requires teachers to construct instruments that best meet the students' capabilities for observing, recording, reading comprehension, and computational skills. Figure 2 illustrates a simple form of peer assessment for Roll and Run in which students record the runs and outs for their team. A sample of a more complex peer assessment appropriate for fifth and sixth graders includes all the categories of skill execution, decision-making and support play (See Figures 3 & 4.); however the student or teacher may still choose to observe only one aspect of game play depending on the time available. Figures 3 and 4 can be simplified for use with third and fourth graders by including only one or two categories, as students at this level may be distracted by assessments with too many categories. These instruments will require some explanation by the teacher, but they are user friendly and merely require a judgment and a tally to record whether game performance was appropriate or inappropriate.

To help check the reliability of peer assessments, teachers may also choose to assess game performance themselves. While some controversy surrounds the accuracy of peer assessments, we recommend the use of multiple formats of assessment to provide the students with a variety of information about the effectiveness of their game play. Our experience suggests that when students intentionally observe their peers, the players who are performing begin to expect more careful scrutiny and thus are more intentional about their performance. Therefore, the teacher only needs to provide prompts and reinforcement regarding the important role of peer assessment to keep all students engaged.

One primary strength of using the GPAI to assess students is that it rewards not only effective skill execution but also good support play and effective decision-making. This creates an inclusive team environment and does not merely reward the most skillful players. Just as with the game, assessment must be designed to accommodate students' developmental abilities. It is our hope that teachers plan, teach, and assess striking and fielding games in ways that promote physically active learning environments and challenging contests.

GPAI Striking/Fielding—Peer Offensive Assessment

Class _____ **Evaluator** _____ **Date** _____

Categories:

**Skill
Execution:**   **<u>Runs</u>**—Batter/kicker/roller sent ball to the field and ran to first outside the baseline and beat the throw to the base.

<u>Outs</u>—Batter/kicker/roller recorded an out by not reaching first base before the throw, illegally running to first inside the base path or by rolling two consecutive foul balls.

Recording: Use a tally to mark the responses. This represents only one facet of game play; however, elementary teachers using the GPAI find it effective to assess only one category per day for younger children using a peer assessment scheme.

Players	Runs	Outs
Jose		
Marie		
Danny		
Kendra		

Figure 2. GPAI Striking/Fielding—Peer Offensive Assessment

GPAI Striking/Fielding—Peer Defensive Assessment

Class _____ Evaluator _____ Date _____

Categories: **Start**—Fielder is in an appropriate starting position (e.g., no runners on, no outs, fielders should play straight away).

Catch and Throw—Player fields ball cleanly and accurately throws ball to first base in time to get the runner.

Decision-making—Fielder makes appropriate decision considering the situation (e.g., no runners, no outs, grounder to second, throw goes to first; sometimes decision not to throw the ball is a good decision).

Back Up—Player provides back up for player fielding ball or covering base.

Recording: Use a tally to mark the appropriate responses in the 'A' category and the inappropriate responses in the 'I' category. Each time a batter comes to the plate, assess whether or not the fielder is in appropriate starting position, backs up the play, makes a good catch and throw and makes an appropriate decision.

Players	Start		Back-up		Catch & Throw		Decision-making	
	A	I	A	I	A	I	A	I
Jose								
Marie								
Danny								
Kendra								

Figure 3. GPAI Striking/Fielding—Peer Defensive Assessment

GPAI Striking/Fielding—Teacher Offensive Assessment

Class _____ **Evaluator** _____ **Date** _____

Skill Execution: **Batting**—sent the ball to a place on the field allowing the batter to arrive safely on base or advanced the lead runner.

   Base Running—ran through first safely or rounded first and arrived at second safely.

Decision-making: **Batting**—attempted to send the ball to a place on the field, to allow batter to arrive safely at first or advance the lead runner.

   Base Running—attempted to run through first safely or round first and arrive at second safely.

Scoring:
   5 = very good performance
   4 = good performance
   3 = average performance
   2 = weak performance
   1 = very weak performance

Recording: View the entire team at bat and judge how well the batter executed the skill performance and whether or not they made a good decision based upon the situation. Place the number 1-5 in the space across from the batter for each category. We recommend using this as a teacher assessment rather than a peer assessment.

Players	Skill Execution		Decision-making	
	Batting	**Base Running**	**Batting**	**Base Running**
Jose				
Marie				
Danny				
Kendra				

Figure 4. GPAI Striking/Fielding—Teacher Offensive Assessment

Table I. Block Plan for Striking/Fielding

Lesson #1—Organize for Roll and Run	Lesson #2—Preventing Scoring
Objective: Students will learn boundaries of their home field playing area, identify team name, review individual roles and play initial game of Roll and Run.	**Objective:** In a 2-vs-2, half-infield game students will execute effective fielding to defend space by cleanly fielding and accurately sending (within one step) the ball to first base ahead of the runner.
Introduction—10 minutes Assign teams and home field. Set up field and equipment. Introduce entrance and exit routine.	**Entry Routine—2-3 minutes** Players report to home field, set up equipment under the direction of the equipment manager and begin playing previous 2-vs-2 Roll and Run game. Reward first team to successfully begin play with an extra out per side.
Team Meeting—8 minutes Teams identify a team name and discuss responsibilities associated with each role. Roles include coach, umpire, statistician, and equipment manager.	**Game Play—5 minutes** Roll and Run *Goal:* Get ball to first base ahead of the runner.
Game Play—5 minutes Play Roll and Run game on their home field. *Conditions:* 2-vs-2, half-infield game, 0 outs, 0 runners. Offense must roll the ball on the ground so that it does not bounce above defenders' knees prior to passing base or fielder. A run is scored when the thrower reaches first base safely, ahead of the throw. Whether safe or out, the runner returns to the safety zone until his/her next turn to roll. Play until offense scores 3 runs or is thrown out 3 times and switch. *Goal:* Roll the ball and reach first base safely.	**Q/A Segment—1-2 minutes** Q: What did fielder have to do to get ball to first base ahead of the runner? A: Catch and throw it to first. Q: How? A: Quickly Q: What are some things that fielders can do to get the ball to first more quickly? A: Move quickly to the ball, scoop with two hands and pull ball into throwing position, stay low, step and follow to first (target).
Closure—2 minutes Reinforce and reward teams demonstrating fair play, knowledge of the boundaries, and proper equipment take down.	**Practice Task—5-7 minutes** Offensive team members throw five consecutive balls to fielder (F1) and run to first on the fifth trial. Fielders rotate and repeat drill. After both fielders have had five trials, they rotate with offensive team members. *Goal:* Smooth transition from catch to throw—no bobbles—throw within one step of first. *Cues:* Feet to the ball, watch it in, scoop to throw position, step and follow to first.
	Game Play—5 Minutes *Goal:* Get more runners out more often than first game.
	Closure—2 minutes Compare final game to initial game and reinforce equipment managers and teams exhibiting fair play.

Table I., contd.

Lesson #3—Support Play

Objective: In a 2-vs-2, half-infield game students will cover first base on a force play using a two-hand target and foot placement on inside edge of base.

Entry Routine—2-3 minutes
Players report to home field, set up equipment under direction of equipment manager and begin activity (i.e., game play, practice drill, or catch & throw with a partner).

Game Play—5 minutes
Roll and Run.
Goal: Get ball to first base ahead of the runner.

Q/A Segment—1-2 minutes
Q: What does player off the ball do to support teammate fielding the ball?
A: Moves to cover first, receives throw, tags first base.
Q: How can the first base play help fielder make an accurate throw?
A: Give a good target.

Practice Task—7-10 minutes
Task: Thrower rolls grounders to infielder, who fields and throws to first base. As soon as first base player sees the throw going to fielder, he/she moves to first and puts foot on inside edge of base and gives fielder a big two-hand target, big hands, arms extended at chest level. The first base player then rolls ball to retriever. Rotate after each defensive player has 5 trials at first then rotate with offensive players.
Coach: Gives feedback on foot placement at inside edge of base.
Goal: Move to base quickly, place foot on inside edge, give a big target, and control the ball.
Cues: Move quickly to cover first, foot on inside edge, big two-hand target, pull ball into body (absorb).

Game Play—5 Minutes
Conditions: Same as initial game. Statistician records runs and outs (see Figure 2.)
Goal: Get more runners out more often than first game. (Spread fielders further apart as they improve.)

Closure—2 minutes
Compare final game to initial game and reinforce teammate support during game play and practice and coach feedback to players.

Lesson #4—Base Coverage

Objective: In a 2-vs-2, half-infield game, students will move quickly to the ball, field cleanly, then run safely to first base and tag the inside edge of the base.

Entry Routine—2-3 minutes
Same as Lesson #3.

Game Play—5 minutes
Roll and Run.
Goal: Get ball to first base ahead of the runner.

Q/A Segment—1-2 minutes
Q: If the ball is rolled toward first base, what should the first base player do?
A: Field the ball then run and tag first base.
Q: What should the other fielder do?
A: Back-up the first base player as he/she fields the ball.

Practice Task—7-10 minutes
Task: Thrower rolls grounders between the players. The first base player fields then runs to first to tag the base ahead of the runner. After fielding the ball, the first base player should take a curved path ("u" or "c") toward the baseline and then run parallel with the baseline to tag the base. The of-the-ball player should back-up and provide support for the player fielding the ball. The first base player then rolls ball to retriever. Rotate after each defensive player has 5 trials at first base, and then rotate with offensive players.
Goal: Get to ball quickly, field cleanly and use a safe, effective path to tag inside edge of base.
Umpire: Calls the play at first
Coach: Gives feedback on tagging inside edge of base.
Goal: Move to base quickly, place foot on inside edge, give a big target, and control the ball.
Cues: Move quickly to ball, catch first, then cover base, curved pathway to base (if necessary) tag inside edge.

Game Play—5 Minutes
Conditions: Throws should be modified to challenge both fielder and runner.
Goal: Get more runners out more often than first game.

Closure—2 minutes
Compare final game to initial game and reinforce accepting umpire's calls and coach feedback to players.

Table I., contd.

Lesson #5—Base Running—Scoring	Lesson #6—Rolling to Scoring
Objective: In a 2-vs-2, half-infield game students run as fast as possible *through* first base.	**Objective:** In a 2-vs-2, half-infield game students will roll and run as fast as possible *through* first base.

Lesson #5—Base Running—Scoring

Objective: In a 2-vs-2, half-infield game students run as fast as possible *through* first base.

Entry Routine—2-3 minutes
Same as Lesson #3.

Game Play—5 minutes
Roll and Run.
Goal: Run to first base ahead of the throw.

Q/A Segment—1-2 minutes
Q: After hitting the ball what should you do to get to first base as fast as possible?
A: Roll and run fast.
Q: What can the roller/runner do to get to first as fast as possible?
A: Get a good start, run hard, run past the base, don't watch the ball—run!
Q: Should you run inside or outside the base path?
A: Outside.

Practice Task—7-10 minutes
Task: All four players start at home plate or three at home plate and one player in the coaching box to encourage runners to run hard through the base and past the cone, which is placed about 10 feet past first base. Players/runners should take off from behind home plate, "drive" knee and opposite arm toward first base. Repeat 5 times each.
Coach: Directs runners to run hard *through*, or past, the base.
Goal: Run to first as fast as possible. Question-and-answer segment on why rules require runner to run outside the base path, and why it is important roll (kick or hit) not to watch the ball as they run to first base.
Cues: Drive knee and arm, eyes down the line, run outside base path, run hard *through* first base.

Game Play—5 Minutes
Conditions: Same game, extra players can coach first base. Umpire can call plays at first base.
Goal: Get to first base ahead of the throw.

Closure—2 minutes

Lesson #6—Rolling to Scoring

Objective: In a 2-vs-2, half-infield game students will roll and run as fast as possible *through* first base.

Entry Routine—2-3 minutes
Same as Lesson #3.

Game Play—5 minutes
Roll and Run.
Goal: run to first base ahead of the throw.

Q/A Segment—1-2 minutes
Q: What's the best way to get a good roll and a good take-off to first base?
A: Not sure.

Practice Within the Game—5 minutes
Task: Return to your game and as you play, try different ways to roll. Watch your teammates too, and see if you can determine one or more ways to roll so that you can get to first base more quickly. Once you've determined a good way to roll and run, practice it on your next few turns. Share your way with your teammates and see if you use some of the same techniques or some different techniques to get to first more quickly.
Coach: Coach can use a stopwatch to time runners and statistician can record times.
Goal: Determine quickest way to roll and run to first base.
Cues: Step left to roll and step (drive) right to run. (Cues may vary with different techniques. Can have players determine their own cues to help each other get the "notion of the motion."

Game Play—5 Minutes
Conditions: Continue game play, same as initial game.
Goal: Get to first base ahead of the throw.

Closure—2 minutes
Discuss the importance of transitioning between skills for smooth, efficient performance.

References

Almond, L. (1986). A games classification (pp. 71-72). In R. Thorpe, D. Bunker, & L. Almond (Eds.). *Rethinking games teaching.* England: University of Technology, Loughborough, Department of Physical Education and Sports Science.

Griffin, L. L., Mitchell, S. A., & Oslin, J. L. (1997). *Teaching sport concepts and skills: A tactical games approach.* Champaign, IL: Human Kinetics.

Mauldon, E. & Redfern, H. B. (1969). *Games teaching: A new approach for the primary school.* London: MacDonald & Evans.

Mitchell, S. A., & Oslin, J. L. (1999). *Assessment series K-12 physical education series: Assessment in games teaching.* Reston, VA: National Association of Sport and Physical Education.

Oslin, J. L., Mitchell, S. A., & Griffin, L. L. (1998). The game performance assessment instrument (GPAI): Development and preliminary validation. *Journal of Teaching in Physical Education, 17,* 231-243.

Siedentop, D. (1994). *Sport Education: Quality PE through positive sport experiences.* Champaign, IL: Human Kinetics.

The Progressive Games Approach to Teaching Expertise in Volleyball

Chapter 4

Theresa Maxwell, University of Calgary, Canada

Introduction

This chapter discusses the incorporation of Teaching Games for Understanding (TGfU) concepts into the net/wall games category through a progressive teaching/learning sequence. Games in this category—such as tennis, badminton, table-tennis, pickle-ball, volleyball, squash and racquetball—share the following characteristics. The fundamental intention of these games is to send the object back to opponents so that they are unable to return it or are forced to make an error (Butler, 1997). The target for scoring is on the playing surface and all players serve and receive the ball (Bunker & Thorpe, 1982). These games take place in relatively restricted spaces.

Net/wall games are tactically simpler than invasion games, and generally include fewer players, resulting in reduced levels of complexity and decision option possibilities. These factors combine to create a direct link between the tactical option chosen, the execution of the skill, and the results of these actions. The reduced numbers of players ensures personal involvement, responsibility, and accountability. Students should therefore be able to learn strategies for playing these games more quickly than is possible in more complex games.

Children link fun with games playing. They view activities as fun when they are able to be actively involved. Activities that are most fun are those that challenge their abilities and include clearly communicated expectations (Rowley, 1996). Yet for many students, participation in games is a frustrating experience. They do not understand the strategies and tactics required, nor are they able to use skills effectively, even if these skills are highly developed.

Coaches, parents, and children accept the assumption that developing skills through drills is boring, and that games are fun (Strean & Holt, 2000). However, games require a fundamental level of skill competency. Children view skillfulness as the ability to employ skills within a game context (Turner, Allison, & Pissanos, 2001). Vickers (1994) showed that students who had a total concept orientation when learning games remembered more and were able to perform better at a later date.

The following teaching/learning structure is offered as an example to address the apparent conflict between the need to develop skills to be successful in a game context and the idea that learning skills is boring because it involves repetition or drills. As one interpretation of the Games for Understanding Approach (Chandler,

1996), this structure focuses on a planned and systematic integration of skills and tactics of the chosen game, moving from a very simple game structure to progressively more complex situations. The four fundamental pedagogical principles of planning the games curriculum as outlined by Thorpe, Bunker, and Almond (1984) are inherent in the proposed structure. The four principles: sampling, modification-representation, modification-exaggeration, and tactical complexity are evident throughout the sequence. Even though the game of volleyball is developed in this example, a similar sequence is applicable for all net/wall games (sampling). The second principle, modification-representation, is evident throughout the document, since the initial game form is determined by the fundamental intent of the adult game. Subsequent game forms are increasingly complex adaptations of this. Exaggeration refers to creating situations that force the learner to use a specified concept or skill in a very directed or obvious manner. This is achieved through rule modifications made by the teacher, which are determined by student needs. Tactical complexity is increased in a sequential manner throughout the learning sequence, with an emphasis on logical expansions of the preceding skills and concepts. Maintenance of the tactical structure of the adult game is crucial to this proposed sequence; the challenge is developing progressive game forms that continually develop this.

Tactical decisions are determined by a combination of the knowledge of tactical options and individual skill competence (Griffin, 1996). Therefore this model integrates the presentation of tactics and technical skill in a manner that demonstrates how the skills are used tactically. Information about the essence of the game through game structure and rules is paralleled with how to achieve the desired outcomes. Students are presented with a selection of appropriate responses to the game condition and then allowed to practice this decision-making relative to the skills being utilized until they develop a level of competency.

Games situations in which students require new decision options from a tactical or skill perspective are initially structured to be fairly simple. Technical skills are taught and included as they are required, to meet the complexity of the game form. This model introduces specific skills only as they are needed to expand the decision options required to achieve a tactical outcome. When drills are incorporated into the template sequence, it is emphasized that these are to improve skills to enhance tactical options. Students recognize them as such because they form the basis of the subsequent game form. The aim is to provide a systematic format for children to become expert players in the chosen game through increasingly more complex game structures. The game of volleyball will be used to demonstrate the structure.

What the Research Says About Expert Players

Normally an expert is defined as the individual who is able to function best in a high-level competitive situation, that is, the player who can employ strategies and tactics in the effective execution of skill. Experts exhibit more sport skill, play more effective shots, and understand the game situations better than novice players. (Blomqvist, Luhtanen, & Laasko, 2000). Logic suggests that the expert acquired these qualities either deliberately or incidentally.

From a perception perspective, experts focus on more meaningful and predictive cues that enhance quick and accurate decision-making (Singer, 1994). Experts anticipate better because they immediately pay direct attention to appropriate cues and extract meaning from those cues regarding opponents' possible intentions of. In addition, experts are significantly more accurate than nonathletes in retaining visual information (Blomqvist et al., 2000).

The knowledge component of games and sport consists of declarative knowledge— factual information including the rules, goals, and subgoals—of the game, and procedural knowledge-the selection of an appropriate action within the context of the game (McPherson & French, 1991). From a knowledge structure perspective, experts make better decisions because they have better procedural knowledge (Turner & Martinek 1999). To be successful in games play, the most pertinent information is knowing the means by which a game is won. High-knowledge individuals understand relations between game states and actions within a game's goal structure. Based on a small set of environmental cues, they are able to anticipate opponents' game-related actions or determine appropriate responses for themselves. Some of these concepts (i.e., creating mismatches, isolating a player, overloading a zone) transfer across sports. Thomas (1994) states that adults spontaneously produce and employ strategies regardless of expertise in a particular activity, suggesting that they have learned these strategies in some other context.

Decision-making is another criterion that distinguishes expert and novice performers. Tactical aspects of sports are based on the ability to make good decisions and execute them. Skilled decision-making in sport is based on the ability to anticipate upcoming events, focus on relevant cues, avoid irrelevant disturbances, and respond as fast as possible (Tenenbaum, 1993). Experience allows athletes to integrate information more efficiently and to increase the probability of choosing the correct response, particularly in fast ball games. This suggests players have had some practice in decision-making and have learned from it. Skilled decision-making is possibly one of the most telling qualities in determining expertise. Singer (1994) found that it was possible to improve both the speed and accuracy of decisions through training, and that subjects learned to transfer anticipatory information presented in one situation to new game situations. Improving the speed of decision-making, and transference of information, results in more complex skill options and improved performance.

Incorporating These Research Findings Into a Learning Sequence

These results frame the proposed learning sequence. A game form that preserves the contextual nature of the real game will be used to present appropriate tactics and skills. Although concepts such as mismatches, overloading, and creating space can be taught through tactical games, the proposed format integrates the learning of tactics with the skills required to execute these for successful game performance. The relevance of specific tactics is evident as the student learns to recognize and practice real-game situations. Technical skill instruction is included as required. Initial learning situations and game forms should not place too great a technical demand on the players in order to ensure their success in game performance. Students need opportunities for repetitive practice of decision options, both tactical and technical.

The game form evolves in a progressive fashion, with increasing complexity in both skill and decision options. The structure of the game allows students to be personally and continuously involved in the game outcome. The personal involvement and game structure, accompanied with appropriate skill development, should result in more fun while their activity expertise increases and learn to play games effectively.

Planning the Program

The first step in implementing this learning sequence is to determine the fundamental intention of the game. In volleyball (and other net/wall games), this is to score by having the ball land in the opponents' court. Combine this idea with a fundamental skill level that encourages—rather than discourages—participation. As a result, the simplest possible learning structure is a game of 1-vs-1 catch and throw.

One-Vs-One Catch And Throw

The basic rule for this game is that a player scores a point if the ball lands in the opponent's court. If students are allowed to determine their own courts, two additional objectives are achieved. First, participants can work at their own comfort level, because the court is only as large as they feel they can cover. Determining their own court size also gives students permission to change these if, in fact, the court size is too large or small for their abilities. Consciously determining court lines forces individuals to be aware of different court dimensions and their own court position, a concept fundamental to volleyball and other net/wall games at all levels. Working one against one ensures that each student is actively involved in the game process, both in the tactical decision-making aspect and the skills required to execute decisions. To be successful, the players must work on aspects that would help them score or prevent the opponent from scoring. To achieve these objectives, the player must work on cue recognition, visual integration, and decision-making in the fundamental aspects of the game. The game form itself provides maximum practice of the skills required to achieve the objective with immediate feedback regarding success.

Outcomes of this structure are immediate and personal. Students quickly learn to place the ball in particular spaces on the opponent's court, which creates scoring opportunities by forcing the opponent out of preferred positions, either through trajectory or speed changes. The ongoing application of various strategies is sometimes limited by students' skill development. The awareness of this limitation, however, often serves as an incentive to practice and improve skill performance. As well as the tactical aspect, the child is developing a sense of responsibility for playing the ball since there is no one else on the court.

The teacher can have footwork and tactical-decision options demonstrated by students who use these skills effectively. If some students are having difficulty with the fundamental skills, instruction, and practice of these can be included. Teachers can set requirements or restrictions dependent on their objectives. If the objective is to emphasize lateral movement skills, teachers should set minimum width requirements for the court; if front and back footwork skills are the objective, teachers should set minimum length dimensions. Feedback should be focused on the tactics or strategies students use, rather than on their technical skills.

Corrections of technical aspects should be made bearing in mind how they will affect the students' tactical decisions.

The next step is to progress the game form toward the adult volleyball game. To approximate the volley position and action, the teacher should require that the ball be caught and thrown only from the forehead area. A violation of this rule will result in a point for the opposition. In order to play with this restriction, players recognize that they must get into appropriate position both on the court and relative to the ball. The effectiveness of the chosen tactic and skill is inherent in the situation and serves as immediate reinforcement and feedback. The teacher can augment this feedback through question-and-answer sessions. Within a short time, students will learn effective movement patterns, scoring tactics, body position, and court dimensions, all without overt teaching and drilling by the teacher. The structure of the full game of volleyball is being presented in a simple, uncomplicated format so that students can recognize the basic elements. All the aspects of expert games players are being presented in a manner relevant to the players, while providing a challenge appropriate to the individuals.

Introduction of the skill of volleying leads naturally from this point. It is easier, quicker, and more efficient to present the mechanics and execution of the volley through a direct-technique approach. Drills involving proper handling should be included. Students would not naturally develop this skill without direct instructions. Students should then be placed in a 1-vs-1 volley game situation. The only change in the rules would be that students must contact the ball with a volley, rather than throwing and catching the ball.

One-Vs-One Volley Game

The students' choices of tactics involving trajectory, speed, and placement are all evident in this game. Students display a variety of tactical aspects without prompting. Technical skills including hand position, knee bend, arm extension, follow-through, and summation of forces are all practiced as the player attempts to score. Poor skill execution has an immediate consequence, so there is an incentive to learn and perform properly, and even to practice outside the game context. Players are actively involved in the volleyball structure display. Playing alone provides maximum practice opportunities, which increase the students' skill learning and development.

At this point, the forearm pass should be introduced. Once again, this is achieved through a technique-and-drill approach. Drill practice should be structured from stationary light tosses, to moving, faster trajectory passes approximating what the student would experience in a game. Reinforce the techniques and mechanics of proper passing during this practice. The position of the body relative to the ball, arm contact, focus, follow-through, and other technical aspects should be reinforced from the perspective of how these impact the player's potential tactical decisions in a game context. The game structure should now progress to a 1-vs-1 situation, where each player is allowed two contacts with the ball.

Two-Contact Volleyball: 1-vs-1

In this game structure, each player is playing against a single opponent, thereby maximizing contacts and reinforcing responsibility and movement patterns, but has two contacts in attempting to score. This change is the beginning of the pass-set-attack sequence in the regular game of volleyball. The normal volleyball sequence is reinforced by requiring that the first contact be a forearm pass and the contact that sends the ball over the net be an overhand volley. Reinforce proper positioning and contact (skill technique) through the rules implemented for the game. Increasing the number of contacts, to a maximum of three per side, introduces the official game structure, as well as increasing the potential decision options of each player.

Outcomes of this activity include recognition of the need for control of the forearm pass, moving into more advantageous positions for the attack, movement after the pass, and reinforcement of the normal volleyball game sequence: pass-set-attack. Personal responsibility for performance is further reinforced. Progressing the game form now requires the addition of an official start to the game.

Add an Official Serve

An accepted volleyball serve technique can be introduced at this point. For beginners, an underhand serve is recommended for simplicity and increased control. Again, this can be taught through a direct approach. The game activity should then incorporate the serve, the forearm pass and the attack. Initially, the serve should be executed from wherever the player can get it over the net to ensure success for the performer and to prevent the lack of skill from causing a breakdown in the game form. As the player becomes proficient in executing serve techniques, the service line can become fixed at predetermined distances from the net. Utilizing service games for accuracy and control is encouraged as a means of providing additional practice without the continuous decision-making required within a volleyball game context. With the exception that all the contacts are by a single individual, this game structure is volleyball in its simplest form. The complexity of the game structure should now be increased by having players work with partners, i.e., two players on each side of the net.

Add a Partner

Once students have achieved a level of competence through 1-vs-1 play, adding a partner increases the game's tactical complexity. Prohibiting consecutive contacts by any one individual requires the players to work together to achieve the game objective of scoring. Students are actively involved in learning communication skills, greater options in setting up the attack, recognizing player positions on the court, cooperation, and coordinated-movement skills. If concepts such as space are not being effectively employed, the teacher should take time to suggest and point out appropriate alternatives. The transition skills of moving from defense to offense are ongoing and are being practiced within a realistic situation both individually and as partners. If a skill deficiency is perceived, the teacher should incorporate skill-development drills, but the primary vehicle for learning cooperative game play should be through games. The teacher should include specific outcome games, such as cooperative games, if there is a deficiency in a particular area. The differences between the objectives of these game forms and that of the fundamental volleyball game should be clearly outlined to the players so they recognize the relationship between different types of games, and so students recognize that rule and structure changes can be used to augment and change the game form to meet the needs of the situation.

At this point in the learning sequence, setting as a skill (high, quick, back, location, etc.) becomes important and should be incorporated, either through drills or rule changes within the game. Cooperative defensive positioning can also be stressed, but is inherent in the structure. Using a one-handed overhand contact for the attack can be introduced as an advanced technique. This type of contact imparts greater speed on the ball but makes it harder to control. The foundations are being laid for deception in the attack.

Depending on the level of play or the skill expectations, the teacher can introduce the spike and tip as attack options. The spike is an attack form that is generally more effective in scoring due of the angle at which the ball is directed (because of the jump) and the speed with which the ball travels because of the type of contact. The tip is an additional adaptation. Again, teaching these skills should be through a technique/drill approach. If the spike is deemed to be too complex for the age or motor ability of the students, the attack can be a one-handed contact without a jump, or simply the volley that the student has been using effectively to this point. If the jump can be incorporated into the volley attack, the preliminary aspects of spiking are being practiced, as is the concept of jump setting. Students should be encouraged to use a variety of attack options. The spike is simply more effective for scoring at higher levels of play.

Blocking as a skill needs to be taught only after players have learned the spike. Blocking is the first line of defense against the spike, and generally is not required until opponents can spike effectively. Once spiking is an attack option, countering defensive skills are required. Basic defensive position and movement skills can be introduced and practiced. The players should once again be put back into the game structure so that they can practice decision-making and perceptual skills, similar to those that would present themselves in a real game situation. The complexity of the game form is then further increased by adding a third person to the team.

Add a Third Person to the Team

With the addition of a third person, attack deception along with basic attack and defensive systems begin to emerge. It is now possible to have a defined setter. The set can be directed to either of the two teammates, spreading out the attack options and allowing for faking opportunities. On defense, short- and long-coverage systems are options to be tried. Possible variations in the attack require commensurate defensive skills practice, including fundamental court position, defensive movement, ball contact, and transition. At this stage, all aspects of the official game are in place, including many of the subgoals used to achieve the primary scoring objective. If the spike has not been taught to this point, it should be included here.

Playing triples, or threes, is a legitimate volleyball game, with all the skills and strategies of the real game. It has added benefits in that each teammember has increased opportunities to contact the ball, and thus enjoys a greater role in every play sequence, both technically and tactically. Individual responsibility for play execution is more apparent and easily determined by the players themselves. The progressive game form for volleyball requires that there be a fourth person added to each team at this point.

Add a Fourth Person

With the addition of a fourth player, back-row concepts are introduced. Rules restricting the back-row player should be similar to those in the normal game of volleyball. Penetrating setter aspects could be introduced at this point. Cooperative team defense and transition are maximized in this situation. The final game form in volleyball would be six players on each side.

Sixes

At this stage, it is relatively simple to incorporate two additional players to bring the game to the official complement. Offensive systems—such as 4-2, 6-0, 6-2, and 5-1—are merely extensions of learning at this point, rather than entirely new concepts. The teacher can determine the system to be used and explain it from the perspective of the previously learned game formats. Serve-receive patterns incorporating the additional people are accommodations of learned patterns rather than new concepts, as are defensive players. The students can play the official game and relying on their practice incorporating the individual skills into the appropriate game sequence. Decision-making and movement patterns have been ongoing. Rather than learning new skills in order to accommodate new players, students need only to make minor adjustments. The transitions between game forms are relevant and logical. Decisions and skills from previous forms are simply augmented in each additional game structure.

Tactical Skill Instruction

Individual skills can, and should, also be taught from a strategies and tactics perspective. Two examples will be used here to clarify this idea—the serve and the spike.

The serve should be taught as an offensive weapon, rather than just a means of putting the ball in play. Teach service for control, using games that would reward precise placement of the ball, i.e., serving golf. Additionally, the players should work in pairs, which increases practice opportunities. In this case, the player should serve at the partner as a target, since it is easier to focus on a target than on an open space. Once competence has been achieved in directing the ball to the target, teachers can direct the students to place the ball away from the receiving partner, who remains somewhat stationary. Teachers can also develop rules or games that provide scoring opportunities only under restricted placement conditions. Asking students to identify and discuss serving options is also an effective strategy in developing the knowledge structure.

The spike is another skill that will be used to demonstrate skills taught from a tactical, strategic perspective. Tactical aspects should be introduced as soon as the student has reasonable approach patterns and arm action. A variety of options and outcomes are suggested. Having the player toss the ball to him/herself to approach and spike, although initially difficult, has a number of benefits. The player learns to adjust the approach and timing to accommodate a variety of types of self-tosses (sets). Because the player is responsible for the toss, ineffective spike execution cannot be blamed on the setter, resulting in the development of a sense of responsibility for proper execution. In addition, the player learns to hit a variety of sets, not just those that are perfectly located. Teaching the initial spiking action on a lowered net results in better technical execution and a sense of success. Once students have achieved a reasonable competency in the technical executions of the spike, they should practice spiking from a toss or set by teammates.

Early in this phase, the player should be required to hit the ball at a target on the opposite side of the net. Focusing on a target teaches the spiker to look at the defensive side of the court rather than focusing exclusively on the ball. Using a player as the target will promote the development of defensive and digging skills on the part of the defensive player. In this way, both the offensive and resultant defensive aspects of spiking are being practiced in a controlled situation. When consistency at hitting the target is achieved, have the target person move as the attacker starts the approach, forcing the spiker to watch the movement and adjust the spike direction. Aiming at a target is initially easier for the beginner than aiming at a space. As competency increases, have the spikers hit away from the person acting as a target. As skill increases in this regard, have the target move later and later into the spike approach while requiring the spiker to adjust the ball trajectory away from the target position. The spiker is forced to watch the defensive display and make a decision as to ball placement. This type of practice not only requires the students to recognize and respond to relevant cues, but also provides opportunities for game-context decision-making. This also becomes an excellent challenge game from either an offensive or defensive perspective.

The next aspect of this sequence would be to add a blocker. After practice in the fundamental techniques of the block, let the blocker have the choice of executing the block or not, as might happen in a game context. If the block is in place, the spiker must tip or soft hit over the block into predetermined areas. If no block is in place, the spiker is required to hit hard, first at a target, then away from the target. Again, the practice of this type of decision-making reflects the competitive game situation and is fundamental to the implementation of tactical options. This progression forces the spiker to be aware of the defensive display, respond to the cues being presented to him or her, make decisions as to the effectiveness of the ball execution and placement, as well as executing the skill. This sequence aids the development of smart attacking, rather than just hitting hard.

It should be stressed that these skills or concepts are not all learned at one time. Each of the concepts or skills is presented in a simple situation and is then enhanced and practiced through the addition of restrictions or additional display aspects. The student is never required to perform skills in complex situations without having had practice and lead-up experiences in both the situations as well as the skill. The focus is always on the tactical aspects, rather than on the skill execution in itself. Reinforcement should also be directed along these lines. Technical correction should be introduced and reinforced as it affects performance or enhances tactical play.

Conclusion

Besides learning strategies and tactics of the game itself, students benefit in many other ways from using a model of this type. Students learn a variety of small-sided games that are legitimate volleyball games, which give students greater recreational and practice opportunities. They learn to adjust rules and boundaries and to alter tactics accordingly. They are not bound by the official rules of the game, but learn to adjust these to their circumstances and needs. Responsibility for decisions and celebration of results becomes personalized. Using a progressive-decision option and game-structure approach to teaching games allows students an opportunity to learn the game structure, practice decision-making in the execution of skills, assume responsibility for their actions, and actively participate in the outcome of those decisions, all of which help them become experts at various levels and increase their desire and competence in the game situation.

References

Blomqvist, M., Luhtanen, P., & Laasko, L. (2000). Expert-novice differences in game performance and game understanding of youth badminton players. *European Journal of Physical Education. 5*(2), 208-219.

Bunker, D. & Thorpe, R. (1982). A model for the teaching of games in the secondary school. *Bulletin of Physical Education. 10,* 9-16.

Butler, J. (1997). How would Socrates teach games? A constructivist approach. *The Journal of Physical Education, Recreation, and Dance. 68*(9), 42-48.

Chandler, T. J. L. (1996). Reflections and further questions. *The Journal of Physical Education, Recreation, and Dance. 67*(4), 49-51.

Griffin, L. (1996). Improving net/wall game performance. *The Journal of Physical Education, Recreation, and Dance. 67*(2). 34-37.

McPherson, S. L. & French, K. E. (1991). Changes in cognitive state and motor skill in tennis. *Journal of Sport and Exercise Psychology. 1,* 26-41.

Rowley, D. A. (1996). *Physical activity through the eyes of six ten-year-old children: A case study.* Unpublished doctoral dissertation, University of Alberta.

Singer, R. N. (1994). A classification scheme for cognitive strategies; implications for learning and teaching psychomotor skills. *Research Quarterly for Exercise and Sport. 65*(2), 143-151.

Strean, W. B. & Holt, N. L. (2000). Players', coaches', and parents' perceptions of fun in youth sports; assumptions about learning and implications for practice. *Avante. 6,* 83-98.

Tenenbaum, G. (1993). Decision making in sport; a cognitive perspective. In R.N. Singer (Ed.), et al. *Handbook of Research on Sport Psychology.* (pp. 171-192). New York: Macmillan.

Thomas, K. (1994). The development of sport expertise; from Leeds to MVP legend. *Quest. 46*(2), 199-210.

Thorpe, R. D., Bunker, D. J., & Almond, L. (1984). A change in the focus of teaching games. In M. Pieron & G. Graham (Eds.), *Sport pedagogy: Olympic Scientific Congress Proceedings, 6,*163-169. Champaign, IL: Human Kinetics.

Turner, A. P., Allison, P. C., & Pissanos, B. W. (2001). Constructing a concept of skillfulness in invasion games within a games for understanding context. *European Journal of Physical Education. 6,* 38-54.

Turner, A. P. & Martinek, T. J. (1999). An investigation into Teaching Games for Understanding; Effects on skill, knowledge, and game play. *Research Quarterly for Exercise and Sport. 70*(3). 286-298.

Vickers, J. N. (1994). Psychological research in sport pedagogy; exploring the reversal effect. *Sport Science Review. 3,* 28-40.

Teaching Invasion Games For Understanding: Game Sense[1] in Field Hockey

Chapter 5

Louisa A. Webb, San Francisco State University, United States

Introduction

[handwritten margin note: comparison made in use in first paragraph]

[handwritten margin note: examples of invasion games]

Conceptually, games can be classified into categories such as invasion games, net/wall games, target games, and striking/fielding games. Invasion games are considered the most tactically complex (Belka, 1994; Werner, Thorpe, & Bunker, 1996). This chapter focuses on the principles of invasion games with field hockey as a specific example. Invasion games—such as hockey, basketball, soccer, and rugby—share the following:

◆ common tactical features of invading territory to make space in attack,

◆ containment of space in defense, and

◆ use of a goal or similar target for scoring. (Kirk & MacPhail, 2002, p. 179)

Wilson (2002) outlines a generic framework of cognitive concepts for invasion games (see Table I). The first step in simplifying the tactical aspects of invasion games is to recognize and understand the similarities among them, as listed above. "These similarities make it possible to identify and describe generic objectives, principles, or themes that govern play, and the tactical decisions that can be applied to all invasive team games" (Wilson, 2002, p. 21). Approaching invasion games from a conceptual perspective simplifies their complexity and also creates a structure that enables sampling, one of the pedagogical principles of Teaching Games for Understanding (TGfU). The principle of sampling suggests that a variety of game experiences can be selected to show similarities among various invasion games (Thorpe & Bunker, 1989; Holt, Strean, & Garcia Bengoechea, 2002, p. 168). Approaching invasion games from a conceptual perspective "provides teachers with the knowledge needed to teach the basic strategy of any invasive game in the physical education curriculum and, most importantly, gives teachers a more global understanding of how games are played" (Wilson, 2002, p. 21).

Wilson's (2002) article provides excellent suggestions for some generic activities to develop students' tactical game knowledge in invasion games. As students develop their abilities, they can also move toward modified versions of invasion games—such as soccer, hockey, basketball, and rugby-to continue the principle of sampling. The aim of this chapter is to provide ideas for the modification of hockey to add to those provided for soccer and basketball (Griffin, Mitchell, & Oslin, 1997; Stevens & Collier, 2001) and rugby (Turner, 2001).

---

[1] Australian Sports Commission. (1997).

The ideas contained in this chapter are based on experience gained through teaching, coaching, and playing hockey. In contrast to a hockey unit plan suggested by Doolittle & Girard (1991), my suggestions focus on possession and advancement aspects of the game of hockey, rather than goal play. My intention is to explore these aspects as a different, yet complementary, component of learning hockey with a TGfU approach. It is my aim for readers to combine the ideas from this chapter with ideas currently available in the literature (Doolittle & Girard, 1991) and by doing so, explore the three objectives of invasion team games (to score points/goals, to retain possession, and to advance) in a hockey unit. This chapter outlines some suggested activities, as well as discussion of issues that arise with the application of TGfU.

It is pertinent at this point to raise one of the issues associated with the application of the TGfU approach. Although there is a growing body of literature on the TGfU approach, there are still many details being negotiated by professionals in the field. The model includes four pedagogical principles of sampling, modification-representation, modification-exaggeration, and tactical complexity (Thorpe & Bunker, 1989; Holt et al., 2002). Sampling and tactical complexity have been referred to previously in this introduction. The principle of modification-representation refers to the way that the modified TGfU game forms represent the adult version of the sport. The principle of modification-exaggeration suggests the use of modified game forms that exaggerate certain aspects of the adult version of the sport to highlight specific tactical concepts. Regarding these two principles of modification-representation and modification-exaggeration, certain issues arise in relation to teaching hockey and what "counts" as TGfU. Associated underlying philosophical questions include "What is a game?" and "How do we differentiate between drills and games?" At either end of the continuum are activities that are very clearly games or drills, but there is a large gray area in the middle. An activity may replicate part of a game context, but it is sometimes hard to discern when the context becomes too narrow to provide understanding. For example, is it essential for the game form to have goals and some concept of scoring to be an appropriate modification-representation of the game of hockey? This is potentially an issue with the first two game forms suggested below. With this in mind, I argue that simple possession games provide one starting point for considering tactics in invasion games, and in hockey in particular. A warm-up and three game forms are described below; issues of application will be revisited at the end of the chapter.

Ideas for Developing Game Sense in Hockey

This section of the chapter outlines five ideas for developing game sense in hockey. The first two ideas provide a possible introduction for a TGfU unit on the invasion game of hockey, including a focus on safety. The other three ideas[2] are game forms for a TGfU unit on hockey. The first game form, Aussie Triangle Hockey, is a modification-representation of hockey without the concepts of goals or scoring. The lack of goals and the 3-vs-1 formation exaggerate the role of attack in maintaining possession. Retaining possession is one of the objectives of attack outlined in Table I. The description of Aussie Triangle Hockey also includes modifications to

---

[2] Acknowledgement for inspiration for some of my ideas are explained in Webb (1995).

make it more complex or less complex. Knowledge of these options allows a teacher to cater for differences in ability within the group while still exploring similar game concepts. The second game form, Crazy Add-On Hockey, provides another progression for a hockey unit. In this game form, each team is larger and the structure of the game allows options for 5-vs-1, 5-vs-2, 5-vs-3, 5-vs-4, or 5-vs-5. The third game form, Go-for-Goal Hockey, is a modification-representation of hockey that includes goals. In the other two game forms, participants score points but not for making a goal. Go-for-Goal Hockey does not specifically emphasize tactics for play around the goal (see instead Doolittle & Girard, 1991), but rather a context of directionality that is suitable for a focus on advancement. This game form is a modified version of hockey with small-sided teams and the same safety restrictions as game forms one and two. All three game forms are described below. Implementation issues for TGfU in the hockey context will be discussed both within the descriptions of the game forms as well as in the conclusion of this chapter.

Introductory Activity

"Touching opposite lines" (McCallum, 1995) is a game that I have found useful for an introductory invasion game lesson. The area for the game depends on the size of the group and whether you are trying to increase the challenge for either the defenders or attackers (modification-exaggeration). One option is a square area, but the game form and decisions can be modified by making the area rectangular. The participants are split into three groups, and at any one time, one of the groups is defending the area. The other two groups work together in attack, attempting to score points by touching any boundary line and then crossing the game area to touch the line directly opposite without being tagged on the way. Attackers are allowed to move around the outside of the boundary and attack from any direction. Each round lasts one minute. At the beginning of each new round, the three groups rotate and the new teams have time to discuss their tactics. Whole-group discussions of the outcomes are useful after each round and at the end of the game. Each attacking and defending team can share the strategies they were attempting and discuss their effectiveness. Other concepts for discussion include defending space, moving into unmarked space (mobility, width), creating overlaps (width), effective perception and deception, overloading defenders' perceptual systems, effective stance for improved perception of defenders, and effective use of skills such as dodging. Questions include: "How could you make it more difficult for the defenders to tag you?" "How could you work better as a team to stop the attackers from scoring?"

Safety with Hockey Stick and Ball, and Other Declarative-knowledge Issues

The next part of the introduction involves familiarization with the stick and ball, and some points about safety. Some teachers are reluctant to teach hockey due to concerns about safety. It is important to have a structure that will address safety concerns. To reduce the possibility of injury from a swinging stick, participants have to keep the stick head on the ground at all times. Therefore, the striking skill to be used is a push pass. The push is one of the striking skills in hockey and the grip is essentially the same as in dribble. Momentum is produced by pushing the ball over space and time—the stick and ball start at, or behind, the rear foot and contact is maintained until the ball passes the front foot. To prevent the ball running up the stick into the face when trapping (receiving), the top of the stick should be held forward from the bottom of the stick. In defense, only interceptions—no tackling or stick contact—are allowed. In agreement with Turner (2001, p. 12) the "contact element of the full-sided game has been virtually removed in order to better facilitate tactical and skill development." These safety suggestions also can be considered as modification-representation and modification-exaggeration game form.

Declarative knowledge in game play includes factual information such as rules. Safety rules should be discussed prior to the game, other rules can be discussed with participants on an as-needed basis. A summary of rules is provided below. One of the issues in the application of a TGfU approach in field hockey relates to rules of stick usage and associated movement-execution constraints. In floor hockey, both sides of the stick can be used to contact the ball, so players can tap the ball from side to side without changing grip. In field hockey, there is a rule that only one side of the stick can be used to contact the ball, so maneuvering the ball involves either moving the feet right around the ball or using a fore-stick and reverse-stick combination called Indian dribble. This is quite a complex fine-motor skill, and so the timing of its incorporation is contentious. Some professionals feel it would be easier for younger participants to use floor hockey sticks and skills as a modification; others feel that the game is fundamentally not a modification-representation of field hockey without the specific nuances of the one-sided stick. An associated issue is the lack of popularity of field hockey in some countries such as the USA. Floor hockey as a modification of ice hockey is more prevalent in the USA. This creates some decisions for the teacher, partly associated with budget. With a limited budget, only floor hockey equipment might be available; however, if the budget is not an issue, teachers could intentionally teach students a new and unfamiliar sport.

Summary of Rules

◆ The bottom of the stick must stay on the ground at all times (push passing only)

◆ No tackling or stick contact (intercept only)

◆ When a player makes an error (ball out of bounds, safety violation) the other team assumes possession of the ball from the place that the error occurred. In addition, the defending team retreats 3 yards from the ball (based on Turner, 2001)

◆ Limited protection of the ball with the body (contrast to basketball)

◆ Optional (see above)—ball can only contact front face of stick

Game Form One: Aussie Triangle Hockey

For Aussie Triangle Hockey, divide the participants into groups of four. Within each group, there should be three attackers and one defender for a 3-vs-1 formation. The aim of the game is to gain or maintain possession, but the exaggerated focus is on maintaining possession. The defender is only allowed to intercept, not tackle. On interception, the defender swaps places with the attacker. A maximum timeframe for the defender and a random rotation can be applied if an interception does not occur within a reasonable time. Different strategic scenarios can be explored through modification-exaggeration of the scoring system. For example, one scoring system could be 1 point for five successful passes and minus 1 point for an interception. An alternative could be 1 point for each pass and minus 10 points for an interception. This will generate a discussion about how players' behavior changes in certain contexts—to become more offensive or more defensive. This is a modification-representation of how hockey players may change their tactics based on the score of the game and the time remaining.

After playing Aussie Triangle Hockey, participants can have the opportunity to change to a more-complex or a less-complex modification. The less-complex modification involves fixing positions around a square area, marked with cones. Attackers start at three of the four cones and the defender works in the middle. Passes are only to be made around the sides of the square, not diagonally across, as this represents an angle of attack that is easily intercepted by the defense. The principle of this modification is that the attacker with the ball must always have an attacker at each adjacent corner of the square so that there are two passing options (in field hockey these are called square and through options). So whenever a pass is made, the third attacker moves to ensure two passing options. This is an example of procedural knowledge in the form of an if-then statement. The cognition of the player would be: "If the ball is passed to the other support player, then I need to move to balance the attack, so the ball carrier has two passing options." This modification-exaggeration focuses on the concept of balance in attack as a subset of the action principle of width (see Table I). Scoring points for passes or interceptions is important for making the activity less like a drill and more like a game. This modification is helpful for participants who might have trouble with the spatial aspects of the original game form and would benefit from the square structure. More complex modifications of Aussie Triangle Hockey include allowing the attackers to move with the ball to introduce the concept of dribbling and playing multiple games of 3-vs-1 within the same large area, so that there is increased pressure on the vision and perception systems.

Questions for discussion of Aussie Triangle Hockey and the modifications include: "What can your team do to maintain possession of the ball?" "How can you score more passing points?" "How can the defenders increase their chance of intercepting the ball?" Concepts include scanning for space, moving into space, deceiving the defender, creating options, changing angles of attack, defending space, and anticipating the attack.

Summary of Aussie Triangle Hockey:

- 3-vs-1 (intercept only)
- Focus on strategic action principles of mobility, advancement, and width
- Rotation on intercept or after 1 or 2 minutes
- Scoring system exaggeration examples
    — 1 point for 5 successful passes, minus 1 point for an intercept
    — 1 point for each pass, minus 10 points for an intercept
- Playing space options
    — Square (e.g., 7-x-7 yards or 10-x-10 yards depending on developmental level)
    — Narrow/wide exaggeration option (e.g., 5-x-10 yards)

Less-complex version:

◆ Simplification of one strategy—always have options on either side of ball carrier
◆ Fix positions around square marked with cones (approximately 5-x-5 yards, depending on developmental level)
◆ Attackers take positions on three of the four cones
◆ Defender starts in middle
◆ As the ball moves (is passed) the nonreceiving player must move (mobility) to balance the attack on both sides of the ball (emphasizing off-the-ball skills)

More-complex version:

◆ Allow dribbling (advancement)
◆ Play multiple 3-vs-1 games in the same space to exaggerate perceptual demands

Game Form Two: Crazy Add-On Hockey

For Crazy Add-On Hockey, the participants form teams of five. In each game, one team of five starts in the defined area (approximately 10-x-10 yards) and will be the attackers in possession of the ball. The attackers are encouraged to stay mobile and communicate with each other. After every minute, one of the defending team players enters the area and tries to intercept the ball. If the attackers maintain possession of the ball, defenders continue to enter the area every minute so that the game progresses from 5-vs-1 to 5-vs-2 and so on, up to 5-vs-5. When the ball is intercepted, the teams change roles. While in attack, teams score points for the number of defenders they have in the area, without losing possession of the ball. Crazy Add-On Hockey continues to develop the game concepts introduced in Aussie Triangle Hockey in a context where players are given time to adjust to increasing pressure. Additional questions include, "How did your game play change as the number of defenders increased?" "What strategies became more important as you got closer to 5-vs-5?"

Game Form Three: Go-for-Goal Hockey

Possession concepts introduced in the first two game forms can be developed further through small-sided games in a rectangular space (e.g., 10-x-12 yards) with goals designated at the ends. Goal options include specified areas (as in hockey or soccer) or dribbling the ball across the baseline in a controlled manner. The presence of goals introduces directionality into the game play, with a focus on advancement, and, in terms of the principle of modification-representation, makes the game form more like the full-sided version of the game. The size and configuration of the small-sided games is flexible. For example, games could be 3-vs-3 or focus on modification-exaggeration with 3-vs-2 or 3-vs-1. The game begins with all players onside, the ball near the middle of the field, and the two teams separated by 3 yards.

In a similar game form, Turner and Martinek (1999, p. 288-89) describe the way this activity can lead to an awareness of passing options (through and square) and also how skill development can be included:

> In Lesson 2 the teacher asked, "What could you do in this situation to help the ball carrier?" The students indicated that the support player should run past the two defenders to receive the pass. The teacher then asked the students, "Is there somewhere that this player doesn't want to be?" The students suggested that positioning directly behind the defender would make receiving a pass very unlikely. A game-related practice, in this instance a 3-vs-1 practice (attacking the end line in a 10-x-10-yard grid), was used to help the students develop a strategy to resolve this predicament. In the second lesson, the teacher then asked the students, "Where else could the receiving player position to assist the passer?" The students indicated that positioning almost square of the passer would provide an opportunity for the passer to set up a give-and-go situation, thereby developing the notion of providing an appropriate angle of support for the passer.
>
> The teacher questioned the ball carrier during the 3-vs-1 practice: "When is a good time to pass the ball while attacking the defender?" The students suggested that if the pass was too early, then the defender had time to get across to the receiver and make a tackle, but if the pass was too late, then the defender would dispossess the attacker. Once the tactic was appropriate, the teacher intervened to teach the skill. In the second lesson, the push pass was taught to the students once they saw the need for it in their games.

Square- and through-passing options make the most sense in a game form that includes a directional context emphasised by goals. Understanding these concepts is enhanced by the progression to Go-for-Goal Hockey from the two previous game forms.

Whereas Aussie Triangle Hockey and Crazy Add-On Hockey are unique variations of activities for teaching hockey in a TGfU unit, Go-for-Goal Hockey is a standard, small-sided game form. There are quite a few good resources that outline teaching ideas for small-sided game forms. The following suggestions are based on Turner (2001):

◆ Draw the defender and pass (3-vs-1)—the ball carrier learns to run toward the defender, the defender has to commit to the ball carrier (or the ball carrier will score), then the ball carrier can slip the pass to either of the supporting players.

◆ Maintain possession—once the participants have experienced scoring success in their 3-vs-1 situations, they should return to their 3-vs-3 games. They will come to understand that an errant, hurried pass that results in an interception will provide the opponents with an excellent scoring opportunity.

◆ Value width on offense—in 3-vs-3 games, participants will see the value of spreading their offense across the field, because it opens up spaces in the defensive line. Furthermore, the ball handler needs to utilize peripheral vision to see the position of teammates in relation to their opponents.

◆ Support play, surprise, and depth—using the tactical concept of width every time can become predictable, so the support players can also utilize surprise and depth.

◆ Include other modifications—the offense can be helped by playing 3-vs-3 plus 1, where an additional neutral player always plays for the team that has possession of the ball, creating an immediate numerical advantage for the offense. An offense can also be awarded an extra point for including a specific tactic that led to a scoring opportunity. Another game modification is to play "walking hockey" (no running is allowed), where tactics and skills other than speed have to be used to deceive the defense.

Summary of Game Concepts

After participating in these game forms over time, students should develop an understanding of the following game concepts (refer to Table I for the action principles and action options).

In attack:

◆ Create as many options as possible to confuse the defender with lots of decisions (width, mobility, advancement, and offensive depth).

◆ Move into space to create a viable option for receiving the ball (mobility, advancement, width, and offensive depth).

◆ Change attack angles according to the position of the defender. Certain angles of attack will be within the defender's reach and the attackers need to take up positions at other angles of attack to create viable options (often square or through).

◆ Deceive the defender with false moves (fakes), disguised moves, or last-minute moves (mobility).

◆ Practice footwork, body fakes, and evasion skills such as dodging (used to evade the defender and move into space) these skills become increasingly important in 3-vs-3 or 5-vs-5 situations (even-sided).

In defense:

◆ Work together for balance or defensive width (expansion), when there is more than one defender.

◆ Position yourself between the ball and the goal (contraction).

◆ Look for cues that will indicate the plan of the attack (perception).

◆ Use footwork to allow you to respond quickly to the attackers' moves (engagement).

◆ Reduce options for the attackers by positioning the body and also by using the environment (e.g., moving them towards sidelines or corners).

Table I. A Generic Framework of Cognitive Concepts for Invasion Team Games

Content Area	Attack		Defend	
Participants and Roles	Offensive Team (possession, attacking) ◆ On-ball attacker ◆ Off-ball attacker		Defensive Team (nonpossession, defending) ◆ On-ball defender ◆ Off-ball defender	
Objectives	◆ Score points, goals ◆ Retain possession ◆ Advance		◆ Prevent points ◆ Regain possession ◆ Prevent advancement	
Action Principles	◆ Mobility ◆ Advancement ◆ Width ◆ Offensive depth		◆ Engagement ◆ Defensive depth ◆ Contraction ◆ Expansion	
Action Options	On-ball Attacker (A1) ◆ Attempt to score ◆ Retain possession ◆ Pass	Off-ball Attackers ◆ Provide depth ◆ Provide width ◆ Advance ◆ Move	On-ball Defender ◆ Prevent scoring ◆ Dispossess A1 ◆ Contain A1 ◆ Channel A1	Off-ball Defenders ◆ Provide defensive depth ◆ Contract ◆ Expand

Wilson, G. E. (2002).

Conclusion

The focus of this chapter was the invasion game objectives of possession and advancement. Two of the suggested game forms exaggerated possession and the third game form exaggerated advancement. Issues were raised that professionals would have to address when choosing a sampling focus on hockey, such as rules regarding stick usage. Two of the suggested game forms did not include goals, and this was raised as a modification-representation issue. This would be a pertinent area for further research. At one end of the scale, Brooker, Kirk, Braiuka, and Bransgrove (2000) found that for children whose prior knowledge of sports was formed through their viewing of professional adult sport on television, any modification was considered to be disappointing and unsatisfying. In contrast, participants in initial stages of TGfU units have expressed that they feel comfortable in possession games, but game forms that included goals put too much pressure on them to execute proficient skills before they had a chance to be develop the skills. These questions still remain:

◆ Is the best form of TGfU game form a small-sided version of a full game with goals?

◆ Does the development of possession skills and strategies always require a directional context?

◆ Is direction essential to ensuring that understanding is transferred to the full-sized game?

◆ Would it be appropriate to begin with possession games and then progress to a game with goals, or does this not qualify as TGfU?

◆ In other words, do the possession games suffer from the same lack of context as traditional drills?

These questions are relevant across most invasion games. Within the group of professionals interested in TGfU, there are broad-ranging opinions and this is an area worth further discussion and research.

References

Australian Sports Commission. (1997). *Games sense: Developing thinking players.* Belconnen, Australian Capital Territory: Author. ***QU: not cited in text-remove?

Belka, D. (1994). *Teaching children games.* Champaign, IL: Human Kinetics.

Brooker, R., Kirk, D., Braiuka, S., & Bransgrove, A. (2000). Implementing a game sense approach to teaching junior high school basketball in a naturalistic setting. *European Physical Education Review, 6*(1), 7-26.

Doolittle, S. A. & Girard, K. T. (1991). A dynamic approach to teaching games in elementary PE. *Journal of Physical Education, Recreation, and Dance, 62*(2), 57-62.

Griffin, L. L., Mitchell, S. A., & Oslin, J. L. (1997). *Teaching sport concepts and skills: A tactical games approach.* Champaign, IL: Human Kinetics.

Holt, N. L., Strean, W. B., & Garcia Bengoechea, E. (2002). Expanding the teaching games for understanding model: New avenues for future research and practice. *Journal of Teaching Physical Education, 21* (2), 162-176.

Kirk, D. & MacPhail, A. (2002). Teaching games for understanding and situated learning: Rethinking the Bunker-Thorpe model. *Journal of Teaching in Physical Education, 21* (2), 177-192.

McCallum, J. (1995). Success in sport: Doing the right thing, in the right place, at the right time. *Aussie Sport Action, 6*(2), 24-25.

Stevens, P. & Collier, C. (2001). Shooting hoops: WallTar as an alternative. *Teaching Elementary Physical Education, 12* (1), 17-19.

Thorpe, R. & Bunker, D. (1989). A changing focus in games teaching. In L. Almond (Ed). *The place of physical education in schools.* London, GB: Kogan Page.

Turner, A. P. (2001). Touch rugby: A tactical twist. *Teaching Elementary Physical Education, 12* (1), 12-16.

Turner, A. P. & Martinek, T. J. (1999). An investigation into teaching games for understanding: Effects on skill, knowledge, and game play. *Research Quarterly for Exercise and Sport, 70* (3), 268-296.

Webb, L. (1995). A few suggestions for PE teachers. *ACHPER Action,* November, 18-19.

Werner, P., Thorpe, R., & Bunker, D. (1996). Teaching games for understanding: Evolution of a model. *Journal of Physical Education, Recreation, and Dance, 67*(1), 28-33.

Wilson, G. E. (2002). A framework for teaching tactical game knowledge. *Journal of Physical Education, Recreation, and Dance, 73* (1), 20-26 & 56.

Teachers' Experiences Using TGfU: Near and Far

Introduction to Chapters 6-10

In this section, the authors made efforts to study TGfU concepts and curriculum in an applied setting. Research with teachers in their classroom implementing TGfU helps move TGfU toward a more research-based practice model. It is important that researchers value the meaning teachers make of TGfU and they explore teachers' successes and challenges with the model.

In Chapter 6, Richard Light, from the University of Melbourne, heads this section and reports on a two-year study in which he examines the experiences of preservice, generalist primary school teachers with TGfU. Many students came to the study with a negative view of games teaching and physical activity. Light's results indicate a shift in their perception. Light attributes their receptiveness and generally positive response to the TGfU approach to the extent to which students were committed to teaching games and the very essence of TGfU itself.

In Chapter 7, Barbara McCahan et al. provide readers with a rather unique application of the TGfU curriculum. McCahan and the students at Plymouth State College reflect upon the TGfU Club formed in 1995, its influence on their pedagogical growth and efforts to mentor underclass students. The outcomes as described are diverse, multifaceted, and student-centered and all have been influenced by the constructivist thinking inherent in TGfU. The various and unique applications of the TGfU approach, beyond the typical physical education program impact on games instruction, should prove fascinating to all educators. Whether analyzing the effects of constructivist thinking on teaching, learning, and professionalism, or reflecting on the physical education curriculum and preservice professional development, the interpretations of the club members provide readers with a multitude of possibilities for the application of TGfU in a wide array of settings.

In Chapter 8, Amandio Graca and Isabel Mesquita examine the conceptions of 16 preservice teachers for teaching sport games in school settings to determine the effects of the recent movement to TGfU curriculum models in Portugal. Results, while not surprising, reiterate the oft-repeated theme that changing teachers' beliefs is difficult. A short-term learning experience may not be enough to effect change to the more-conceptual TGfU curriculum.

The next two articles are similar, since they attempt to ascertain specific outcomes emanating from the experiences of preservice teachers with TGfU. First, in Chapter 9, Eileen Sullivan (USA) and Karen Swabey (Australia) conduct a cross-cultural study in which preservice teachers were assessed on their teaching effectiveness and the scope of TGfU practices. They found that the TGfU approach can help teachers become more effective in a variety of ways and enhance learners' engagement, both reflectively and conceptually. Finally, in Chapter 10, Shelley Sweeney, Amy Everitt, and James Carifio attempt to ascertain changes in attitude and understanding of the TGfU approach. They interviewed a small group of undergraduate students both before and after completing an activity-based TGfU course. General findings indicated an intriguing relationship between students' desire for control and their attitudes toward TGfU. The investigators plan to continue their work and to focus on students' specific level of knowledge about TGfU and its interaction with unique characteristics of future movement educators.

All chapters should prove interesting to the reader, professional, and pre-professional alike. More importantly, however, the works briefly reviewed in this implementation section should help professionals gain information and build an agenda for future analysis and review.

Preservice Primary Teachers' Responses to TGfU in an Australian University: "No Room for Heroes"

Chapter 6

Richard Light, University of Melbourne, Australia

Introduction

There has been growing interest in the application of learning theory to sport and physical education over the past decade (Kirk & Macdonald, 1998; Rink, 2001; Kirk, Brooker, & Braiuka, 2000). Despite this development, the dominant approach adopted by physical education teachers continues to draw on what Kirk and Claxton (1999) describe as "antiquated" skill-acquisition theory to focus on the development of technical proficiency in sport skills. As they suggest, it is indeed "astonishing" and disappointing that promising and innovative ideas such as TGfU have met such resistance in schools. Two decades after Bunker and Thorpe (1983) first published their TGfU (Teaching Games for Understanding) model, and despite several efforts to promote it in Australia, it has yet to make a significant impact on the teaching of games in schools. Butler (1996) argues that if we are to succeed in initiating change in schools, we need to listen to teachers' concerns about innovative approaches such as TGfU and the ways in which they challenge their existing beliefs and conceptions of physical education teaching. The research on Physical Education Teacher Education (PETE) socialization (Armour & Jones, 1998; Dewar, 1989; Macdonald & Tinning, 1995) suggests we also need to consider the values and attitudes toward learning in physical education that preservice teachers bring with them. This needs to include generalist primary school teachers and they bring quite different dispositions toward the teaching of physical education and sport than PETE students typically do. If teacher education programs encourage change in the way physical education is taught in schools then we need to better understand the ways in which the beliefs, attitudes, and personal histories of engagement in physical culture, which preservice teachers bring with them, shape their responses to innovative approaches such as TGfU.

Focused on preservice generalist primary school teachers' responses to TGfU in an Australian teacher eduction program, this paper examines the ways in which their prior experiences of, and dispositions toward, physical activity shaped their responses. Unlike typical PETE students, many brought with them negative attitudes toward sport and physical education and indicated that they did not intend to teach games or sport on a regular basis as practicing teachers. However, their responses to TGfU were generally very positive and made a significant impact on their inclination to teach games and how they would teach them. This was very much related to their own subjective experiences of the TGfU unit and the extent to which they were wholly engaged in games—cognitively, physically, and socially.

...od, and Procedure

...search reported in this chapter—conducted over two years at a leading research ...sity in Australia—forms part of an ongoing, longitudinal study. It is focused on ...er-education students in their second year of a four-year undergraduate Bachelor ...ucation degree in which health and physical education was a single, 36-hour ...ulsory subject in the first two years of the degree. It was offered as an option ... the latter two years of the degree. Academic requirements for entry into the program were relatively high. Data were generated from questionnaires, in-depth interviews, and observation. The semester began with a two-week unit of work on teaching athletics, using a conceptual approach, which was followed by a four-week TGfU unit covering one major game per week. There was only one formal lecture on the conceptual approach used in the athletics and games classes. The games taught were basketball, field hockey, kanga cricket, and volleyball. Educators got a broad picture of the student participants by reviewing the 152 questionnaires that students completed before and after the TGfU unit. Following the first questionnaire, 20 students were chosen at random each year and asked to take part in in-depth, semi-structured interviews. The interviews were conducted during and after the TGfU unit.

Social Analyses of Physical Activity

Building on the work of Apple (1979), Kirk (1999) argues that meaningful social analyses of physical education view the subject as a particular form of social activity, which takes place within larger institutional arrangements and social contexts. This suggests that meaningful analyses of physical activity, such as learning in games, need to account for the situated nature of learning and the interaction between social dynamics such as gender, class, and culture. Kirk (1999) suggests that recovering the term "physical culture" would help us believe that physical education is intimately related to other social phenomena and recognize it as a social practice. However, much research in the physical education field continues to focus only on the development of psycho-motor competencies. Rather than highlighting the complexities of learning, this research tends to be simplistic and one-dimensional (Kirk, 1999). Such approaches fail to adequately consider the social, cultural, and institutional contexts within which physical education is practiced and where learning takes place. They also neglect to focus on the ways in which the knowledge and dispositions that learners bring with them impacts learning.

Griffin and Placek (2001) suggest that teacher educators need to consider the knowledge that students bring with them and the way that they apply this to learning. The following section outlines not only the knowledge, but also the attitudes, the embodied histories of engagement in physical culture, which preservice teachers brought to games classes that use the TGfU approach. It then examines the ways in which this prior knowledge and sets of dispositions shaped students' experience of TGfU and their responses to it. In particular, it looks at the impact of TGfU on their intentions to teach games as practicing teachers, their views on the educational value of games, and the pedagogy they intended to adopt.

Dispositions to, and Prior Experience of, Games

As the work of Lortie (1975) suggests, teacher education students' schooling experiences are central to their decision to become teachers and in the development of their beliefs and values in relation to education. While there is a body of literature on PETE socialization, little such research has been conducted on generalist primary teachers and their attitudes to physical education. In Australia, these teachers deliver much of the primary-school physical education. Preservice primary school teachers are not socialized into the same "subjective warrant" (Dewar & Lawson, 1984) that PETE students typically are. For the student teachers in this study, whose experiences of sport and other physical activity were more varied, health and physical education comprised only one, 36-hour-per-semester subject and they were exposed to constructivist approaches to learning in other subject areas such as mathematics education, science education, and literacy. They were predominantly female (82%) with 91% of the participants between the ages of 18 and 21. A quarter of the students reported not enjoying sport and physical education at school, 15% had a negative attitude toward sport and 29% were not involved in sport while at university. Their own experiences of games and sport at school emerged as the most significant factor in their disinclination to teach games and sport as practicing primary-school teachers. Prior to the TGfU unit, only 56% of students indicated that they intended to teach games and sport regularly in their classes.

PETE students entering the gym typically display physical confidence and enthusiasm and, at times, a touch of arrogance. While a considerable number of students in this study also approached the games unit with enthusiasm, others were ambivalent, some were apprehensive. Their experiences of physical education were embodied in movements and postures. With slumped shoulders and a limited occupation of space, they milled at the back of the gym in small, supporting groups. When given the chance, many were quick to articulate their anxiety:

> *I hated PE at school, I was never any good at sport and I was always* last picked for teams, and always humiliated by the PE teachers. I really *tried to think of a way out of the sport classes...There wasn't really* any way out. ("Anna," 19)

Unlike those students who entered the gym and immediately wanted to start shooting baskets, a large number of students arrived late, some of the females were dressed in tight jeans and platform shoes. The clothing and body language made it clear that they were not looking forward to the games class. Subsequent interviews indicated that they saw little value in physical education and had little intention of teaching it on a regular basis. Their own negative experiences of physical education at school emerged as the primary reason for their disinclination to teach physical education. It was not only the female students that had been alienated from physical education, as "Marco" makes clear:

> *For me, physical education was boring and unfulfilling. I was never* really athletic and was not interested in sport...the bigger and more active students always dominated. I'd be walking around the outskirts of the court or the sports field being ignored while the main action was taking place on the other side. ("Marco," 21)

Ennis (1999) argues that team sports taught using a traditional approach allow confident and aggressive males to dominate games and to marginalize girls and the less-skilled, less-aggressive boys. Many of the females' personal accounts of physical education at school confirmed this. While there were some who enjoyed sport and physical education, a significant number described their experiences as being unsatisfying, intimidating, and even humiliating. Many of the females who did not enjoy physical education at school specifically outlined the ways in which they had been intimidated by large, aggressive boys who dominated activities and by teachers' stress on performance as the most significant factor contributing to their dislike of physical education:

> The bigger boys in the class would just take over and push us out of the way and the teacher wouldn't do anything. They'd be showing off to their mates and trying to be real heroes and most of the girls would just give up. (Jasmine, 20)

Interviews indicated that for many students, their experience of physical education at school significantly shaped their view of its place in the curriculum and their intention, or otherwise, to include games or other physical activity in their teaching.

Experiences of TGfU as Students: Engaging Mind and Body

There were five students who had been exposed to TGfU at school, but for the other students, their introduction to TGfU began with a two-hour session on basketball that I taught. I could feel the enthusiasm develop during the session as the students who initially had been so reluctant began to engage in the activities. They began to move, to look around, to talk, and to think. As the class progressed, they became more animated, more physically active, and increasingly prepared to contribute to the team discussions on tactics. These students were not just participating but were increasingly engaged in the games. The subsequent interviews confirmed my observations and my sense of their increased engagement:

> I was really surprised how much fun I had. I'm not exactly the most skillful person in the world, but this way of teaching sport lets you get involved mentally. TGfU showed me how to use my intelligence. I was no longer beaten before the game started. I am still not that great at throwing or catching the ball properly all the time, though these skills did improve. Rather, I had more chance of placing it strategically in defense or in attack. ...learning basketball this way gave me a feeling of achievement and satisfaction that I have never experienced in sport. (Katherine, 19).

The majority of the students interviewed related their enjoyment of the TGfU unit to their cognitive engagement in the game. They noted the ways in which the emphasis on the tactical dimensions of games allowed them to understand the game and to be involved as a valued member of the team. This was perhaps most noticeable in the session on kanga cricket, a modified form of cricket. As is the case with most physical education classes, there was considerable disparity in skill levels, experience, and enthusiasm for sport-related activities. Some of the males in the class played cricket previously and were highly skilled, yet many of the girls

saw cricket as a "guys' game" and knew little about it. Despite th
ability, the class's growing game awareness and inclination to eng
discussions meant that they were inclined to try and meet such c
more-skilled cricketers said that the emphasis on tactics and colle
solving kept them interested. The less-able and less-enthusiastic
degrees, able to compensate for a lack of skill through their cogni
and their contribution to the development of tactics and strategies.

> I had no interest in cricket and can't play it at all. No skills. Before the
> cricket workshop I was sure it would be really boring, but after the
> lesson I found that I enjoyed it. This session was different. The little
> team conferences made your opinion valued, not just the skillful
> players. It was empowering to be allowed to decide as a team what
> our strategies would be, as opposed being told what to do by the
> teacher. (Kim, 19).

Questionnaires indicated that all but 11% of the students enjoyed their introduction
to TGfU. This translated into a significant increase in students who intended to include
games in their teaching. While 56% intended to make games a regular part of their
teaching prior to the TGfU unit, 76% intended to do so following it, 20% intended
to teach games occasionally and 4% did not intend to teach games at all. While
there was a significant shift in intention to teach among those who had intended to
teach games only occasionally before the TGfU unit, those who did not intend to
teach games at all proved more intransigent. The students interviewed from this
group brought with them strong and deeply embedded attitudes to physical activity
that were largely unrelated to the consideration of educational value. The few
students interviewed who were determined not to teach games or sport were all
female. Some of them spoke of their dislike of getting "sweaty and smelly" from
exercise and physical effort. Culture seemed to play a significant part in the negative
attitudes that several of the females in this group expressed and displayed. They
were from Southeast Asian cultures and said that during their schooling they were
actively discouraged from physical exertion. While many students enjoyed the social
interaction involved in collective problem solving, the effect of culture made one
student's experience quite different. "Amy" said that she would have enjoyed the
verbal and physical interaction had the others been relatives or friends. She did not
like interacting with people who were not "close" to her. These students' culture
and their life experiences of physical culture were clearly central to their disinclination
to teach physical activity as practicing teachers. The data also suggests that the
strong predispositions toward physical education that they brought with them
profoundly shaped their experiences of TGfU and their disinclination to teach games.

When the students were asked about the strengths, if any, of TGfU, most emphasized
its propensity to engage learners of all levels and to make all students feel valued:

> I think the main strength of TGfU in schools is that children don't
> need to have any particular ability in the sport, or knowledge. But,
> they are still all included. Everyone is actively participating. After
> seeing the way that TGfU works, I feel much more confident in my
> ability to teach sport. (Anthony, 20)

This, I suggest, reflects the students' own experiences of TGfU, and for many of them, the way in which it addresses their own negative experiences of games and sport at school. For many of them, their understanding of the TGfU approach to include learners of differing competency arose from their own subjective experience of the TGfU unit:

> This is just the best way to teach games. Everybody's included and there is no room for heroes. I've experienced it, and it works. I told many people about it. The only thing wrong with TGfU is that it wasn't around when I was at school. (Christine, 20)

Experiences of TGfU as Teachers

Students who taught physical education after they participated in the TGfU unit generally reported some concern and even resistance from teachers. These teachers expressed concern with the lack of attention to skill development, and this was most pronounced with teachers who specialize in health and physical education. A few students did, however, report positive experiences of teaching TGfU and of supportive teachers. Many of these teachers recognize the student-centered, constructivist approach used as the same that they used in their classroom teaching.

While not necessarily representative of the group, there were three interesting accounts of teaching games in three distinctly different settings. All three student teachers had some problems implementing TGfU, but reported being very satisfied with the experience. "Jane" decided to take up the challenge of teaching an unfamiliar game by teaching Australian football at a school in Chicago. Although her students knew nothing of Australian football, she found that they were able to apply their knowledge of other games, soccer in particular, with enthusiasm. She was very pleased with, and encouraged by, her first attempt at using TGfU. Her supervising teacher was very supportive.

"Mary" taught touch rugby in a remote aboriginal community in South Australia. She described her teaching as successful because the students were engaged and playing cooperatively. Only two of her students had ever seen rugby and they were more familiar with Australian football and soccer. She found that, although they were limited in their ability to articulate their knowledge, they exhibited great understanding in the way they played:

> Their skill level is really high but their explanation of tactics and decision-making through the English language was limited. I had to use demonstrations instead of explanations. Only a few could explain decisions in English, but they showed really good understanding when they actually played the games. They react better to visual clues. (Mary, 20)

Mary reported that students' limited command of English restricted their ability to articulate an understanding of the tactical dimensions of play, what Thomas and Thomas (1994) refer to as declarative knowledge. They were, however, able to display a considerable mastery of the games in practice. The performance of indigenous players at the elite level of Australian football or rugby is typically distinguished by uncanny "vision" and anticipation. Rugby's famous Ella brothers were said to have a "supernatural ability to anticipate each other" (Tatz, 1987, p. 91). This may suggest that Mary's indigenous students learned and displayed understanding in ways that were culture specific, I would suggest that this is something that needs to be considered in future research on TGfU and learning in games.

"Dianne" was placed in a metropolitan primary school in Melbourne and asked to coach netball. The other coach was a state netball player and was having trouble getting enough girls to participate. Normal training was very much focused on technique and included passing up to hundred times and punishment for dropped balls. Dianne tried to follow this approach but had the same problem of low attendance. She decided to try TGfU and found that she had more than enough for two teams within a week:

> I stopped the game a number of times and asked questions, which involved the girls suggesting different strategies. Students tried out different positions, had fun, practiced skills within a game, talked a lot about strategies, and made their own decisions and experimented with these. The girls asked if we were going to do the same sort of thing for the next training session and I said yes. The next session, I had two whole teams. It really was successful and the girls enjoyed it and continued to turn up and have fun. (Dianne, 20)

Responses from those student teachers who had the inclination and opportunity to implement TGfU during their teaching experiences, indicated that they felt their first attempts had been successful. While few of them considered learning in their assessment, most judged success in terms of student participation, enjoyment, and the extent to which TGfU engaged all learners. Significantly, most felt comfortable taking a TGfU approach and saw it as a way of delivering student-centered learning in physical education.

Discussion

Kirk (2001) contends that resistance to TGfU is particularly evident among primary school generalist teachers. He suggests that this is largely due to their lack of experience and competence as game players. On the other hand, this study indicates that the preservice primary school teachers involved seemed more amenable to the TGfU approach than we might typically expect PETE students to be. The data suggests that this might be due to a personal realization of its educational worth and the provision of a methodology through which this might be realized. Although some successfully taught using TGfU, the teachers have yet to negotiate the difficulties that arise from adopting innovation as beginning teachers and the resistance they are likely to meet. The relatively short duration of the students' exposure to a constructivist approach to physical education teaching is also a limiting factor in drawing conclusions from this study. As an ongoing, longitudinal study, this research will ideally provide more insight into this issue. These differences may also point to the need to account for cultural and institutional differences in such studies. The Southeast Asian cultural background of some of the girls in this study and the responses of Mary's aboriginal students to TGfU certainly indicate that culture is an important factor. As the work of Lave and

Wegner (1991) suggests, learning is deeply situated in cultural and social contexts. Certainly culture emerged as a significant factor for some students in this study.

The generally positive responses of the student teachers to TGfU are clearly linked to their subjective experience of, and engagement in, the games played in the unit. For many, this was also intimately tied to their personal experience with physical activity in schools. While the majority of students pinpointed the inclusive nature of TGfU as its greatest strength, the data suggests that the ways in which the TGfU approach highlights the cognitive dimensions of play was central to student enjoyment of, and engagement in, games. Emphasizing the cognitive aspects of games facilitated social interaction through group discussion and collective problem solving. It also encouraged increased movement due to the motivation that this generated.

As Griffin and Placek (2001) argue, it is important that, as teachers or teacher educators, we understand the knowledge students bring to the gymnasium or field. Educators need to be aware of the ways in which the knowledge that learners bring with them is organized and applied to learning in new situations, and the ways in which their prior experiences shape this. I would suggest that this is equally important in the preparation of preservice teachers. This study's future teachers' conceptions of physical education, their experiences of it, and the knowledge that they brought into the TGfU unit, were of pivotal importance in their interpretation of the experience. In the case of the generalist primary teachers in this study, it is not only a question of influencing what pedagogy they might adopt in teaching physical education but also whether or not they teach it at all. There is now evidence of a move for a back-to-basics approach to education in Australia. As a reaction to an increasingly crowded curriculum, the Minister for Education in the state of Victoria recently raised the possibility of dropping the requirement for compulsory hours of sport and physical education in schools.

The TGfU approach provided a more wholly engaging and appealing learning experience for the students involved. Most of them felt more inclined to teach games regularly as a result of their own games experience in the unit. After listening to young men and women talk and reading over transcripts, it struck me how personal many of their experiences of games seemed to be. Some who had been "humiliated" at school and found physical education "boring" and "unfulfilling" spoke of being "liberated," "empowered," and of feeling a sense of "achievement and satisfaction." Others were surprised to discover the thinking involved in playing games and the way in which this made games interesting. As one student teacher said in an interview, "I was really surprised how much you had to think in games." Student teacher responses to TGfU indicate that, given appropriate pedagogy, games can simultaneously develop cognitive, social, and physical learning. This seemed central to their understanding of TGfU and their positive responses to it. This encourages a more holistic view of learning in games.

Kirk, Brooker, and Braiuka (2000) and others have argued that cognitive function and physical action are intimately interrelated and this represents long-overdue recognition that skill execution cannot be separated from decision-making and perception. I would take this a little further to suggest that, indeed, thinking in games is not separate from action or the body's movement in games. Action is not so much a product of thought nor thought a product of action because thought is bodily action. As Ilyenkov (1976) suggests, thinking is action considered at the moment of its performance, thought is not structured only in a "mind" that is somehow separate from the body (Merleau-Ponty, 1962). Such a view illuminates the potential that games hold for learning and encourages a more holistic conception of people's engagement in games. Engagement in games can offer students, not only ways of acting and thinking, but also ways of being. The TGfU approach to games teaching allows the teacher to create the context within which such cognition can occur and to see games as an indissoluble blend of thought and action.

References

Apple, M. (1979). *Ideology and Curriculum.* London: Routledge and Kegan Paul.

Armour, K. & Jones, R. (1998). *Physical Education Teachers Lives and Careers.* London: Falmer Press.

Bunker, D. & Thorpe, R. (1983). A model for the teaching of games in secondary schools. *Bulletin of Physical Education, 19,* 5-8.

Butler, J. (1996). Teacher responses to teaching games for understanding, *Journal of Physical Education, Recreation, and Dance, 67(1),* 28-33.

Dewar, A. (1989). Recruitment in physical education teaching: Toward a critical approach. In T. Templin & P. Schempp (Eds.), *Socialization into physical education: Learning to Teach* (pp. 39-58). Indianapolis: Benchmark Press.

Dewar, A. & Lawson, H. (1984). The subjective warrant and recruitment into physical education. *Quest, 36,* 15-25.

Ennis. C. (1999). Creating a culturally relevant curriculum for disengaged girls. *Sport, Education and Society, 4(1),* 31-50.

Griffin, L. & Placek, J. (2001). The understanding and development of learners domain-specific knowledge: Introduction. *Journal of Teaching in Physical Education, 20* (4), 299-300.

Ilyenkov, E. (1976). *Dialectical logic: Essays in its history and theory.* Moscow: Progress Publishers.

Kirk, D. (1999). Physical culture, physical education and relational analysis. *Sport, Education and Society, 4*(1), 63-73.

Kirk, D. (2001, August). Future prospects and directions for TGfU. Paper presented at international conference: Teaching for Understanding in Physical Education and Sport, New Hampshire, USA.

Kirk, D., Brooker, R., & Braiuka, S. (2000). Teaching games for understanding: A situated perspective on student learning. Paper presented at the meeting of the American Educational Research Association, New Orleans.

Kirk, D. & Claxton, C. (1999). Learning, excellence and gender: Promoting girls' participation in physical education and sport. Paper presented at the BAALPE Annual Conference, University of Wales Institute, Cardiff, July 1999.

Kirk, D. & Macdonald, D. (1998). Situated learning in physical education. *Journal of Teaching in Physical Education, 17,* 376-387.

Lave, J. and Wenger, E. (1991). *Situated learning: Legitimate Peripheral Participation,* New York: Cambridge University Press.

Lortie, D. (1975). *Schoolteacher: A Sociological Study.* Chicago: University of Chicago Press.

Macdonald, D. & Tinning, R. (1995). Physical education teacher education and the trend to proletianization: A case study. *Journal of Teaching in Physical Education, 15,* 98-118.

Merleau-Ponty, M. (1962). *Phenomenology of Perception.* London, Routledge.

Rink, J. (2001). Investigating the assumptions of pedagogy. *Journal of Teaching in Physical Education, 20,* 112-128.

Tatz, C. (1987). *Aborigines in Sport.* Adelaide, South Australia: The Australian Society for Sports History.

Thomas, K & Thomas, J. (1994). Developing expertise in sport: the relation of knowledge and performance, *International Journal of Sports Psychology,25* (3), 295-312.

A Constructivist Approach to a Major's Club: Helping P.E.T.E. Students Transition to Professionals

Chapter 7

Barbara McCahan, Shawn Croteau, Laura Liard, Elizabeth Ballard,

Chad Mitchell, Laurie Murphy, Joy Butler

INTRODUCTION

In response to the challenges in higher education today, the strategic plan at Plymouth State College, NH, focuses on four themes: student success and satisfaction, academic vitality, community consciousness, and effective use of resources. The college's efforts of faculty, departments, and the administration are now working to nurture activities that support these themes. The formation and support of majors' clubs is such an activity. The Department of Health, Physical Education, and Recreation hosts several such clubs with the goal of helping students make connections between curricular and co-curricular activities to support students' experiential learning and their development as practitioners.

The purpose of this chapter is to demonstrate the effectiveness of one major's club in the professional development of several future Physical Education teachers. The following is a discussion by a group of students from the Teaching for Understanding Club, which was founded by faculty member Joy Butler in 1995 to enable Physical Education Teacher Education (PETE) students to discuss constructivism in teaching outside the classroom.

The club provides a forum for students to participate in academic discussions with faculty and peers, to experiment with the application of theory in real-life teaching situations, and to develop professional presentations. The club allows students to compare and contrast various teaching models for movement and games education in a safe, supportive setting. Many of the meetings are open discussions using the democratic process and Roberts' Rules of Order. Others are activity sessions where students test different teaching styles and models. The club also organizes service-learning outings that provide opportunities to practice teaching children outside the context of the curriculum. In the early years, the TfU Club implemented several after-school events with community children and groups (such as the local Boy Scouts) for games and educational gymnastics. Later, a more formal, ongoing program was developed (the proceeds are dedicated to helping the club finance travel to conferences). The club's activities have blossomed to include participation and presentations at local, regional, national, and international conferences. Presentations have included both practical and theoretical sessions based on their work as a club, including: *"Danish Longball—An Introduction to Striking Games," "Turning Students On To Games," "Teaching Territorial Games," "Academic Majors' Club: Strategies for Success, Start Up, Development, and Professional Benefits,"* and *"A Constructivist Approach to a Majors' Club: Helping PETE Students to Transition to Professionals."* Additionally, the executive members have presented panel discussions and lecture sessions at Eastern District Association meetings in Philadelphia and at the AAHPERD Annual Meetings in Boston, MA; Cincinnati, OH; and San Diego, CA. These presentations were group efforts, with guidance from the faculty advisors and balanced participation among presenters.

It is noteworthy that the threads of constructivist philosophy are woven throughout the fabric of the club's structure and evolution. All students, on their own developmental path, are building their own meaning and broadening their understanding of professionalism. Connections are made between motor learning and development, biomechanics, physiology, and concept-based teaching while performing and planning club activities. As young professionals, they are also learning the value of academic discourse, mutual respect, and mentoring to build a legacy and share knowledge. The following are the students' own reflections on the benefits of club participation in their development from students to professionals.

Student Reflections

Constructivism (Elizabeth Ballard—Teacher Certified December 2002)

I was first introduced to constructivism in my second-year physical education classes. I initially struggled with the concept of constructivism. It was not until I joined the TfU club and watched as more experienced students tried different teaching approaches that I started to grasp the abstract concept.

My definition of constructivism now includes the concepts of 1) facilitating active learning, 2) sharing ideas in a safe environment, 3) building meaning from experiences, and 4) questioning "why?" I summarize my personal definition with the quote *"Give a man a fish and he will eat for a day. Teach a man to fish and he will eat for life."* My approach to teaching has been permanently impacted by my participation with the TfU club.

So how does constructivism apply to our club? First, the club was founded on the principles of democracy and inclusion. Secondly, it is adaptable to the interests and needs of its members. Third, connections develop between theory learned in the classroom and practical application and discussion. Additionally, our mentoring system gives us a chance to truly learn through the process of helping others to learn.

We have identified four general areas of club activities that support our transition from students to professionals. These are: 1) comparing learning theories and teaching models, 2) making academic and curricular decisions, 3) testing different teaching styles, and 4) discussing assessment methods. The papers that follow will discuss some of these areas and others including growth areas for PETE students and professional development.

Learning Theories and Teaching Models (Laura Liard—Teacher Certified)

My thoughts about the influences of the TfU club activities on my transition to professionalism are centered on our discussions and activities comparing *learning theories and teaching models.* As undergraduate PETE students, we struggle with understanding the variety of teaching and learning theories presented to us. We have our own experiences from the PE classes and athletics of our elementary and high school years, and we have found ways to reconcile these two perspectives. Many of us have been in athletics for years and were "brought up" with teaching and coaching that was mainly "product-oriented" and teacher-centered. Our philosophical discussions in the club often deal directly with these "Behaviorist versus Constructivist" issues. As constructivists, we look at, and work, with the contrasts between these general theories. The following lists summarize some of the features of behaviorists and constructivists:

Behaviorist
- Teacher-centered instruction
- Learning "how-to" but not "why"
- Product orientation
- Passive, restricted learning

Constructivist
- Student-centered instruction
- Taking ownership of learning and knowledge
- Process orientation
- Creative, interest-directed learning

Since most of us had so much first-hand experience with the behaviorist approach in our younger years, it has been challenging to work with the constructivist processes in the club activities. We have been challenged to let go of some of our habitual behaviors and try new ways of doing. Each part of the learning process has required thinking about how we were taught, what we are setting out to do in our classes, and curriculum and how we can best accomplish it.

Making Academic and Curricular Decisions (Shawn Croteau—Teacher Certified 2001)

In the TfU club, we not only discuss *how* we are going to teach, but also *what* we are going to teach. The discussions and teaching activities of the club help each of us to formulate our own personal teaching philosophies. This, in turn, gives us a basis for evaluating the priorities that we feel need to be set in a curriculum. In the after-school programs for example, we have a chance to mesh our philosophy with the interests and needs of our students, helping us to decide what concepts and skills we cover and how these are to be addressed. These are curricular decisions.

Reflecting on my high school physical education experience back in 1976-81, I can now see that my teacher was, for whatever reasons, the stereotypical "gym" teacher. He always stayed within his comfort zone, often "rolled out the ball," had a *laissez-faire* attitude, avoided conflict, and thought he was doing his job by keeping the students "happy." Territorial games constituted the majority of the curriculum and tended to exclude the less-skilled players. In contrast, I visited the same school 20 years later as a PETE student and noted an incredible difference. The new PE teachers, gung-ho on health and fitness, offered a curriculum that included classes such as Fitness for Life, CPR, First Aid, and Weight Training. Games represented less that half the curriculum and there was a general attitude that there is insufficient

(2001)

…ch skills and that the students "didn't want to do drills anyway." Their … was simply to keep the students active.

… one thing that I have learned from my participation with the TfU club, it is …ents of all ages dislike drills if they are without a context of understanding …e drills are either too challenging or not challenging enough. Students want to …t mostly they want to be successful in meeting challenges set before them.

In our after-school club programs, we applied constructivism at several levels. We used a modification of the classification system first published by Bunker and Thorpe (1982) to organize a games curriculum. We then incorporated a systematic introduction of concepts and skills for a "building" effect. The conceptual system we used is illustrated in the following chart:

Games Classified by Concepts

TARGET	FIELD/RUN	NET/WALL	TERRITORIAL
Archery	Baseball	**Net**	Basketball
Bowling	Cricket	Badminton	Football
Croquet	Danish Longball	Pickleball	Handball (team)
Curling	Kickball	Table-tennis	Hockey:
Golf	Rounders	Tennis	field, floor, ice
	Softball	Volleyball	Lacrosse
			Netball
		Wall	Rugby
		Handball (court)	Soccer
		Paddleball	Ultimate Frisbee
		Racquetball	
		Squash	

The system organizes games into four basic categories, from the simplest concepts (target games) to the most complex (territorial games). The concepts in these categories are discussed by Butler (1996 and 1997). Our curricular approach was to present a set of modified games to address concepts at a developmentally appropriate skill level for the children in our programs. This allowed them to develop a conceptual understanding of the games at a skill level that lets them play. As a result, they were active learners, not just skill robots. The younger students began with target games, which helped them develop spatial understanding together with throwing, catching, and kicking skills. These fundamentals provided the basis for more the conceptually advanced games. As different games were introduced, skills to fit the games were addressed.

It is this conceptual approach that allows for a spiral curriculum—introducing selected games from different concept groups and later revisiting the concepts group using a different game. The concepts can be transferred and applied to other games. As children mature, the categories feed into each other and provide a framework in which to develop more sophisticated skills. For example, being able to defend an open court in tennis is similar to being able to defend court space in basketball zone defense, which is similar to covering open space in paddle ball or even four-square.

While these concepts seem simple, and we can easily tell students about these concepts and how they can be transferred, our technique was to use guided discovery. It was our belief that students will gain and retain understanding much more effectively when they learn by doing and discovery. This process allows each child to "build" their own meaning based on their history of experiences. Without this connection, students tend to make a habit of looking to the teacher/coach for direction rather than being responsible for their own learning.

At another level, we as the PETE students, were engaging in our own process of learning by doing, as we planned and implemented this after-school program. This same learning by doing and "building" on knowledge also came into play as we prepared presentations. In the future, the club will look at several curricular questions such as: "What position should dance, educational gymnastics, and recreational activities hold in a school PE curriculum?" "How can we design a curriculum that supports constructivism?" "How can we allocate time to various activities and units?" "What do our students really need to learn and how can we best meet those needs?" Discussion of these and other topics help us to feel comfortable with the challenge of change and with our future roles as practitioners.

Testing Different Teaching Styles (Chad Mitchell—PE Major—Graduated in Spring 2002)

In the process of becoming professionals, PETE students are clearly expected to become knowledgeable. True professionals are also innovative and versatile. My experiences with the TfU club have given me an opportunity to think about and discuss a wider variety of issues and ideas than I could ever do in my classes.

One issue we have addressed in the TfU Club is the question of how and when to apply different teaching styles. The club activities provided a safe environment for me to sample and practice various styles including problem-solving, guided discovery, cooperative learning, peer teaching, and the direct command style. Some of the club meetings are devoted to learning and playing games and role-playing as teachers. At other times, as we work on presentations, we use cooperative learning within smaller groups. In the after-school programs, we have a chance to refine our skills using command style when necessary and guided discovery whenever possible.

With a solid footing in the constructivist philosophy, we strive to develop a repertoire of styles. We practice applying these in various contexts and through our own process of trial, error, and discovery as we become professionals.

Growth Areas for PETE students (Laurie Murphy— Junior PETE and Athletic Training)

There are four areas of growth that our club members feel are important for transition from student to professional: 1) social growth, 2) career preparation, 3) community, and 4) civic mindedness and academic development. I have come to appreciate the benefits of participation in a major's club, such as our TfU club, include opportunities for growth in all these areas. For me, the area of social development has been especially important.

As a first-year, relatively inexperienced student, I had no idea of the variety of career choices available to me as a Physical Education major. I joined the club mainly because of the influence and recommendation of friends who were in the club. Through club participation, I have learned that I am capable of making a difference to a group. My thoughts and actions have an impact and I can contribute significantly to the club's achievements. As a consequence of participating in the club presentations and teaching programs, I have discovered personal leadership assets and have had opportunities to apply and develop these assets. I have also discovered that I can develop theories and solve problems, write curriculum, and manage children in a teaching environment. These are big realizations in the life of a first-year student!

The TfU club's academic activity at professional conferences has also been a significant boost to my self-confidence both as a speaker and a thinker. I am learning what it means to be "academic" and that the concepts I am learning about in class have an application in a real-life context. Being in the club has strengthened my decision-making skills and my self-discipline. I have learned to focus, to finish projects under pressure, and to network with my fellow students and the faculty. I find myself seeing career goals more clearly, which influences every aspect of my school experience.

Professional Development (Laura Liard—Teacher Certified in 2001)

Of particular benefit to me has been the growth of career skills that I have experienced while being a member of the TfU club. The group has given me opportunities to build my resume and professional portfolio, to practice leadership and public speaking, and to be on both sides of the mentoring experience. As an officer of the club, I have come to better understand group dynamics and how to help a group set and accomplish goals.

Being a naturally shy person, I have probably experienced the most growth in the area of oral presentation. Working with a group to develop professional presentations has been a safe way for me to "leave my shell" and develop speaking confidence. It has been especially interesting and informative to be in contact with club alumni who have secured teaching positions and continue to stay in touch with the club and even participate in professional presentations. This is an important part of the mentoring and networking process that reaches past the boundary of graduation.

Shawn Croteau—Speaking as TFU Club President (Teacher Certified Spring 2001)

For the past year I have been the president of the TfU club. This role has been invaluable in helping me to master the skills related to the art of governance— organization, delegation, and motivation. It has been within my jurisdiction to be in charge of elections, agenda planning, budgeting and fundraising, interactions with the college student government, and with our faculty advisors. The TfU club is a very active group and I have come to understand the demands of commitment to such a group.

Not only have we as club members benefited from our activities, but the club has also had a positive impact on the local community. The teaching/recreational activities that we provided for the Plymouth Parks and Recreation program were well received by the parents and children and we had many repeat customers. In addition to the after-school programs, our community outreach included programs for the local Boy Scouts and a special "Parent's Night Out." We have learned that "it's not just about us."

The experiences I have had in this club have helped me as a student, as a developing teacher, and as a person. I have been able to gain a deeper understanding of the information in my coursework, I have mastered many types of technology related to professional presentations, but most importantly, I have experienced the pleasure of working with a group. We have shared ideas, questioned, and taken and given feedback. We have motivated each other to produce work that we could never do alone with a synergy that benefited all. On important matters, we discussed issues and came to decisions based on consensus. At the same time, we have built friendships and feelings of accomplishment. The club has stimulated me intellectually, which has been reflected in my academic achievement. We have come to feel that we can continue to work together as teachers to make a difference.

Conclusion

Barbara McCahan—Club Co-Advisor

It has been a continual pleasure to work with the TfU club and these fine students. The benefit of club participation for a faculty advisor is a big dose of gratification from witnessing students' personal and professional growth. According to Angeles Arrien, author of "The Fourfold Way" (1995), the role of the "Teacher" is that of a quiet observer—one who simply facilitates learning through careful listening and strategic questioning, both hallmarks of constructivism. As the club members graduate and enter roles as teachers, they continue to influence the club as alumni members. Their influence helps move the club forward and keep it on top of current issues in education. Future topics for the club's consideration will include: how to integrate a constructivist teaching for understanding into the existing PE culture, how to assess the impact of this approach, and how this philosophy can be applied in other areas besides games.

Truly through this club, Dr. Butler, the HPER department, and Plymouth State College are supporting student success and satisfaction, academic vitality, and community consciousness. I have no doubt that these students will be among the future leaders in the physical education arena.

References

Arrien, A. (1995). *The Four Fold Way: Walking the Paths of the Warrior, Teacher, Healer and Visionary.* San Francisco: Harper and Row.

Bunker, D. & Thorpe, R. (1982). A model for the teaching of games in secondary schools. *Bulletin of Physical Education, 18,* 7-10.

Butler, J. (1996). Teacher responses to teaching games for understanding. *Journal of Physical Education, Recreation, and Dance 67*(9) 17-20.

Butler, J. (1997). How would Socrates teach games?—A constructivist approach to teaching games. *Journal of Physical Education, Recreation, and Dance 68* (9) 42-48.

Physical Education Teachers' Conceptions About Teaching TGfU in Portuguese Schools

Chapter 8

Amândio Graça, University of Porto, Portugal

Isabel Mesquita, University of Porto, Portugal

Introduction

The current reality of sport games in physical education school curricula is swinging between hope and condemnation; inclusion and segregation; enthusiasm and alienation; renovation and retirement. We read Ennis and we plunge into criticism about discriminatory abusive practices (Ennis, 1996); about noncompliance and impoverished curriculum (Ennis, 1995); about fear and disengagement (Ennis et al., 1997). And although she pictured a gloomy PE sport games scenario for us, she does not dismiss sport games, as she believes (Ennis, 1999) that the Sport for Peace curriculum holds promise for reconnecting disengaged students with sport-based PE.

The full-blooded resurgence of the Teaching Games for Understanding (TGfU) model and the interest it has received, not only for curriculum developers, but also and chiefly for empirical researchers, conveys optimism for the placement of sport games within PE curricula. In the same way, the diffusion of curricular materials and the research findings on the Sport Education Model also transmit a positive message for the future of sport games and PE in schools (Hastie, 1998).

The TGfU model has fueled changes in several directions. A major one was the shift of the teaching focus away from technical execution to tactical understanding, which anticipates comparative studies of technical-vs.-tactical approaches (Rink, French, & Tjeerdsma, 1996; Turner & Martinek, 1995). Another direction was game reduction or game modification, which contributed to redesigning the perennial debate concerning the whole-vs.-partial game by downsizing the complexity of the whole game to the level of students' capacity of discernment. This became an essential frame for the sport education model design (Siedentop, 1996).

Game reduction and modification could maintain a direct link to full games and respective skill and strategy fundamentals. The more radical move of game creation, on the other hand, seems to be more prone to divorce from the transmission of traditional forms of sport games by stressing game categorization and generalization. As Laursen (1996) said:

Games-making introduced a shift in the conceptual structure because it focused on the common properties of games and left the "great games" out of focus as being just a few games among an endless number of possible games that could be created (p. 3).

The focus on student tactical decision-making ("What to do?" "When to do it?") has become associated with problem-solving skills, student- or activity-oriented strategies, and indirect teaching approaches. This direction, particularly its constructivist orientation to teaching and learning, intersects movement education perspectives for teaching games (Rovegno, 1993). Meanwhile, the association between tactical learning and indirect teaching, sometimes taken for granted, has been questioned (Rink, et al, 1996). Furthermore, the polarization of direct and indirect teaching styles seems less clear and obvious than has been suggested (Rovegno, 1999).

In Portugal, the official curriculum guide has an eclectic orientation, which, when combined with tradition, is likely to produce a kind of smorgasbord of multiple, short-duration activity units usually in traditional sports. In general, the brief time allocated for subjects prevents the consolidation of learning, which works to trap the student's experience within an endless vicious circle (Siedentop, 1996; Rink et al., 1996). By tradition, team-sport programs include two supposedly interconnected agendas: the first one concerned with basic skills progressions and the other with full-game play experience. The best programs in the first agenda implement a well-stepped sequence of basic skills and well-governed direct instruction. They stress modeling, practice, and feedback within a business-oriented climate. The worst programs in this agenda include meaningless, boring, and disconnected drills, and poor or misleading learner assistance. On the other hand, the best programs in the second agenda could take advantage of systematic scaffolding of students' play, or an active teaching of strategies and action rules and principles, while the worst programs in this agenda do not benefit from any teacher assistance, or they are ill served by authoritarian or faulty instruction. Nevertheless, even counting on the best profile of both agendas we fear that:

The abrupt leap from isolated skill practice to full-game play is likely to degrade the learning students may have made in the first moment, *as the context of application of the skills in the full game greatly exceeds the narrow frame they have been practicing before. (Graça & Januário, 1999, p. 1)*

Requests for the reform of teaching sport games in Portuguese schools have been voiced by several authors in the last few years (Garganta, 1994; Graça, 1994; Tavares, 1994; Mesquita, 1991; 1994). Most preservice and inservice methods courses, inspired by TGfU ideas, have changed the traditional focus into an approach more oriented to the integration of technical and tactical components within a frame of modified and simplified game forms. Conceptual perspectives of teaching games and curriculum guidance congruent with those perspectives were published in a manual entitled "Teaching Sport Games" (Graça & Oliveira, 1994), which was well-received by PE teachers.

The plea for sport games instructional reform is now a couple of years old. Nevertheless there are no systematic data about the consequences of this effort. The purpose of this study was to gather information about the way teachers perceive the teaching of sport games in schools.

Method

Participants and Settings

The study involved 16 physical educators who were attending a 50-hour in-service teacher education course about teaching sport games in schools. The course was oriented by university sport game methodologists and took place at a secondary school, 30 km away from Porto. It is necessary to acknowledge that those attending the course were motivated not only by intrinsic interest in its content, but also by their need to meet legal requirements for career progression. This may have influenced the sample.

The teaching experience of this group ranged between 7 and 25 years, with a mean value of M=14.13±6.18. Only three teachers worked with upper elementary classes (5-6). All the others taught more advanced grade levels (7-12). Twelve out of 16 teachers refer to their coaching experience (all but one with more than six years of coaching experience, and mainly in the same sport they participated in as athletes. Seven of these teachers were involved with sport games (volleyball—four; soccer—two, and tennis—one). Six out of 16 teachers also reported a significant experience as sport games players (more than six years).

Data Collection

On the first day of the course, teachers answered a written questionnaire, in which they were asked about their conceptions of teaching sport games in school settings. The questionnaire was actually an adaptation of an interview script used in previous research (Graça, 1997). We acknowledged that although the way data were collected could favor parsimony and economy of time and resources, it also could produce a severe impact on the amount and depth of information that would be shared. There was, most importantly, no possibility of interaction, and this ruled out the possibility of probing, rephrasing, or redirecting the respondents' answers. Written skills and other constraints also combined to restrict the information delivered.

Questions in the study were based directly on the components of pedagogical content knowledge from Grossman's conceptualization of the following construction (Grossman, 1990): (a) the knowledge and beliefs about the purposes of teaching a subject at different grade levels; (b) the knowledge of the students' understanding, conceptions, and misconceptions of particular topics in a subject matter; (c) the curricular knowledge, concerning the curriculum materials available for teaching particular subject matters, as well as the knowledge about both the horizontal and the vertical curricula of a subject; and (d) a final component, including the knowledge of instructional strategies and representations for teaching particular topics.

Data Analysis

Answers to all questions were transcribed verbatim and introduced in the Nudist 4.0 computer program for qualitative data analysis. The material was codified according to the categories depicted by Grossman's pedagogical content knowledge conceptual framework. Inside each category, we tried to identify and to weigh similar, divergent, or opposing ideas among the teachers' conceptions. Themes and patterns generated by these tactics did not preclude the use of auxiliary theoretical frameworks to assist data display and interpretation. Looking from different angles at the same material may produce a more complete or accurate picture of the issues under analysis. For instance, we looked through Kurz's meanings of sport involvement conceptual framework (Kurz, 1988) to analyze the purposes for teaching sport games (Figure 1).

Data analyses were aligned with the more descriptive branch of tactics for meaning generation (Miles & Huberman, 1994), namely (a) detecting themes and patterns, (b) conceptually grouping data, (c) counting, and (d) contrasting and comparing. In addition, the Kruskal-Wallis nonparametric statistics were employed to test whether there is any difference among teachers' groups on the amount of units of information they delivered about learning topics.

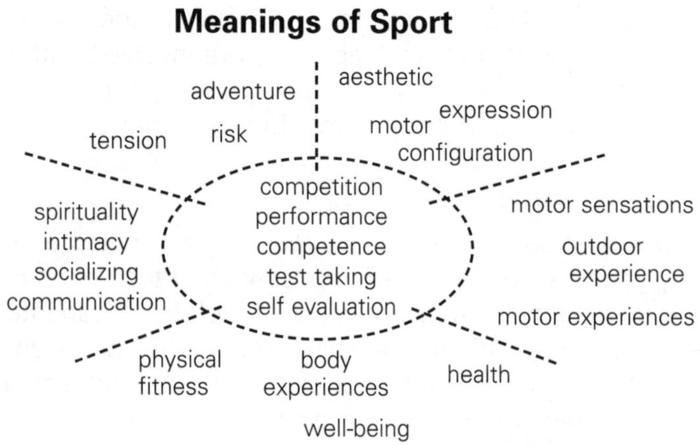

Meanings of Sport

Figure 1. Meanings of sport involvement conceptual framework (Kurz, 1988, p.161)

Results

About Purposes

Looking for the rhetoric the teachers used to justify the inclusion of sport games within PE curricula, it could be seen that teachers unanimously referenced the ideas of cooperation, teamwork, or group spirit (Table I). All but two teachers reported skill development, learning, or acquisition. Eleven out of 16 teachers cited purposes related to knowledge and to ethics. However, references to knowledge deserve further interpretation, since they appear more related to practical or procedural purposes rather than intellectual ones. Quotes of ethical purposes were related to respecting and accepting others, to compliance with rules, and to fair play.

Table I. Purposes quoted by teachers (n), and order of quotation (mean rank)		
Purposes	**References**	**Mean rank**
Cooperation	16	1.81
Skill	12	2.33
Knowledge	11	3.63
Ethics	11	3.50
Pleasure	8	3.91
Lifetime	8	3.36
Fitness	6	2.85
Experience	3	2.00

Pleasure and lifetime purposes were evoked by only half of the teachers, and curiously, the majority of teachers did not include fitness and health in the list of their main purposes in teaching sport games in schools. Cooperation was not only the most consensual purpose, but also the one that ranked first more often. Skill was also well-placed in the overall rank, whereas, fitness and experience occurred in few responses from the teachers (they tend to take precedence when they are spelled out).

The triangulation of the data with Kurz's meanings of sport framework saturated two purpose categories: (a) one that joins the ideas of competition, performance, competence, test taking, and self-evaluation; (b) another that comprises the ideas of spirituality, intimacy, togetherness, socializing, and communication. All teachers referenced purposes within both categories. The remaining meanings of sport were either underrepresented (well-being, 7; motor experiences, 3 out of 16) or completely absent, which may be partly a result of the combination of factors intrinsically attributable to sport games, and failure to consider approaches to games from a more holistic perspective.

About Curricular Content Conceptions

The full game remains a central point of reference for these teachers (Table II). All but one teacher included full games in their program designs. In the same way, 13 out of 16 teachers referred to closed-skill practice. Meanwhile, reduced-game forms and game-like practice were both recorded in more than half of the interviews. This panorama may suggest an approximation to a different picture of those approaches criticized by Rink (1985), which jumped directly from closed-skill practice to full-game play.

Table II. Practice forms framing teachers' team sport programs					
Practice forms	**Full game**	**Reduced games**	**Pre-sportive**	**Game-like**	**Skill drill**
N teachers	15	10	4	9	13

Pedagogical argumentation for including simplified game forms converges with the TGfU starting point for matching game form with student capabilities. As one teacher said:

> Considering the motivational factor, they love the full game, but on account of success, and considering technical and tactical components, I think they cope better with reduced game forms (approaching full game). [Américo: 34 - 36]

Now, looking for the teachers' individual curricular content structure (Table III), we found dissimilarity in teachers' statements about order and the status afforded to particular content and activity forms.

Teachers*	Curricular content structure	Approach
M. Armanda	Pre-sportive; skill practice; full game	
Marlene	Pre-sportive; skill practice; full game	
Emílio	Pre-sportive; skill practice; full game	Skill-
Moura	Skill practice; full game	full game
Pedroso	Skill practice; full game	
Telma	Skill practice; game-like practice; full game	
Alda	Pre-sportive games; skill practice; reduced games toward full game	
Helia	Skill practice; game-like practice; full game	Skill-
Francisco	Skill practice; game-like practice; reduced games; full game	reduced
Sonia	Skill practice, game-like practice; reduced game, referee [full game]	games-
Verónica	Skill practice; reduced games toward full game	full game
Josefina	Game-like practice; reduced games	
Américo	Reduced games toward full game; game-like practice; skill practice	Reduced
Armanda	Game appreciation; reduced games towards full game; skill practice	games-
Cristiana	Rules introduction; reduced games; game-like practice; full game	full game
Gavina	Rules introduction; reduced games; game-like practice; full game	

Table III. Curricular content structure of teachers' team sport programs

*Teachers' names are fictitious

Synthesis of perceived patterns of curricular content structure generated three tentative groups. A first group was comprised of those teachers who did not report the use of reduced-game forms, and who appear to prefer a traditional bottom-up approach. A second group valued reduced-game forms but integrated them in a more developmental step-by-step configuration. Their developmental structure resembles the games stages proposed by Rink (1993). A third group seemed to take reduced game forms as a precursor to curriculum development. This group seems to share some key concepts of the TGfU model, such as the precedence of tactics over technique, the primacy of modified game forms, and the consideration of game appreciation.

A glance over the topics teachers emphasized most in their answers (amount of units considered) suggested a prevalent concentration on technical elements (Figure 2). Tactics came second. The apparent differences between groups, suggested by graphic display, did not reach any statistically significant level anyway (nonparametric statistics, Kruskal-Wallis test).

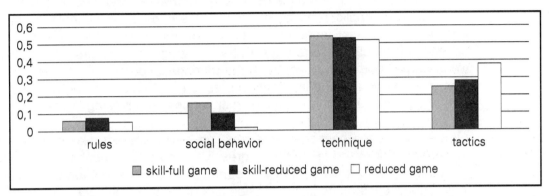

Figure 2. Relative amount of text units dedicated to learning topics (mean values per group)

Nevertheless, from these results one cannot infer that the groups ascribed the same importance to tactics, if they did not differ in the amount of units taught, they differed in the priority they assigned to each particular topic.

About Instructional Strategies and Learners' Comprehension

In general, teachers were somewhat vague and sketchy in their responses concerning their preferred instructional strategies, which contrasts with the amount of considerations they produced about problems related to student involvement and learning in physical education classes (Table IV).

Table IV. Teachers' perception about what makes learning difficult or easy.
Group 1: Bottom-up, no reduced forms group; Group 2: Bottom-up, reduced forms;
Group 3: Top-down, reduced forms

	What makes learning difficult				What makes learning easy			
	Group 1	Group 2	Group 3	Sum	Group 1	Group 2	Group 3	Sum
Relationship	1	2	2	5	-	-	-	-
Motivation	2	2	-	4	4	2	1	7
Background	5	2	4	11	2	2	4	8
Program	2	1	2	5	5	4	3	12
Technical	4	2	1	7	2	2	3	7
Tactical-technical	3	3	4	10	2	2	1	5

The source of difficulties more widely acknowledged by the pool of teachers (11 out of 16) was concerned with students' attributes and capacities, such as background, prior experience, heterogeneity, gender-specific difficulties, readiness, and pre-requirements to learning.

The tactical-technical demands of sport games were identified as major obstacles to learning accomplishment by a considerable number of teachers (10 out of 16). Acquiring and consolidating the basic skills of the game were reported as a major difficulty by seven teachers, four of them belonging to the first group (closed skills to full-game approach). In contrast, the third group of teachers (top-down approach) was more prone to underline tactical pressures, such as playing off the ball, getting free of defense, adapting to changing situations, and placing in space and time.

Almost half the teachers cited problems concerning student relationships as obstacles to learning. For example, selfish aggressive interactions resulted from differences in skill levels and from gender issues. Five teachers specified curricular and instructional constraints like extension and diversity of subject matter, shortness of the time allocated to specific activities, difficulty to attend to individual problems and scaffold the learning progression of the low-paced students. Finally, only four teachers associated motivational reasons to students' problems in learning and involvement in sport games activities. The list of arguments related to success of learning and participation in sport games PE education class teachers presented was remarkably shorter than the list related to student difficulties.

Adequacy of learning environment, individualized instruction, game-like practice, and reduced game forms were pointed out as program facilitators of learning. Half the teachers considered the homogeneity of student skill, prior experience with, or dispositions towards, games as positive background characteristics. Almost half of the teachers believed that students love the sport games, competition, and competitive situations. In fact, love of the game, together with having a reduced number of students per class, and having the classes paired by skill level were the single arguments more often commonly quoted by teachers as ways to sustain and improve helpful learning conditions.

Conclusions

1. The teachers of the study upheld traditional values associated to the sport games. Ethical values, such as cooperation, and practical values, such as skill, ranked higher in their purposes for teaching sport games.
2. The full game remains the representative game form among the teachers. However, most of them recognized the reduced-game form as a worthwhile mediator to reduce game complexity.
3. Teachers seem to espouse different curricular content models to frame instruction of sport games. They could be divided in three tentative groups according theirs stand towards reduced games and content development: A traditional technique-to-full game model group; a developmental skill-to-modified games-to-full games model group, and a tactical-to-technique, reduced games-to-full games model group.

4. Heterogeneity among students, gender specific difficulties, and associated differential response to activities were perceived as the main obstacles to the success of learning in sport games PE classes.

5. Although not fully discarded, the traditional approach seems to be in a process of giving place to alternative teaching games approaches apparently influenced by TGfU and skill-development concepts. It is a clear sign of change that teachers are concerned with tactical awareness, problem-solving, and decision-making skills, along with the effective development of students' game play performance.

References

Ennis, C. (1995). Teachers' responses to noncompliant students: The realities and consequences of a negotiated curriculum. *Teaching & Teacher Education, 11,* 445-460.

Ennis, C. (1996). Students' experience in sport-based physical education: [More than] apologies are necessary. *Quest, 48,* 453-456.

Ennis, C. (1999). Creating a culturally relevant curriculum for disengaged girls. *Sport, Education and Society, 4*(1), 31-49.

Ennis, C., Cothran, D., Davidson, K., Loftus, S., Owens, L., Swanson, L., & Hopsicker, P. (1997). Implementing curriculum within a context of fear and disengagement. *Journal of Teaching in Physical Education, 17,* 52-71.

Garganta, J. (1994). O ensino do futebol [The teaching of soccer]. In A. Graça & J. Oliveira (Eds.), *O ensino dos jogos desportivos [The teaching of sport games]* (pp. 97-137). Porto: Portugal: CEJD/FCDEF-UP.

Graça, A. (1994). Os comos e os quandos no ensino do jogo [The hows and the whys in the teaching of games]. In A. Graça & J. Oliveira (Eds.), *O ensino dos jogos desportivos [The teaching of sport games]* (pp. 27-34). Porto, Portugal: CEJD/FCDEF-UP.

Graça, A. (1997). *O conhecimento pedagógico do conteúdo no ensino do basquetebol [Pedagogical content knowledge in the teaching of basketball].* Unpublished Doctoral Dissertation. University of Porto, Portugal.

Graça, A., & Januário, C. (1999). Personal curricular models of teaching basketball in school. In J.-F. Grehaigne, N. Mahut, & D. Marchal (Eds.), *1999 International AIESEP Congress.* Besançon, France: IUFM de Franche-Comté.

Graça, A. & Oliveira, J. (1994). *O ensino dos jogos desportivos. [The teaching of sport games]* Porto, Portugal: CEJD/FCDEF-UP.

Grossman, P. (1990). *The making of a teacher: Teacher knowledge and teacher education.* New York: Teachers College.

Hastie, P. (1998). Skill and tactical development during a sport education season. *Research Quarterly for Exercise and Sport, 69,* 368-379.

Kurz, D. (1988). Was suchen die Menschen im Sport? Erwartungen und Bedürfnisse der Zukunft. In Deutscher Sportbund: Menschen im Sport 2000. Schorndorf, Hofmann Verlag. (as cited in Bento, J. O. (1995). *O outro lado do desporto. [The other side of sport]* Porto: Campo das Letras).

Laursen, P. (1996, November). *A case-study of games understanding in PETE.* Paper presented at the AIESEP International Seminar, Lisboa, Portugal.

Mesquita, I. (1991). O ensino do voleibol na escola. *[The teaching of volleyball at school]* Horizonte, 43, 31-37.

Mesquita, I. (1994). Proposta metodológica para o ensino do Voleibol *[Methodological proposal to the teaching of volleyball].* In A. Graça & J. Oliveira (Eds.), *O ensino dos jogos desportivos [The teaching of sport games]* (pp. 167-201). Porto, Portugal: CEJD/FCDEF-UP

Miles, M. & Huberman, M. (1994). *Qualitative data analysis: an expanded sourcebook* (2nd ed.). Newbury Park, CA: Sage.

Rink, J. (1985). *Teaching physical education for learning* (1st ed.). St. Louis: Times Mosby College.

Rink, J. (1993). *Teaching physical education for learning.* (2nd ed.). St. Louis: Mosby.

Rink, J., French, K., & Tjeerdsma, L. (1996). Foundations for the learning and instruction of sport games. *Journal of Teaching in Physical Education, 15,* 399-417.

Rovegno, I. (1993). The development of curricular knowledge: A case of problematic pedagogical content knowledge during advanced knowledge acquisition. *Research Quarterly for Exercise and Sport, 64*(1), 56-58.

Rovegno, I. (1999). What is taught and learned in physical activity programs: the role of content. In J.-F. Grehaigne, N. Mahut, & D. Marchal (Eds.), *1999 International AIESEP Congress.* Besançon, France: IUFM de Franche-Comté.

Siedentop, D. (1996). Physical Education and Educational Reform: The case of sport education. In S. Silverman & C. Ennis (Eds.), *Student learning in physical education* (pp. 247-267). Champaign, IL: Human Kinetics.

Tavares, F. (1994). O processamento de informação nos jogos desportivos colectivos. In A. Graça & J. Oliveira (Eds.), *O ensino dos jogos desportivos* (pp. 35-46). Porto, Portugal: CEJD/FCDEF-UP

Turner, A. & Martinek, T. (1995). Teaching for understanding: A model for improving decision making during game play. *Quest, 47*(1), 44-63.

Comparing Assessment of Preservice Teaching Practices Using Traditional and TGfU Instructional Models: Data from Australia and the United States

Chapter 9

Eileen C. Sullivan, Boston University, United States

Karen Swabey, University of Tasmania, Australia

Introduction

The increased interest and visibility of constructivist learning theory, specifically the Teaching Games for Understanding (TGfU) approach in physical education, provided the impetus for this study. Typically, games have been taught using the traditional method of a technique or a skills approach which, for many students and pre-service teachers, has not stimulated their interest and has resulted in poor game playing (Griffin, Mitchell, & Oslin, 1997). The teacher typically teaches an introductory activity, usually a demonstration, provides a series of structured drills to practice and enhance skill development, and then game playing occurs at the end of the lesson. In other words, a skill from the activity is selected, the skill or skills are taught, and then the students apply the learned or practiced skills to game situations or an actual game. With the traditional approach, the skills become the goal of the lessons and the tactical awareness and cognitive skills for effective game playing are often underemphasized and undermined (Gabriele & Maxwell, 1995). Instead, an approach that focuses on game appreciation and the development of tactical awareness, would meet the needs of the students (Thorpe, Bunker, & Almond, 1986). This approach, called Teaching Games for Understanding (TGfU), aims to expose students to game-like experiences very early in their learning through offensive tactics, defensive tactics, game decisions, and skill acquisition. The traditional approach uses the part-whole-part approach to teaching skills while the TGfU approach models the whole-part-whole method of teaching so students visualize and practice the whole of the game, then learn the parts (Butler, 1997).

The controversy over the strengths of each approach, traditional and TGfU, is vibrant within the current literature. The need to expose pre-service teachers to both approaches was the central inquiry for the researchers, who all teach in a university setting. Pre-service teachers need to acquire the ability to teach a broad range of teaching approaches to ensure that the needs of their students will be met (Tinning, Macdonald, Wright, & Hickey, 2001) It was the aim of this study to examine the two teaching approaches through the lenses of our pre-service teachers. Pre-service teachers, who were more familiar with the traditional approach, but who were receptive to learning about the TGfU method, were asked to plan and teach classes using the two approaches. Systematic observation instruments provided quantitative data to examine the differences between the approaches, and comments from the supervising teachers supported the pre-service teachers' concerns about how to improve their teaching.

Objectives of the Study

The purpose of this study was to analyze the teaching practices of pre-service teachers from two different countries, using two different games-teaching approaches. Each pre-service teacher was asked to plan and then teach two traditional-approach classes and two Teaching Games for Understanding (TGfU) classes with a selected sport or skill theme. The two instruments selected, the Teacher Performance Criteria Questionnaire (TPCQ) and the Educational Games Observational Rubric (EGOR), provided data about the pre-service teachers' teaching behaviors and teacher effectiveness, as well as the range of teaching practices with 10 constructivism-oriented practices. The validation of the TGfU approach was a central component of the study, as the pre-service teachers were less familiar with this approach than the traditional approach. Corresponding trends and variances with pre-service teachers from the two countries were highlighted.

Research Design

Two pre-service teachers from each country, who were teaching as part of their practicum experience, were asked to participate in the study. All pre-service teachers were teaching at elementary schools and their cooperating teachers were agreeable in allowing them to teach a selected theme or sport to two different fourth/fifth grade classes. Each pre-service teacher taught two lessons with a traditional approach and then two lessons with a TGfU approach to a different fourth/fifth grade class. The pre-service teachers had full responsibility for planning and implementation of the lessons. Assistance was not provided by the cooperating teachers. Each pre-service teacher taught a different skill or sport (Australia: scooperball and basketball; United States: volleyball and throwing/catching skill theme). To clarify, pre-service teacher #1 from Australia taught two traditional lessons of scooperball, and then two TGfU lessons with scooperball. Pre-service teacher #2 from Australia taught two traditional lessons with basketball and then two TGfU with the same sport. In the United States, pre-service teacher #1 used volleyball for the four lessons and pre-service teacher #2 taught a throwing/catching theme for four lessons, two traditional and two TGfU.

The supervisor and researcher for the study observed each lesson by taking meticulous notes and recording behaviors, outcomes, and other qualitative data. Immediately following each lesson, the pre-service teachers self-assessed their teaching behaviors with the Teacher Performance Criteria Questionnaire (TPCQ) and the supervisor assessed the pre-service teachers' behaviors with the same instrument. The supervisors provided adequate positive and constructive feedback comments, but the pre-service teachers were asked to use reflective teaching practices to attempt to improve their lessons. When the pre-service teachers taught their TGfU classes, the supervisor recorded the number of tasks for each dimension of the constructivist teaching practice. The coding form and training manual was provided by the developers of the EGOR system (Chen & Rovegno, 2000).

TGfU Approach

The pre-service teachers from both Australia and the United States were introduced to the TGfU approach during a designated skills and methods class. This introduction was limited and the familiarity with the approach should be considered fundamental. They were all provided with a packet of readings (Butler, 1997; Chen & Rovegno, 2000; Griffin, Mitchell, & Oslin, 1997; Turner & Martinek, 1999) and the researchers provided additional one-on-one assistance for the pre-service teachers to learn about TGfU concepts. The pre-service teachers, though, were the ones who developed their own lesson plans for each of the classes.

Data Collection: Description of the Observation Instruments

Instrument I. Teacher Performance Criteria Questionnaire (TPCQ)

Rosenshine and Furst (1971) investigated teacher effectiveness through accumulated process-product studies, which attempted to relate distinct teaching variables to results in student achievement. The 11 variables identified and defined in Rosenshine and Furst's work were then applied to Cheffer's and Keilty's (1981) design of a 16-question instrument and a four-point Likert scale that could assess teacher behavior across the disciplines. Of the 11 variables in the Teacher Performance Criteria Questionnaire (TPCQ), the first five received strong support, so two questions were developed to measure these variables. The remaining six had less support, so one question per variable was generated to reflect the content of the variable. The reported 86.7% content validity, 83.0% internal consistency, 96.0% reliability rating, and an 89.0% rater agreement supported the conclusion that the TPCQ was a valid, reliable measure of teacher effectiveness based on 11 variables.

Although research with the instrument was abundant (Butler, 1993; Cardoza, 1990; Sullivan, 1997, 1998, 1999, 2000), there was a need to revisit the instrument with critical examination of the descriptions of the variables. In 1999, Sullivan revised the wording on two of the variables, and made limited changes to the directions of the instrument. A 94.4% content validity was reported with the revised TPCQ (Sullivan, 1999).

The TPCQ is a reliable and valid method of measuring teacher effectiveness (Cheffers & Keilty, 1981; Sullivan, 2000). The TPCQ is a three-page instrument with one page for the listing of the variables and two pages for the 16 questions. The 11 TPCQ variables assessed are: Clarity, Variability, Enthusiasm, Personal Efficiency, Opportunity to Learn, Accepting and Encouraging, Use of Criticism, Use of Structure and Summary Comments, Question Technique, Probing, and Difficulty Level of Instructions. The 16 questions address these variables and below each recorded question is a space to circle a 4 (Always), 3 (Mostly), 2 (Occasionally), or a 1 (Never) on the Likert scale to describe and rate the teacher or student behaviors. A complete copy of the instrument is available from the authors. The authors have successfully applied the TPCQ instrument for research purposes, but it is also an effective tool for reflective teaching practices with students teaching pre-practicums, peer teaching assignments, as well as for assessments in the field when students teach in their final practicum.

The TPCQ instrument can be used as research tool to collect data on the defined teaching variables. Teachers can opt to use TPCQ for self-assessment, an evaluator can assess a teacher's lesson, or a colleague could use TPCQ to provide feedback. In addition, TPCQ data has been used for triangulation assessment data (Sullivan, 2000). Triangulation assessment data, with TPCQ coding from the teacher, a colleague or peer, and a supervisor, provides further analysis of teaching behaviors through the eyes of two coders as well as the teacher herself/himself. In using triangulation data, the TPCQ can provide similarities, patterns, discrimination trends, and content for reflective teaching discussion with the subjects or teachers.

How TPCQ Was Used in This Study

The pre-service teachers and the supervisors used the TPCQ to assess teaching behaviors for the traditional and the TGfU approach. The pre-service teachers self-assessed their teaching immediately following each lesson. The supervisor used the TPCQ to assess the pre-service teachers' teaching of the two approaches. Data displayed the consistency of recorded 4s, or the Always category, the variables with the recorded 1s or the Never category, as well as comparisons between the two approaches. Similarities, differences, and trends between the Australian and the United States data are included in the results.

Instrument II. Educational Games Observational Rubric (EGOR)

Based on the Science Classroom Observation Rubric (Burry-Stock & Oxford, 1994), Chen and Rovegno (2000) designed the Educational Games Observational Rubric (EGOR) to collect data comparing expert and novice teachers' constructivist-oriented teaching practices. The instrument was designed to "assess the extent to which a teacher's teaching practices are associated with expertise in teaching educational games" from constructivist perspectives (Chen & Rovegno, 2000, p. 360). A coder rates and quantifies the number of teaching practices that adhere to a category and then makes a decision about the score for each teaching practice. Ten constructivist-oriented teaching practices were sectioned into three EGOR categories: (1) Engaging Students in Active and Self-Regulated Construction of Knowledge, (2) Activating Students' Prior Knowledge and Emerging Relevance, and (3) Facilitating Students' Social Interaction Among Groups and Joint Problem-Solving Settings. A five-point rating score was recorded for each of the teaching practices in each category. A score from one—indicating none of the tasks, statements, or teachers' responses showed evidence of the definition—to five—where almost all of the responses show behaviors indicative of the definition-was marked on the coding sheet. Internal consistency of the 10-item EGOR was 88.0% and an interobserver agreement was reached with validation, but the developers of the instrument worked with the coders until a 100% agreement was achieved for their research with expert and novice teachers (Chen & Rovegno, 2000, p. 361).

How EGOR Was Used in This Study

The two researchers used the EGOR instrument to evaluate the teaching practices of the pre-service teachers teaching with the TGfU approach. Each of the two TGfU lessons for the two pre-service teachers from Australia and the two from the United States were coded with the EGOR categories. Data from Australia and the United States were analyzed for each of the 10 items in the three categories of constructivist-oriented teaching practices. Evidence of similarities, differences, trends, and high (5) and low (1) evaluation scores were noted. The EGOR scale was not used to evaluate the traditional approach because the instrument was not designed to assess traditional teaching.

Results and Discussion

TPCQ Results

Table I and Table II display the TPCQ percentage results for scoring a 1 (Never) to a 4 (Always) for the 11 defined teaching variables. Table I, TPCQ results for the traditional approach, displays the United States supervisor rating a 4 (Always) behavior 9.4% of the time and the Australian supervisor rating a 4, 12.5% of the time. Thus, the majority of the scores fell in the 3 category (Mostly), for both countries. The supervisors' rating of a 1 for a teaching behavior that was not demonstrated by the pre-service teachers, stood at 9.4% for the United States and 3.1% for Australia. The majority of the self-assessment scores for the pre-service teachers fell within the Mostly (3) category for both countries. It was interesting to note that the pre-service teachers in Australia and the United States rated themselves with exactly the same number of 4s (Always) in the traditional approach—15.6% or 10, 4 ratings of the 128 questions. Table II, TPCQ results for the TGfU approach showed similar findings with the traditional approach, with the majority of ratings in the 3 (Mostly) category for the supervisor and the self-assessment by the pre-service teachers. In Australia, the 4 (Always) category was statistically lower with the TGfU approach. The Australian supervisor rated eight 4s with the traditional approach, and four 4s with the TGfU approach. The Australian pre-service teachers moved from 10, Always (4) ratings with the traditional approach to five Always (4) ratings in the TGfU approach.

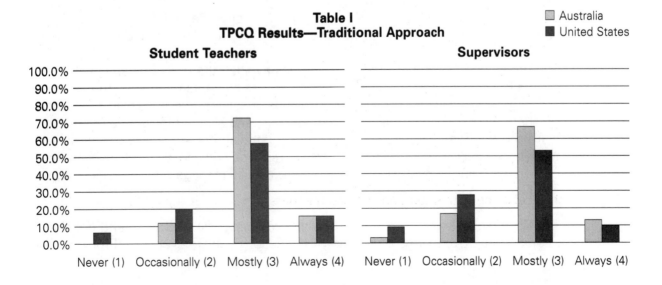

Table I
TPCQ Results—Traditional Approach

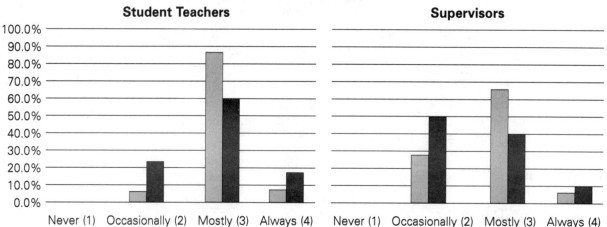

Table II
TPCQ Results—TGFU Approach

 Australia
 United States

Student Teachers   **Supervisors**

The percentage of 4s, 3s, 2s, and 1s with TPCQ indicates a range of teaching behaviors, but the high percentage of 3s (Mostly) for the four pre-service teachers in both countries confirms effective teaching practices. Further examination of the TPCQ variables addresses the teaching behaviors of the pre-service teachers. With the traditional approach for the Australian data, the pre-service teachers rated a 4 (Always) for their teaching behaviors with questions 7 and 8 (Personal Efficiency), question 9 (Opportunity to Learn), as well as question 12 (Use of Criticism). The Australian supervisor rated 4s with the Personal Efficiency variable and the Use of Criticism TPCQ variable, too.

The United States TPCQ variable/question analysis for the pre-service teachers' traditional approach indicates question 5 (Enthusiasm) and question 12 (Use of Criticism) with the highest rating of 4s. The United States supervisor, as well as the pre-service teachers, rated Enthusiasm and the Use of Criticism with 4s when assessing the traditional approach. Enthusiasm is a teaching behavior, which has been identified as an ingredient of effective teaching across the disciplines and in physical education (Carlise & Phillips, 1984; Parson, 2001). As the TPCQ results indicated, the pre-service teachers' enthusiasm was evident through their interest, excitement, and involvement. Their verbal and nonverbal teaching behaviors showed they were enthusiastic about their teaching, the lesson, and the students.

The pre-service teachers from both countries avoided the use of harsh criticism to control the classes. They provided feedback to their students throughout the lessons and they did not have to display negative words or actions. The Australian pre-service teachers were efficient, organized with lessons, and allowed for their students to learn the material. The United States and Australian pre-service teachers, when teaching the traditional and TGfU approaches displayed enthusiastic teaching behaviors, both verbally and nonverbally, and they were able to manage their classes without harsh criticism.

The TPCQ 4s (Always) that were recorded for the TGfU approach, and not the traditional approach, were questions 14 (Question Technique) and 15 (Probing). The pre-service teachers from the United States and Australia showed improvement in the use of questions (Question #14 on the TPCQ instrument reads: "Did the teacher use a variety of questioning techniques of the material presented?"). The United States TPCQ data revealed that the pre-service teachers' and the supervisor's codes shifted from 2s (Occasionally) to 3s (Mostly) and in one instance from 3 (Occasionally) to 4 (Always) from the traditional to the TGfU approach. The Australian data for TPCQ question 14 remained consistent with two 3s (Mostly) for the traditional and the TGfU approach for one pre-service teacher, but the second teacher moved from 2s (Occasionally) to 3s (Mostly). In summary, there was an increase in the use of questions by the pre-service teachers in both countries when they taught with the TGfU approach.

Of particular significance, was the improvement of all TPCQ codings by the pre-service teachers and the supervisors for question 15, the use of probing. The TPCQ instrument defines probing as "the teacher's ability to elicit 'in-depth' answers from students in a manner which encourages further elaboration by the student or another student. Teacher also initiates questions of this sort to encourage student elaboration on various content levels." (Cheffers & Sullivan, 2000). The United States data indicated pre-service teacher number one shifting from 1 (Never) codes for the traditional approach lessons to 3s (Mostly) for the TGfU approach lessons. The supervisor was in complete agreement with the pre-service teacher's codes here. Pre-service teacher number two rated himself 3s (Mostly) for the traditional approach teaching and 4s (Always) for the TGfU lessons when the supervisor recorded 1s (Never) for the traditional approach and 3 (Mostly) for the TGfU approach. Australian codes for TPCQ question 15, probing, like the United States data, shifted from 2s (Occasionally) and 3s (Mostly) for pre-service teacher number one and from 3s to 4s for pre-service teacher number two. The Australian supervisor TPCQ coding increased a category for both student teachers, from 2 to 3 and 3 to 4 for pre-service teacher number one and from 3 to 4 and 1 to 3 for pre-service teacher number two when comparing traditional and TGfU lessons.

The pre-service teachers used more questions during their teaching when they taught using the TGfU approach. They were asking questions about the content at hand, inquiring about how students could improve performances, as well as probing about techniques the students were using to design their own situations or drills. More pre-service teacher questions with the TGfU approach agree with Butler's (1993, 1996) findings of experienced teachers implementing a TGfU approach after exposure to the methods. Butler reported that there was an increase in the number of questions by teachers who taught implementing a TGfU approach, and the range of the cognitive-level questioning was higher. TPCQ data from this study matches this finding; the pre-service teachers teaching with the TGfU approach used probing questions as they encouraged students to reflect on skills, drills, strategies, and tactical knowledge.

The high number of 4s with the TPCQ variable, Personal Efficiency or class management, also corresponds with another of Butler's (1993, 1996) results where teachers are more apt to apply higher-level questioning techniques with TGfU classes than traditional teaching. Managerial or task-directed questions (TPCQ variable of Personal Efficiency) are greater with a traditional approach than a TGfU approach, as found in this study, too.

Clarity, another variable of the TPCQ instrument, shifted from 3s (Mostly) to 2s (Occasionally) for the pre-service teachers and the supervisors from both countries when comparing the traditional to the TGfU approach. Clarity is defined as "the clear presentation of information and direction as reflected by the appropriateness and delivery of the content of the lesson." (Cheffers & Sullivan, 2001, TPCQ instrument, p. 1) The pre-service teachers were less familiar with the TGfU approach, thus they were more apt to be inconsistent with teaching the content, and less clear with the presentation.

TPCQ results indicated that the pre-service teachers often rated themselves higher than the supervisor. Although it was beyond the scope of this study, TPCQ data could be analyzed to find trends with the coding by comparing the self-assessment codes from the pre-service teachers with the supervisors' coding. If the cooperating teachers were included in the assessment component, there would be a triangulation assessment piece to the research. Here, TPCQ data showed that more than one-third of the TPCQ codes by the pre-service teachers ranked higher than the codes by the supervisor. This was consistent for both the United States and the Australian TPCQ data. This trend correlates to findings by Sullivan (2000) with TPCQ triangulation assessment for self-assessment, peer assessment, and professor or supervisor evaluation.

EGOR Results

The Educational Games Observation Rubric (Chen & Rovegno, 2000) assesses the constructivist teaching approach, the Teaching Games for Understanding approach. Table III displays 100% agreement between the countries with a 4 rating (over half the tasks showed evidence) for two sections of Category I, Engaging Students in Active and Self-Regulated Construction of Knowledge: the active engagement section, and elaboration of ideas about movement variety. The pre-service teachers from Australia and the United States were successful in providing opportunities for their students to become active learners and engaged in the process through designing/modifying games or in game-like situations. Furthermore, the consistency of all 4s for the second section of elaboration of ideas shows that the pre-service teachers encouraged their learners to extend their use of skills during game-like settings.

Table III
Educational Games Observation Rubric (EGOR) Results
for Student Teachers #1 And #2 Teaching TGfU Classes
(Australia and United States Data)

	Student Teacher #1		Student Teacher #2	
Category I: **Engaging Students in Active and Self-Regulated Construction of Knowledge**	AUS. Class1-2	U.S. Class1-2	AUS. Class1-2	U.S. Class 1-2
Active engagement (A)	4 4	4 4	4 4	4 4
Elaboration of ideas about movement variety (B)	4 4	4 4	4 4	4 4
Self-regulation of movement quality (C)	2 3	2 2	2 3	2 3
Facilitating students' self-responsibility (D)	2 2	2 2	2 2	2 2
Critical thinking about movement quality (E)	2 3	2 3	2 3	3 3
Category II: **Activating Students' Prior Knowledge and Emerging Relevance**				
Use of metaphors, examples, images (F)	1 2	1 2	1 1	1 2
Connecting to prior knowledge and experiences (G)	2 2	3 3	2 2	2 3
Category III: **Facilitating Students' Social Interaction Among Groups and Joint Problem-Solving Settings**				
Sharing ideas about movement variety (H)	2 3	2 3	2 2	2 3
Discussion about movement quality (I)	2 2	2 2	2 2	2 2
Facilitating partner or group work (J)	5 5	5 5	5 5	5 5

Coding/Rating Scale for EGOR (Chen & Rovegno, 2000):

5-almost all the tasks, statements, or teachers' responses show evidence of the definition

4-over half of the tasks, statements, or teachers' responses show evidence of the definition

3-about half of the tasks, statements, or teachers' responses show evidence of the definition

2-less than half of the tasks, statements, or teachers' responses show evidence of the definition

1-none of the tasks, statements, or teachers' responses show evidence of the definition

Although the Australian and United States data showed the same scores in five sections, the high and the low ratings are the most essential to this study. The only 5s (the highest rating) were recorded with the section, facilitating partner or group work. The pre-service teachers, although they were novice TGfU teachers, were capable of "guiding students to think about how well they can work together productively and cooperatively" (Chen & Revegno, 2001, EGOR Manual) While the pre-service teachers were comfortable guiding learners to work and play together in groups, they were the least comfortable or knowledgeable about "using appropriate, interesting, and captivating metaphors, examples, and/or images that are relevant to students' real world experiences and/or levels of cognitive understanding" (Chen & Rovegno, 2001, EGOR Manual)

Beginning teachers, and especially pre-service teachers in teacher preparatory programs, have been encouraged to use reflective teaching practices to improve their teaching behaviors (Kirk, 1995; Tsangaridou & O'Sullivan, 1994). The EGOR results in this study point to the fact that pre-service teachers are inexperienced when using metaphors in their own teaching practices. Yet, if these pre-service teachers used reflective teaching methods with metaphors, it would assist with their understanding of pedagogy. Recent research has indicated that metaphors, defined as "implicit comparison(s), one(s) which call attention to similarities between two things by speaking of one thing as if it were another" (Petrie, 1980), could function to operate as insights, discoveries, arguments, models, and theories to assist with the development of a pre-service teacher. Carlson's (2001) more recent research into the use of metaphors with pre-service teachers supported Petrie's beliefs, as it found that the teachers began to conceptualize their beliefs about teaching and learning. The researchers involved in this current study believe further research into this area is essential and would add to the body of knowledge surrounding both this current research into teaching approaches used by pre-service teachers as well as enhancing our knowledge about one important element of the assessment areas used in both assessment tools.

While there was some improvement from the first TGfU class each pre-service teacher taught to the second class, it is beyond the scope of this study to elaborate about the depth of improvement. The pre-service teachers increased their scores in 5 of the 10 sections and stayed at a constant score in the other half of the sections. The foundation of this research design-that of teaching the pedagogical differences between a traditional and a TGfU approach to pre-service teachers—would be beneficial to all physical education students in teacher education programs.

EGOR results in this study were consistent with detailed findings in Chen and Rovegno's work (2000) with experienced and novice teachers teaching TGfU classes. The expert teachers in the study had a better understanding of how to link or connect students' prior knowledge to new learning and they were able to use metaphors to enhance learning. The Australian and United States EGOR results here confirmed that pre-service or novice teachers do not use metaphors, examples, or images, but rather they are more likely to ask questions directly related to the learning task at hand.

Limitations and Recommendations

The focus of this investigation centered on the analysis of pre-service teachers' teaching practices using a traditional approach and a TGfU approach. Four pre-service teachers, two each from two different countries were the subjects. All four pre-service teachers were students of the supervisors at their respective universities, where most of their methods classes focused on the traditional approach. Thus, the TGfU approach was a novel teaching method for the subjects. The researchers were interested in analyzing teaching behaviors with the two approaches. Could the pre-service teachers effectively learn and teach the TGfU approach? What were the trends or differences between the two approaches? How did the results compare between the two countries?

The instruments used to collect the necessary data answered the research questions but there were limitations. TPCQ (Cheffers & Sullivan 2000) was a valuable tool to record effective teaching behaviors for *both* approaches. TPCQ was used for the traditional and the TGfU approach, so there was consistency. The EGOR instrument (Chen & Rovegno, 2000) was administered as a means of validating the TGfU approach only and *not* the traditional approach. The categories of EGOR provided information about the extent to which the pre-service teachers were using constructivism teaching methods and a ranking of their expertise, or lack of expertise, in teaching the TGfU approach. One limitation of the study was that EGOR could not be used as a tool for the traditional approach. When further research is conducted with traditional and TGfU approaches, researchers need to authenticate and validate the traditional as well as the TGfU approach.

It is suggested that other researchers affirm and provide data to define the parameters of the traditional approach. Butler (1993) used Cheffers' Adaptation to Flanders Interaction Analysis System (CAFIAS) to compare and contrast "Technical Teaching Style" and "Tactical Teaching Style," which in this study are called traditional and TGfU approaches. CAFIAS is a systematic observation assessment instrument, which allows researchers to record verbal and nonverbal interaction by the student and teacher in the classroom or gymnasium. It is recommend CAFIAS be used to validate or define the traditional, as well as the TGfU approach, for future research studies.

Suggestions and recommendations to expand the scope of this study include the following: (1) videotape all lessons, (2) randomize teaching approaches so TGfU and traditional approaches are taught in a different sequence, (3) include control groups, (4) supplement quantitative date with reflections from the pre-service teachers' journals or interviews, (5) include the cooperating teachers' assessments, (6) use a systematic observation system to record the level of involvement of the students, (7) replicate the study with other grade levels, and (8) validate the approaches studied with interaction analysis systems.

Conclusions and Implications for Teaching

The pre-service teachers from both countries displayed similar teaching characteristics when they taught lessons with the two teaching approaches, the traditional approach and the Teaching Games for Understanding approach. The quantitative and qualitative results from the assessment tools elicited a variety of responses, which showed that the pre-service teachers demonstrated enthusiastic teaching behaviors for both approaches and they avoided the use of harsh criticism. Clarity, or the clear presentation of content, was more evident with the traditional approach than the TGfU approach, but this could be due to the lack of familiarity with the TGfU approach. The most limiting teaching behavior for the pre-service teachers during the TGfU lessons was their inability to use metaphors and examples to link learning with prior knowledge.

The use of questions and probing techniques improved when the pre-service teachers taught with the TGfU approach. Not only did they ask more questions, but also they attempted to use probing question techniques with small groups, the entire class, and individual students. Probing questions like, "How did you get the scoooperball to go higher?" or "How can you throw to your teammates to move the ball forward better?" were probing questions used by the pre-service teachers to give their students the opportunity to discover for themselves solutions to problems. In essence, the pre-service teachers were engaging students so that they could make better decisions about their game-playing and skill performance.

Becoming more knowledgeable about the Teaching Games for Understanding approach has assisted the researchers in the realization that pre-service teachers need to be introduced to the most-current, as well as traditional, methods of teaching. Teacher educators should continue to teach the need to engage learners through the use of effective teaching practices as well as sound methodologies. There is a particular need to teach our undergraduate students how to use metaphors, examples, and ideas by connecting past experiences to new learning. Few would debate that reflective teaching is fundamental to sound teaching and improved teaching.

The pre-service teachers from the United States and Australia that participated in the study were willing to take the risk of learning and teaching a new approach. The researchers commend them for learning, trying, and improving their teaching with the traditional and the TGfU approach. The benefits of using reflective teaching practices, being aware of why, how, and when to ask critical questions results in effective teaching behaviors and learners who are involved in the learning experience.

Practitioners and pre-service teachers should be introduced to self-assessment and evaluation observation tools in order to facilitate reflective teaching. The Teacher Performance Criteria Questionnaire (TPCQ) (Cheffers & Sullivan, 2000) and the Educational Games Observation Rubric (EGOR) (Chen & Rovegno, 2000) are valid, reliable, appropriate, simple to use, and inexpensive observation tools for the supervisor, pre-service teacher, and/or cooperating teacher. We plan on continuing our research with teaching approaches, effective teaching behaviors, and the need for beginning teachers to learn how to use metaphors and connect past learning experiences to make the content more relevant for their students or learners. Our pre-service teachers represent future teachers and we need to equip them with the tools they need to meet the needs of their students. Exposure and teaching practice with the TGfU approach should be included in their suitcase of teaching knowledge they carry into the field.

References

Burry-Stock J. A. & Oxford, R. L. (1994). Expert science teaching educational evaluation model (ESTEEM): Measuring excellence in science teaching for professional development. *Journal of Personnel Evaluation in Education, 8,* 267-297.

Butler, J. (1993). Teacher change in sport education. *Dissertation Abstracts International. 54, (02A), 0457.* (UMI No. 9318198).

Butler, J. (1996). Teacher responses to teaching games for understanding. *Journal of Physical Education, Recreation, and Dance, 67* (9), 17-20.

Butler, J. (1997). How would Socrates teach Games? A constructivist approach. *Journal of Physical Education, Recreation, and Dance, 66* (9), 42-47.

Cardoza, P. & Cheffers, J. T. (1990). "Describing a student, beginning teacher and experienced teacher behaviors." *Proceedings AIESEP: Foundation for promotion of physical health.* Jyvaskyla, Finland, 1990.

Carlise, C. & Phillips, D. (1984). The effects of enthusiasm training on selected teacher and student behaviors in pre-service physical education teachers. *Journal of Teaching in Physical Education, 4,* 64-75.

Carlson, T. (2001). Using metaphors to enhance reflectiveness among pre-service teachers. *Journal of Physical Education, Recreation, and Dance, 72* (1), 49-53.

Cheffers, J. & Keilty, G. (1981). Developing valid instrumentation for measuring teacher performance. *International Journal of Physical Education, XVII* (2).

Cheffers, J. & Sullivan, E. (2000). *Instruction Sheet for the Teacher Performance Criteria Questionnaire, TPCQ.* Available through the authors at Boston University.

Chen, W. & Rovegno, I. (2000). Examination of expert and novice teachers' constructivist-oriented teaching practices using a movement approach to elementary physical education. *Research Quarterly for Exercise and Sport, 71,* 357-372.

Chen, W. & Rovegno, I. (2001). *Manual for scoring and coding sheets. Educational Games Observation Rubric.* Supplied by the authors of the instrument, Temple University.

Gabriele, T. & Maxwell, T. (1995). Direct versus indirect methods of squash instruction. *Research Quarterly for Exercise and Sport, 66,* A-63.

Graham, G., Holt/Hale, S., & Parker, M. (1998). *Children Moving: A reflective approach to teaching physical education.* Mountain View, CA: Mayfield.

Griffin, L., Mitchell, S., & Oslin, J. (1997). *Teaching sport concepts and skills: A tactical games approach.* Champaign, IL: Human Kinetics.

Kirk, D. (1995). Action research and educational reform in physical education. *Pedagogy in Practice, I* (1), 4-21.

Parson, M. (2001). *Enthusiasm and feedback: A winning combination!* PECentral, Jan. 2001. http://www.pecentral.org/climate/monicaparsonarticle.html

Petrie, H. F. (1980). Metaphor and learning. In A. Ortony (Ed.). *Metaphor and thought* (pp.436-461). Cambridge: Cambridge University.

Rosenshine, B. & Furst, N. (1971). Research on teacher performance criteria. In B. Smith (Ed.): *Research in teacher education: A symposium.* Englewood Cliffs, NJ: Prentice-Hall.

Sullivan, E. (1999). *Evaluating teachers and coaches: The teacher performance criteria questionnaire (TPCQ) revisited.* Proceedings of the AIESEP World Congress, Besancon, France.

Sullivan, E. (1998). "Reflective Writing With Non Major Student Teachers in a University Physical Education Program." Proceedings of World Sport Science Congress, AIESEP, "Education for Life." Adelphi University, New York.

Sullivan, E. (1997). Self Evaluation of Non Major Student Teachers in a University Laboratory Physical Education Program. *Proceedings of AIESEP Singapore,* Paper presented at Association International of Physical Education and Sport, World Conference on Teaching, Coaching and Fitness Needs in Physical Education and Sport Sciences. Nanyang Institute of Education, Nanyang Technological University, Singapore.

Sullivan E. (2000) *Variation with the implementation of the teacher performance criteria questionnaire (TPCQ): Self, supervisor and triangulation assessment.* Paper presented at the AIESEP. World Sport Science Congress, September 3, 2000, Rockhampton, Australia.

Thorpe, R., Bunker, D., & Almond, L. (1986). *Rethinking games teaching.* Loughborough, Leicester: Department of Physical Education and Sports Science, University of Technology.

Tinning, R., Macdonald, D., Wright, J., & Hickey, C. (2001). *Becoming a physical education teacher.* Frenchs Forest, New South Wales: Pearson Education Australia.

Tsangaridou, N. & O'Sullivan, M. (1994). Using pedagogical reflective strategies to enhance reflection among pre-service physical education teachers. *Journal of Teaching in Physical Education, 14,* 13-33.

Turner, A. & Martinek, T. (1999). An investigation into teaching games for understanding: Effects on skill, knowledge, and game play. *Research Quarterly for Exercise and Sport, 70* (3), 286-296.

Teaching Games For Understanding: A Paradigm Shift For Undergraduate Students

Chapter 10

Michele Sweeney, Salem State College, United States

Amy Everitt, Salem State College, United States

James Carifio, University of Massachusetts-Lowell, United States

Introduction

Morris and Stiehl (1999) assert that the most common approach to teaching games in the United States is to teach to a single standard-designed game. This approach emphasizes the teaching of predetermined skills and strategies to be performed at a certain level before the game can be played and appreciated. Although this instructional approach has traditionally been the practice of choice among physical educators and coaches, it is currently being met with criticism. Pedagogical leaders who value the diversity of prior experiences among learners are critical of this "skill-first," rigid instruction. They believe that learning is a complex process where learners interpret new information differently based on their individual prior experiences. This process challenges the teacher to provide a learning environment where the knowledge construct of each individual learner leads to the same common understanding. Otherwise known as constructivism, pedagogical leaders influenced by this teaching model have conflicts with the single-standard design. They believe that it is not necessary to obtain a certain skill level in order to appreciate and play games, valuing game appreciation over skill development. Furthermore, constructivists focus on the students' experience within the game and not the game itself.

Teaching Games for Understanding (TGfU), a constructivist-based approach, highlights a student's tactical awareness of the game instead of the single-standard design. The TGfU approach encourages students to solve tactical problems by providing cognitive and psychomotor connections between skill development and conceptual understanding. The focus of the approach is to utilize the game knowledge that a player has already acquired as a foundation to enhance further personal understanding of the game.

Affective connections are also encouraged with this approach. The TGfU approach engages players to be problem solvers in constructing personal meaning of the game. This lends to active learning and socialization between players, critical components in creating an environment that is conducive to a conceptual understanding of the game.

Several studies have investigated the ability of preservice and novice physical education teachers to assimilate a constructivist approach to teaching. Rovegno (1992, 1998) and Chen and Rovegno (2000) discovered repeatedly that preservice and novice teachers have common struggles. Rovegno (1992) found that it was difficult for undergraduates to comprehend how individual lessons linked to larger, conceptual understandings. Specifically, preservice teachers did not have sufficient subject matter knowledge of the constructivist-based approach in order to develop connections or relationships across individual lessons. Rovegno (1998) also discovered that novice teachers, when learning to teach a constructivist movement approach, were uncertain how to facilitate in a less-structured environment. They were unsure when to ask questions in order to engage the learner and when to intervene and provide information to the student. The common practice reported was for novice teachers to either direct students in the activity, allowing for minimal student input, or to provide little to no teacher direction for fear they might violate the approach (Chen & Rovegno, 2000). Research is still in its infancy regarding the assimilation of a constructivist-based approach with preservice and novice teachers.

Another area of inquiry revolved around changes in undergraduates' beliefs about teaching and learning. There was an interest to investigate whether certain beliefs about teaching and learning strongly correlated with a more comprehensive understanding of the TGfU approach. Perry's (1968) work found that on entering college, students believe that knowledge is simple, certain, and handed down by authorities. His work assumed that personal epistemology is one-dimensional and changes according to specific developmental stages. Schommer (1990) however believed that personal epistemology was multidimensional and discovered, through questioning 266 undergraduate students, that their beliefs indeed reflected many factors. Schommer's work revealed four significant dimensions of epistemological beliefs labeled as Fixed Ability, Simple Knowledge, Quick Learning, and Certain Knowledge. Fixed Ability reflects attitudes on the ability to learn, ranging from the belief that learning is innate and established to evolving over time. Simple Knowledge reflects an individual's perceptions on the structure of knowledge, ranging from a belief that knowledge exists in isolated bits to complex concepts. An individual's understanding of the speed of learning, ranging from quick to gradual is reflected in the dimension of Quick Learning. The dimension of Certain Knowledge represents an individual's beliefs about the stability of knowledge, ranging from an attitude that knowledge never changes to an attitude that knowledge is always changing.

Schommer (1990) also explored personal variables that might predispose students to certain epistemological beliefs. She found that the number of college classes taken correlated highly to a belief that knowledge is uncertain and ever-changing. Schommer suggests that greater exposure to higher education will assist in changing one's epistemological beliefs about knowledge and learning.

Believing in the value of the experience and individual differences in knowledge construction, faculty at an urban public college outside Boston, felt a need to expose their students to a new games approach. Consequently, the higher-education curriculum was revised. Skill-based activity classes were replaced with courses emphasizing the TGfU model. Assuming that most of the students had a great deal of exposure to the traditional skill-based approach, this conceptual model would be unique. The original skill courses included soccer, basketball, and volleyball in one course. A second course included the game skills of lacrosse, field hockey, and softball. In a third course, tennis and badminton were taught. The selection of the activities in the original three courses was based largely upon instructor's expertise and traditional school curriculums. The objective of the three courses was to teach as many game skills as possible. College instructors expressed frustration with the inability to provide students with adequate instructional and skill-acquisition time for the number of skills needed to play the games.

With the new curriculum focus on TGfU, the content of the three courses was revised. No longer is the choice of curricular activities teacher-selected or games instructed according to a skill-based approach. Instead, the courses were entitled, and activities selected according to the shared intention of the games. In one course, territorial/invasion games and their related concepts are the focus of instruction. A second course includes striking games and target games, with an emphasis on their corresponding concepts. In a third course, the focus is on the conceptual understanding of net/wall games. This approach allows for an emphasis on the understanding of tactical concepts that correspond with many different sports. Exposure to strategies such as "maintaining possession" allows students to understand, perform, and teach the tactical theme across a variety of territorial games. With the TGfU approach, only the specific equipment, rules, and procedures of the game would need to be introduced. Philosophically, the distinctive features of the TGfU approach paralleled the beliefs of the college faculty. However, pedagogical strategies became problematic. Questions were presented with regard to how students, who have been taught a predominately skill-based approach, would come to understand the TGfU approach.

The purpose of the study was to investigate the attitudes and possible future assimilation of undergraduate students toward the TGfU approach. Furthermore, the researchers attempted to describe how students perceive knowledge and learning.

Methods

Participants

This study was conducted in an urban four-year institution of higher education with 17 undergraduate students. Participants were enrolled in a 16-week activity-based TGfU course, 10 students during the fall 2000 academic term, and 7 students during the spring 2001 academic term. Of the 17 participants, there were 10 males and 7 females. Not all of the students' primary vocations were teacher education, although all intended on using pedagogical skills in some capacity. Other areas of concentration include coaching and fitness/wellness.

Materials

Data was collected using three different measures including interviews, Burger and Cooper's (1979) Desirability of Control Scale, and the Learning by Connections Scale (Sweeney & Everitt, 2000).

Interviews

Interviews with the seven students enrolled in the spring 2001 course were conducted on three separate occasions throughout the academic term. Because of the infancy of this investigation, the 10 students enrolled in the fall 2000 course were not interviewed. Interview questions were designed to identify individual preferences and attitudes toward teaching methodologies and learning styles, prior knowledge of teaching, and attitudes toward the TGfU approach (Appendix A). Each of the interview sessions was recorded on audiotape and later transcribed.

Desirability of Control Scale

The Desirability of Control Scale is a 20-item inventory that measures individual differences in the level of motivation to control the events in one's life (Burger & Cooper, 1979). Students rated their degree of agreement to the 20 statements using a seven-point scale. Individuals with high scores on the scale have a high desire for control and are described as decisive, assertive, and generally seek to influence others. High-desire-for-control people tend to react to a challenge with greater effort and persistence primarily because they feel threatened by the possibility of not being able to complete the task (i.e., threatened by failure).

Low-desire-for-control people demonstrate characteristics of nonassertiveness, passiveness, and indecisiveness. They prefer to have most of their decisions made by others. Burger and Cooper (1979) report a reliability coefficient of .80 for the Desirability of Control Scale.

Learning by Connections Scale

In order to further describe and measure students' attitudes toward the TGfU approach, the Learning by Connections (LBC) scale was developed (Sweeney & Everitt, 2000). Similar to the Desirability of Control, the LBC consists of 20 items with a seven-point scale, allowing students to rank their degree of agreement with statements regarding the TGfU approach. High scores on the LBC scale indicate a favorable attitude toward TGfU and a strong likelihood that the student would assimilate the approach in the future. Low scores on the LBC indicate that the student has an unfavorable attitude toward TGfU and would probably not incorporate the approach in their teaching in the future.

During its development, the LBC scale was reviewed and assessed by a panel of experts in the field of physical education pedagogy. Preliminary factor analysis results indicate that the LBC is valid. Analysis and improvement of the scale is ongoing.

Data Collection and Analysis

During the fall 2000 academic term, 10 students participated in a 16-week undergraduate activity course that focused on the TGfU approach. Territorial/invasion games were specifically highlighted. Students were cognitively challenged about TGfU and learned territorial/invasion games through the approach. In addition, students were provided the opportunity to utilize the TGfU approach in peer-teaching experiences. At the conclusion of the academic term, students were asked to complete both the Desirability of Control scale and the LBC scale.

In the spring 2001, seven students who were enrolled in another 16-week undergraduate TGfU activity course volunteered to participate in the study. Both the fall and spring courses were taught by the same instructor, however, emphasis of the spring course was placed on striking and target games, as opposed to territorial/invasion games. As with the fall, students were asked to complete the Desirability of Control scale and the LBC scale at the conclusion of the academic term. In addition, these seven students were interviewed individually on three separate occasions throughout the academic term, at the beginning, mid-term, and conclusion of the course. Interview questions were designed to identify individual preferences toward teaching methodologies and learning styles, as well as any subsequent changes in attitude and understanding with regard to the TGfU approach. Each interview was recorded on audiotape and later transcribed for analysis. The interviews were conducted by a second researcher who was not involved in the teaching or evaluation of students enrolled in the TGfU activity course.

Interviews were assessed using an analytical scoring scale (Carifio & McBride, 1977). Two researchers using a five-point scale (see Table I) assessed major concept areas relative to epistemological beliefs and the TGfU approach. An interrater reliability coefficient of .80 was achieved between the researchers. The results of each of the three interviews were compared to determine if any changes in epistemological beliefs, knowledge, and attitudes toward the TGfU approach occurred over the course of the academic term. Pearson correlations were used to analyze the relationship between students' desire for control as measured by the Desirability of Control scale and their attitudes toward the TGfU approach as measured by the LBC.

Table I. Interview analysis: Concept areas assessed

Epistemological Beliefs:

1	2	3	4	5
Passive Learner				Active Learner
1	2	3	4	5
Skill Based				Conceptual Based
1	2	3	4	5
Teacher Centered				Student Centered
1	2	3	4	5
Knowledge is Simple				Knowledge is Complex

Attitudes Toward TGfU:

1	2	3	4	5
No knowledge of TGfU				Knowledge of TGfU
1	2	3	4	5
TGfU is ineffective				TGfU is effective

Results and Discussion

The TGfU approach incorporates student-centered learning and the teacher's role is that of a facilitator rather than a provider of information. Allison and Barrett (2000) describe teachers who favor a constructivist approach as someone who views the teacher and learner working together toward a common goal. In this type of educational environment, there are no struggles by the teacher for control of student learning within the classroom. Therefore, it was hypothesized that students who were identified as having a high desire for control would be less likely to utilize the TGfU approach. Results of this study showed that there was a significant relationship between desire for control and the LBC scale $r = 0.73$ ($p < .01$) (see Figure 1). However, the results indicated just the opposite of what was hypothesized. Students identified as having a high desire for control indicated that they would be *more likely* to utilize the TGfU approach.

To clarify the interpretation of the Desirability of Control scale, a person who scores high is considered to have a high desire for control and possesses characteristics that include high aspiration levels, a tendency to select higher-level tasks, and reacts to challenges with great effort. One might conclude that these characteristics are essential to students who favor the TGfU approach in their own teaching. Philosophically and pedagogically different than the common traditional approach, the adoption of the TGfU approach may pose real challenges for students. By its nature, it requires high-order thinking skills and sophisticated pedagogical skills such as effective management, questioning, and facilitation strategies. Therefore, it would be reasonable to consider that students with a high desire for control may have a more favorable attitude toward the TGfU approach.

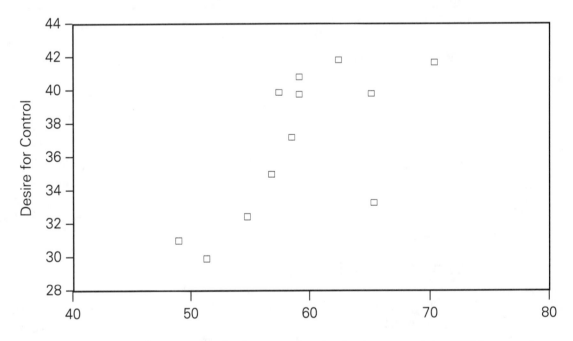

Figure 1. Relationship between desire for control and attitudes toward the TGfU approach.

Furthermore, the LBC is based solely on the students' own interpretation of their knowledge of the TGfU approach. The instrument was not initially designed to measure knowledge of the approach, but rather the attitude toward its use and effectiveness. A misconception and inexperience with the use of the TGfU approach by students may also have accounted for the unexpected findings.

Finally, correlations for epistemological beliefs between interviews conducted at the beginning and conclusion of the academic term were significant $r = 0.78$ ($p < .05$). This indicates that students' epistemological beliefs were similar throughout the 16-week TGfU activity course. A person's beliefs about teaching and learning develop over years and the results parallel the researchers' hypothesis that a 16-week course would not significantly change attitudes.

In conclusion, the relationship between the desire for control and the attitudes toward the TGfU approach is intriguing. Closer scrutiny of the interpretation of high and low desire for control, and how it relates to the assimilation of the TGfU approach is currently being investigated so that educators might better understand how students come to realize the effectiveness of constructivist-based instruction. Further investigations are currently focusing on specific interviewing and other critical assessment techniques to determine students' level of knowledge about the TGfU approach. Student learning styles are also being considered to gain a better understanding of personal characteristics that may lend to a favorable attitude toward the TGfU approach. Finally, the relationship between the epistemological beliefs of undergraduate students and utilization of the TGfU approach is being investigated.

References

Allison, P. & Barrett, K. (2000). *Constructing Children's Physical Education Experiences: Understanding the Content for Teaching*. Needham Heights, MA: Allyn and Bacon.

Burger, J. M. & Cooper, H. M. (1979). The desirability of control. *Motivation and Emotion, 3*, 381-393.

Carifio, J. & McBride, B. (1977, April). *Empirical results of using an analytic versus holistic scoring method to score geometric groups: Linking and assessing Greeno, Bloom, and Van Hiele's views of students' ability to do proofs*. Paper presented at the Annual Conference of the American Educational Research Association, Chicago, IL.

Chen, W. & Rovegno, I. (2000). Examination of expert and novice teachers' constructivist-oriented teaching practices using a movement approach to elementary physical education. *Research Quarterly for Exercise and Sport, 71*, 357-372.

Morris, G. & Stiehl, J. (1999). *Changing kids games* (2nd ed.). Champaign, IL: Human Kinetics.

Perry, W., Jr. (1968). *Patterns of development in thought and values of students in a liberal arts college: A validation of a scheme*. Cambridge, MA: Bureau of Study Counsel, Harvard University. (ERIC Document Reproduction Service No. ED 024315).

Rovegno, I. (1992). Learning a new curricular approach: Mechanisms of knowledge acquisition in pre-service teachers. *Teaching and Teacher Education, 8*, 253-264.

Rovegno, I. (1998). The development of in-service teachers' knowledge of a constructivist approach to physical education: Teaching beyond activities. *Research Quarterly for Exercise and Sport, 69*, 147-162.

Schommer, M. (1990). Effects of beliefs about the nature of knowledge on comprehension. *Journal of Educational Psychology, 82*, 498-504.

Sweeney, M. & Everitt, A. (2000). [Validation of the learning by connections scale]. Unpublished raw data.

Appendix A

Interview Questions

Pre-Course Interview

1. What do you think you will get out of this course? What are your expectations?
2. How do you prefer to learn?
3. Have you ever taught before?
4. If yes to #3, how do you present information/material to your students?
5. Tell me about your favorite teacher.
6. How did they present information? What was their teaching style?
7. Tell me about your least favorite teacher.
8. How did they present information? What was their teaching style?
9. Are you aware of the TGfU approach?
10. If yes to #9, can you explain it?

Post-Course Interview

1. How do you feel about the course now that you have completed it?
2. Did your expectations of the course change?
3. What is TGfU? Can you describe it?
4. Is the TGfU approach effective?
5. What are your beliefs about teaching and learning?
6. Who do you think controls knowledge?
7. Who/what is the source of knowledge?
8. Is knowledge simple or complex?
9. What are more important, skills or concepts, when teaching a game?

Exploring the Construction of Knowledge for Student Learning

Introduction to Chapters 11-13

The authors in this section attempt to bridge the gap between the theory and practice of Teaching Games for Understanding (TGfU). A prime objective for the student to internalize is the inherent connection between constructivism and TGfU. The broad notions of understanding though experience (John Dewey and others) and game epistemology form the basis of the following readings. The reader will also see obvious connections between experiential learning, TGfU, and constructivist pedagogy.

Wells and Wells (1992, p.8) identify the foundations of the constructivist process as:

1. The recognition of the active nature of learning, manifested in the opportunities for the learners to set their own goals, and plan and carry out the activities necessary to achieve them.
2. The recognition of the social nature of learning, manifested in the encouragement of the collaboration of learners in all aspects of their work and in the guidance and assistance provided by the teacher.
3. The recognition of the affective foundation of thinking and learning manifested in the positive values of empathy, curiosity, caring, and risk taking.
4. The recognition in the holistic nature of learning, manifested in the spontaneous integration of information and strategies.
5. The recognition of the central role of language, both in the medium through which learning takes place and as the means for collaboration and integration. This is manifested in the encouragement of learners' purposeful use of their linguistic resources, both spoken and written.

These articles present the reader with two types of information that lead to a successful explanation of Teaching Games for Understanding (TGfU). On the one hand, you will read entries from three sets of researchers who will articulately describe the process of "learning" the TGfU model. On the other hand, you will be processing another critical set of data within a constructivist paradigm: that of the participants as they become aware and transformed into active learners, capable (and needful) of self discovery as a primary means of acquiring knowledge.

In all of the articles in this section, the authors attempt to relate the theory of specific TGfU teaching with general constructivist pedagogy. You will be introduced (or re-acquainted in many cases) to terminology that distinguishes a TGfU classroom.

Much of the language associated with TGfU is familiar across the education spectrum. Colleagues in elementary and secondary education share the need of physical educators and coaches to connect with the student. Parallel literatures are abundant.

In chapter 11, Kath Howarth and Jeff Walkuski explain the differences between skills-oriented and TGfU approaches to teaching. One of the first missions of the reader might be to look at the definitions that the researchers use for these two models and read between the lines for those missing and needed elements (connections and transitions that bridge student knowing and application). It is important to note that the authors point out that the research has not indicated a "winner" between the paradigms. The important aspect of the article remains that continued inquiry is important to understand the roles that the specific approaches play in the total milieu of physical education pedagogy.

Howarth and Walkuski describe an intervention involving preservice teachers and the shifts in teaching focus that occurred over a few months. Some of the shifts were more profound than others, but the self-reporting style of inquiry resulted in or led to greater pedagogical understanding for the subjects as well as the researchers.

Nathalie Mahut and her colleagues in chapter 12, using the game of badminton, describe the formalities of teacher-centered and student-centered learning. They use the terms "situated action," "reflective attitude," and "reflective horizon" to emphasize the PETE program at the University of Franche Comte. Students, aged 12 and 13, are asked to debate and interpret performance of badminton skills in the context of games situations. As you will see, the results yield important information relating to empowerment of students-an important outcome of TGfU learning.

Jean-Francois Richard and Linda Griffin present the reader with two assessment tools that complete the pedagogical troika of planning, action, and assessment. Too often, excellent planning and class activity are lost if not adequately monitored and assessed. The authors introduced the Team Sport Assessment Procedure (TSAP) and the Game Performance Assessment Instrument (GPAI).

Readers should focus on the connections between the student and teacher data-collection techniques offered in these two instruments. How "flexible" are the tools and why (especially in the constructivist/TGfU format) is this so important? Richard and Griffin also emphasize Cohen's notion of the continuity between learning outcomes, teaching strategies and assessment. The paper treats assessment not as an end but as a process. It is our intention that the reader studies these papers separately and together, melding concepts as well as looking for individual idiosyncrasies.

References

Wells C. & Chang-Wells, G. (1992). *Constructing Knowledge Together.* Portsmouth, NH: Heinemann.

Teaching Tactical Concepts with Preservice Teachers

Chapter 11

Kath Howarth, SUNY College at Cortland, United States

Jeff Walkuski, SUNY College at Cortland, United States

Teaching Tactical Concepts With Preservice Teachers

The attainment of sport-skill competence and proficiency are concerns of physical educators and the field of physical education (National Association for Sport and Physical Education, 1995). The debate however continues over the methods by which students are taught these sport skills, the underlying assumptions regarding the type of teaching method employed, and the ultimate goals of such instruction (Rink, French, & Tjeerdsma, 1996; Gréhaigne, Godbout, & Bouthier, 1999). An interesting point sometimes hidden in the debate about approaches to the teaching of games is that most ways of presenting games and sports are successful and motivating if presented by effective teachers (Rink et al., 1996). This study was designed to look at the change, if any, which occurred in preservice teachers' knowledge of tactical concepts as a result of a required games course.

The typical pedagogical orientation to sport and games teaching uses direct teaching and follows a drill, mastery, modified-games approach with attention to tactics followed by the game proper (Gréhaigne et al., 1999). As argued by Placek, Griffin, Dodds, and Briand (1998) the skill-oriented approach, devoid of any specific focus on tactics, has been the dominant pedagogy when examining various standard and popular texts in the area of physical education pedagogy. A skill-oriented approach has not been without its detractors (Fleming, 1994, Turner & Martinek, 1995). Specific concerns have revolved around the apparent erroneous assumption that a skills-based approach leads to the ultimate attainment of a skill and tactical base that will allow a learner to fully engage in the broad context of a sporting endeavor. Researchers have pointed out that the skills-based approach is often detached from its sporting context and leads to pedagogic episodes that have little inherent value and meaning for students (Turner & Martinek, 1995).

Advocates of the teaching games for understanding approach argue that the skills-based approach often leads to low motivation and low levels of skillfulness and tactical understanding (Werner, Thorpe, & Bunker, 1996). Inherent in the understanding approach is the view that games fall into particular categories of common tactics and goals which are transferable across games within the same category (Ellis, 1983; Werner & Almond, 1990). In the tactical approach, students are first guided through a particular game form, recognizing the particular "problems" to be solved. Students are introduced to rules that govern play within the game (e.g., the size of a goal, the number of players, the constraints and advantages of the playing space). After a more formal introduction of skills is undertaken, students return to the game form (Werner et al., 1996).

Questions have arisen regarding the utility of the games for understanding approach. It is critical to note that research in this area has been characterized by differing results and limitations regarding the types of game classifications used, the length of intervention, and the types of subjects employed. The research base examining the tactical approach has not produced emphatic data to indicate that this approach is superior to the traditional skills-based approach. It is not clear that such an approach does indeed allow for both the development of contextual skills and tactics and if the student as well as the teacher can develop the "why" with little direct attention to the "how" (Fleming, 1994).

Research in this area is still evolving and there appears to be no unified or agreed-on methodology to examine the impact of the tactical approach. In an early study examining the effects of a tactical and traditional approach to the teaching of a six-lesson badminton unit with students between the ages of 12 and 13, no differences were found between the groups either in skill or knowledge (Lawton, 1989). Turner and Martinek (1992) reported similar results in their study that examined the use of both approaches in a six-week hockey unit. Turner and Martinek described that the groups in the study did not differ in measures of procedural and declarative knowledge, control, execution, or decision-making. The authors attributed the results to the limited timeframe in which the study was undertaken.

Expertise, or the ability of an individual to unconsciously or automatically perform a given skill, has been examined extensively (Vickers, 1990). Early research has indicated that the expert has a greater ability to solve problems in a variety of settings than the novice, yet is typically unable to explain how he/she is able to do it. Experts have also been described as having "a high altitude overview" (Vickers, 1990, p. 27) that allows them to call upon small bits of relevant information to solve a problem (as opposed to a novice who typically collects a large amount of irrelevant information when attempting to solve a problem).

Experts, in general, typically possess three cognitive characteristics that differentiate them from the novice (Vickers, 1990). The first of these includes the ability to group or chunk information into sizeable integrated units. Another characteristic of the expert is his/her ability to hierarchically organize information as opposed to the novice (Vickers, 1990). The expert organizes information in such a way that skills, strategies, or concepts are richly interconnected and described. Experts also differ from novices in the way that they organize knowledge and make decisions (Vickers, 1990). Research has shown that experts tend to chunk information into large units that are hierarchically organized.

These phenomena have been illustrated in sport settings. Allard and Burnett (1985) report on Allard, Graham, and Paaralu's research, which asked varsity and intramural basketball players to recall set play situations and random game positions in basketball. Participants were shown slides providing only brief glimpses of different phases of play. Varsity players (experts) but not intramural players (novices) were able to reconstruct the tactics or plays shown. When slides were presented lacking tactical sense, however, both groups performed the same. Allard and Burnett attributed the ability of expert players to have superior recall of structured game situations to the possibility that such athletes develop perceptual strategies based on the pattern or structure of the game.

In an unpublished study reported in Vickers (1990), Housner and Griffey (1985) examined knowledge structures of novice and expert badminton players and found that experts were better able to make interconnections between strategic concepts than novices. Experts also were shown to utilize a more efficient, solution-based strategy when examining game situations.

Housner and Griffey (1985) examined planning and teaching behaviors of novice and expert teachers. In respect to planning, expert teachers attempted to acquire a more detailed view of a teaching situation than novices. Expert teachers also made more planning decisions, interacted more with students, and possessed a larger bank of ideas than the novices. Expert teachers also focused more on subject matter when teaching and were less influenced by the students like or dislike of the lesson than the novice.

One of the most interesting challenges for teachers of any age group, whether novice or expert, is to discover the level of domain-specific knowledge prior to the beginning of instruction, and to understand how to help learners restructure the knowledge base through conceptual change (Dodds, Griffin, & Placek, 2001; Placek et al., 1998). Using research in science education on alternative conceptions, Griffin, Dodds, Placek, & Tremino (2001) looked at domain-specific knowledge of seven tactical problems in soccer with sixth-grade students. They analyzed the students' naïve conceptions of the tactical scenarios in order to document early, novice conceptions of a game. These conceptions, it was argued, could be different from concepts authenticated by experts, or they may be incomplete versions of these concepts. Students' prior experience and sources of information about soccer played into the ways in which they understood tactics, and they showed different levels of domain-specific knowledge. This area of research is particularly interesting for teachers who are presenting contrasting and new concepts to learners that challenge their previously held conceptions and require them to change domain-specific knowledge. The study of sixth graders illustrated the complexity facing any teacher when planning the instructional environment.

This complexity increases when instruction is planned within a teacher-education program. Not only are preservice teachers likely to come to activity classes with a variety of experiences of the activities, but also with alternate conceptions of how to teach that activity. Therefore, as participants, they could fall into the novice or expert categories and, as preservice teachers, experience varying levels of cognitive dissonance when faced with a model of teaching sports that uses a very different knowledge base from their own. Placek and Griffin (2001) suggest that:

> The difficulty of teaching tactics may explain why physical education sports and games curricula remain firmly grounded in the teaching of isolated skills. In addition, we suggest that teachers lack knowledge about how to teach tactics. There is also the hurdle of convincing teachers that teaching tactics is an important part of physical education (p.404).

It was with these issues in mind that preservice teachers were given the same seven tactical soccer scenarios as were given to the sixth graders (Griffin et al., 2001) to ascertain their domain-specific knowledge during the time they took a tactical concepts class in which they were introduced to the tactical model. In this way, the underlying knowledge structures could be examined in an effort to understand more about preservice teachers' prior knowledge and competing conceptions of teaching sports and games.

Purpose

As part of a larger project, the purpose of this study was to examine preservice students' construction of tactical concepts pre- and post-participation in a tactical concepts course. Specifically, the research was designed to examine the following research questions: a) What was the effect of a tactical concepts course on preservice students' knowledge and application of tactical concepts? b) What was the effect of a tactical concepts course on the language used by preservice students when describing tactical situations in soccer?

Method

This exploratory study set out to ascertain the level of domain-specific knowledge held by preservice teachers when faced with seven tactical scenarios, based on soccer, at the beginning and the end of a tactical concepts course. Qualitative data was collected through two interviews. Participants explained the scenarios as if they were teaching students in a school setting. Participants also manipulated moveable markers on a white board to illustrate their solutions to each tactical scenario.

Participants and Setting

The participants of the study were eight volunteer undergraduate physical education students of at least junior status from a required tactical concepts course within a Department of Physical Education at a small comprehensive state college in the northeast United States. The sample consisted of three females and five males with varying degrees of experience in the playing of, and the teaching and/or coaching of, soccer. All participants had taken at least the first required methods course offered within the preservice program. Data for the purposes of this report were collected at the beginning and end of the tactical concepts course. Students were scheduled for data collection on an individual basis. The collection of data occurred in a large private room where students were presented with various scenarios in soccer using a three-by-five-foot white board marked out as a soccer field with colored moveable markers representing offensive (red) and defensive (blue) players. A smaller black marker represented the ball. The white board was placed on a table in front of the subject, while the second researcher orally presented seven tactical problems and manipulated the colored markers to represent the tactical problem with the assistance of the first researcher. The tactical problems were those used by Placek et al. (1998), which were a) maintaining possession of the ball, b) attacking the goal, c) creating space in attack, d) using space in attack, e) defending space, f) winning the ball, and g) bunching up. For each of the scenarios, the participants were asked to explain how they would describe the play/tactics of the particular scenario to naïve high school physical education students. Participants were encouraged to manipulate the markers on the white board as they verbally described their solutions to the tactical problem. All responses were videotaped for later video and audio analysis using an RCA model CC4352 camcorder mounted on a tripod. Of particular interest for the purposes of this paper is the scenario "4-vs-4 - bunching up," the last scenario presented (see Figure 1). This scenario was analyzed at the completion of the data collection and will be further discussed in this paper.

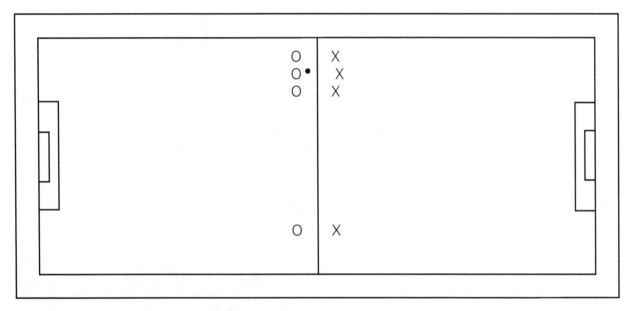

Figure 1. 4-vs-4 bunching up scenario based on Griffin et al. (1997). Symbol "O" represents the offensive players, symbol "X" represents the defensive players, and symbol "•" represents the ball. Play is from reader's left to right

Analysis of Data

At the completion of the research project, both researchers independently viewed the videotaped responses of the subjects from the pre- and post-teaching data-collection sessions. The researchers independently transcribed the participants' verbatim verbal responses to the "4-vs-4 — bunching up" scenario and diagrammed the subjects' physical movements of the markers. The researchers then met to discuss the data collectively. This process was repeated three times over a three-week period. By the third meeting, both researchers were in total agreement in regard to the transcription of each participant's verbal responses and the topography of the physical movements of the markers. After the third meeting, all verbal responses and the participant's physical movement of the markers were transcribed. Verbal responses were considered for their instructional usefulness. A global solution, such as "spread out," recognizes the required solution but is of very little help to players who are bunching around the ball. Richer descriptions were identified as those that help players understand the tactical concept more fully and give them specific help. A rich description would give a player specific movement suggestions with a reason, for example, "Drop back to give support." Combination solutions were also noted where both offense and defense were included in the solution, such as, "Try to get this player away in the hopes that the defense will follow." Such combination solutions would be helpful because they explain what the defense would do as a result of their actions in offense (or vice versa). Giving reasons for suggested movements was noted as adding to the usefulness of the solution for instructional purposes, for example, "When defense are together, they are more likely to steal the ball."

Results

Results from this phase of the study will be reported using three specific levels of focus. The first level describes the levels of verbal solutions given by the participants to the problem of bunching up. The second level describes the levels of manipulation of moveable markers on the white board. Finally, the levels of participants' conceptions of the scenario from a tactical viewpoint are identified, as are the levels at which they gave reasons for the solutions they provided.

Verbal Solutions

Participants were asked in each interview to describe what they would tell a class of students when they saw the scenario of bunching up. They gave a variety of descriptions, "They are like bumble bees, they all want to be near the ball" and "They're going after the ball. They all want to be part of the action. They all want to kick the ball." They were encouraged to go on talking until they had no other solutions. Every participant identified the problem and immediately offered the solution of "Spread out."

There was a difference however in the number and richness of the solutions given to solve the problem. Although the number of solutions did not increase significantly for most students between the first and second descriptions of the scenario, the specificity of the solutions did. For example one participant who, in the first interview stated, "By spreading out you make runs. Create space for others to move through" and in the second interview he stated, "They must learn to spread out and move the ball. Get a better opportunity to get the ball. This person, drop back to give support. This person, (move) into the middle. This person makes a corner run."

Only one participant showed a real change in terminology and used the terminology demonstrated in course handouts, the text, and by the instructor. Some students did not become more specific in terms of what each player should do, but their overall descriptions became clearer. One participant in the first interview said, "Bunching up is bad. Not making the defense play harder. Spread out and move around." In the second interview, the same participant explained the term "bunching up" more clearly by relating it to the size of the field and the ease by which the defense could regain possession of the ball. She said, "The soccer field is very big. So bunching up is to no purpose. Spread out and use the field. Move; scatter the defense a bit. [It's] easy to intercept. Spread out. Create space and passing lanes."

Manipulation of Moveable Markers

In addition to verbal solutions, participants' manipulation of markers on the white board was also of interest, in particular, any change in the number of moves made from the first to the second interview. Most participants manipulated the markers more in the second interview. One of the most fluent and knowledgeable students in the first interview increased from 3 moves by the offense in the first interview to 10 moves on the board in the second interview. Another participant stayed about the same in number of moves, but in the second interview explained a global tactical plan (the use of lanes to help students space out) as he moved the pieces on the white board.

In the second interview, participants also tended to see the whole field more clearly. For example, in the first interview, several did not touch or refer to the isolated offense and defense on the opposite side of the field in the bunching-up scenario. In the second interview, these same participants brought in the opposite-side players into their solutions.

Understanding of the Scenario and Reasons for the Solutions

Descriptions of the scenario not only varied in the amount of detail, but also in terms of the global view of the tactical situation. Some students saw the situation as affecting both offense and defense at the same time and even when they were asked about offense, brought in the defensive viewpoint. For example, one male participant stated during the first interview "by spreading out [the offense], you make the defense work harder." During the second interview, the same participant stated "...middle run so you have the defense moving, this will make more space for this [offensive] person." Others only described what the offense should do and rarely related this to the defensive role. One female participant, during her first interview, provided nontactical statements such as "move away a little bit," in describing what the offense should do while not relating it directly to the defense. The same participant's response, during the second interview, showed little change as she again used nontactical statements such as "stay in the back," in describing what the offense should do. This tendency did not seem to change from the first interview to the second.

This tendency to view the offense and defense either dependently or independently was reflected in the manipulation of the moveable markers. Some students moved the offense and defense together or sequentially. Other students moved only the offensive pieces. For example, while describing the offense, one male participant, during the first interview, moved only the offensive pieces for a total of five moves, while during the second interview, he only moved only the offensive pieces for a total of two moves. Another male participant, describing the offense, moved the offensive pieces four times and defensive pieces four times together during the first interview. This same participant during the second interview moved the offensive pieces six times and the defensive pieces four times when describing what the offense should do during the second interview.

In describing the solutions, students showed variation in the detail in which they explained their reasons for the moves they made on the board. For example, a male participant exhibited a more global, tactical view during the first and second interview, primarily during his description of the offensive strategy as he moved the pieces. Comments such as "spread out," "create space," and "working the ball on offense is all about moving without the ball" were typical of the quality of his responses during both interviews. This tendency to explain, or not explain, the reasons for the moves, did not change much from the first to the second interview.

A Rubric for Levels of Tactical Understanding for Teachers

Using the data collected from this initial sample of preservice teachers, we constructed an initial rubric to show four levels of tactical understanding based on the one scenario, bunching up (see Table I). This is speculative and we will need to test it further on other scenarios already taped with the same preservice teachers. Preservice teachers with the most fluent and richest descriptions of how to help their students solve the tactical problem of bunching up in soccer identified the problem and the global solution easily. They clearly described verbally what each player might do, what general tactical solutions might be suggested (e.g., create passing lanes, triangle formation) and gave reasons for each solution) e.g., "try to get this player away in hopes that the defense will follow"). They related their solution to the defensive plan (e.g., "defense not as close together—space them out. When defense are together they are more likely to steal the ball"). They also matched their verbal description to their manipulation of the moveable markers, thus giving a visual, as well as verbal, explanation of how to solve the problem.

Table I. Rubric for assessment of preservice teachers' tactical concepts knowledge				
	Verbal Solutions	**Manipulate Solutions**	**Interplay of Offense/Defense**	**Reasons for Solutions**
Level 0	Does not recognize the tactical problem, or identifies it incorrectly	No manipulation of moveable markers	1—one-sided focus (offense or defense) 2—includes offense and defense	A—no reasons given for actions proposed B—incorrect reasons given C—correct reasons given
Level 1	Global solution identified (e.g., Spread out)	Manipulation of moveable markers reflects global solution	As above	As above
Level 2	Global solution identified and richer description is given (2 or fewer moves are described)	Manipulation of moveable markers reflects global solution and richer description is given (2 or fewer moves are made)	As above	As above
Level 3	Global solution identified and richer description is given (3 or more moves are described)	Manipulation of moveable markers reflects global solution and richer description is given (3 or more moves are made)	As above	As above

The rubric offered in Table I represents these initial ideas about how preservice students could be assessed and helped to improve their ability to identify and present tactical problems and solutions in a game situation. Further research is needed to test the rubric out on other scenarios already recorded with the same set of students, and also on scenarios described by expert teachers, to see if it does indeed capture their expertise in teaching tactical concepts in physical education classes.

Discussion

These interviews with preservice teachers showed a range of levels of understanding of a typical tactical scenario they would meet when teaching invasion games in schools. This was apparent during the first interviews and it was clear that, although there were some improvements in levels of understanding in individual students, the tactical-concepts class did not serve as an equalizer. In other words, it did not allow those who started at a lower level of understanding to catch up with, or close the gap between themselves and other more experienced students.

Teachers and coaches who are experts show expertise by "chunking" information. They also exhibit the ability to organize information hierarchically. These abilities eventually impact the decision-making process (Vickers, 1990). Chunking refers to the way in which an expert remembers information as large chunks that allow them to make associations and connections and take a global overview based on small pieces of information. Experts group these chunks into a plan, or hierarchy, which is stable and from which they can select information according to the situation. These aspects are shown to be different in experts when compared with beginners. It was apparent in the ways in which our preservice teachers talked about the "bunching up" scenario that they varied in their ability to group information and state it clearly as teachers in relation to a specific tactical problem. The tactical-concepts course is a work in progress relative to its potential to prepare preservice teachers to teach with confidence using this particular teaching model.

Implications and Directions for Further Research

To reiterate the findings of this study, it was found that this sample of preservice teachers had different knowledge structures when describing the scenario "4-vs-4-bunching up" and results were consistent from pre- and post-teaching episode interviews. There were some improvements in levels of understanding in individual students, however, the tactical concepts class did not serve as an equalizer between students of differing initial levels of tactical understanding. The other scenarios, and the post-course interviews, may help the authors refine the rubric further and develop different strategies for the teaching of a tactical concepts course. Further research is needed to apply the rubric on other scenarios already recorded with the same set of students, and also on scenarios described by expert teachers to see if it does indeed completely capture their expertise in teaching tactical concepts in physical education classes. This particular avenue of research may allow for further refinement of the proposed rubric. One consideration regarding the teaching of the tactical concepts course is to require the students, after playing a game, to immediately verbalize solutions to a given scenario, for example, how to use a 3-vs-2 situation to advantage as offense. The purpose would be to enhance their ability to communicate verbally the solutions to a problem many of them can easily solve physically.

Further research is needed to examine the impact of a tactical-concepts course on preservice students. Such research must address the permanence of such a course on these students' understanding and application of the model. As the model begins to be used more widely in schools, we as teacher educators must fully understand the impact of the model in preservice teachers' construction of knowledge structures pertaining to the instruction of sport-based curriculum and whether we can influence a conceptual shift in how our future teachers can effectively present content to their students.

References

Allard, F. & Burnett N. (1985). Skill in sport, *Canadian Journal of Psychology, 39*(2), 294-312.

Dodds, P., Griffin, L., & Placek, J. H., (2001). Chapter 2. A selected review of the literature on development of learners' domain-specific knowledge. *Journal of Teaching in Physical Education, 20,* 301-313.

Ellis, M. (1983). *Similarities and differences in games: A system for classification.* Paper presented at the International Association for Physical Education in Higher Education (AIESEP) Conference, Rome, Italy.

Fleming, S. (1994). Understand 'understanding': Making sense of the cognitive approach to the teaching of games, *Physical Education Review, 17*(2), 90-96.

Gréhaigne, J.F., Godbout, P., & Bouthier, D. (1999). The foundations of tactics and strategy in team sports. *Journal of Teaching in Physical Education,18,* 159-174.

Griffin, L., Dodds, P., Placek, J. H., & Tremino, F. (2001). Middle school students' conceptions of soccer: Their solutions to tactical problems. *Journal of Teaching in Physical Education, 20,* 324-340.

Housner, L. D. & Griffey, D. C. (1985). Teacher cognition: Differences in planning and interactive decision making between experienced and inexperienced teachers. *Research Quarterly for Exercise and Sport, 56*(1), 45-53.

Lawton, J. (1989). Comparison of two teaching methods in games. *Bulletin of Physical Education, 25*(1), 35-38.

National Association for Sport and Physical Education. (1995). *Physical education standards: Moving into the future.* Reston, VA: AAHPERD.

Placek, J. H. & Griffin, L. (2001). Chapter 9. The understanding and development of learners' domain-specific knowledge: Concluding comments. *Journal of Teaching in Physical Education, 20,* 402-406.

Placek, J. H., Griffin, L., Dodds, P., & Briand, J. (1998, April). *Children's Views of Bunching Up": A Field Study of Naïve Conceptions in Soccer.* Paper presented at the annual meeting of the American Educational Research Association, San Diego, CA.

Rink, J. E., French, K. E., & Tjeerdsma, B. L. (1996). Foundations for the learning and instruction of sport and games. *Journal of Teaching in Physical Education, 15,* 399-417.

Turner, A. P. & Martinek, T. J. (1992). A comparative analysis of two models for teaching games (Technique Approach and Game-Centered [Tactical Focus] Approach). *International Journal of Physical Education, XXIX*(4), 15-31.

Turner, A.P. & Martinek, T.J. (1995). Teaching for understanding: A model for improving decision making during game play, *Quest, 47,* 44-63.

Vickers, J. N. (1990). *Instructional design for teaching physical education.* Champaign, IL: Human Kinetics.

Werner, P. & Almond, L. (1990). Models of games education. *Journal of Physical Education, Recreation, and Dance, 61*(4), 23-27.

Werner, P., Thorpe, R., & Bunker, D. (1996). Teaching games for understanding: Evolution of a model. *Journal of Physical Education, Recreation, and Dance, 67*(1), 28-33.

The Construction of Student Tactical Knowledge in Badminton

Chapter 12

N. Mahut, University of Franche Comté, France

G. Chevalier, University of Franche Comté, France

B. Mahut, University of Franche Comté, France

J.F. Gréhaigne, University of Franche Comté, France

Introduction

Research on physical education teacher education (PETE) is an international endeavour. PETE's subject matter is essentially based on teaching/learning systems, on the teacher missions about student motor-skill acquisition. This tendency can be identified by the present North American school that develops teacher-centered studies. The purpose of this study was to describe the tasks system and to define instructional settings where teachers formulate how students learn (Astolfi & Develay, 1989; Theureau, 1992).

Recently, there has been a growing interest within European research field toward student's motor-skills learning, from the student point of view. This renewal in the questioning constitutes more than an innovation or a simple originality; it represents a real evolution for the didactic domain (Vergnaud, Halbvacks, & Rouchier, 1978; Brousseau, 1998; Fayol, 1997). In the pedagogical research field, one can observe two tendencies:

1. The *teacher-centered studies*, which describe the task system and the teaching settings. The organization and the conception of learning conditions are considered as determinant for acquiring motor skills (Rink, French & Tjeerdsma, 1996). A learning activity is the manifestation of a logical operative system based on symbolic representations (Cowley, 1997; Rumelhart & Ortony, 1977) and on predetermined elements of the setting (Doyle, 1986; Tardif, 1998).

2. The *student-centered model*, emerging in Europe, seeks to access the student's own activity when he/she is elaborating learning strategies (Vermersch, 1978). The constructivist approach of sport pedagogy insists on the active role of the student as a representation system. This pragmatic conception of teaching, based on a double *ecological and semiotic model*, is emerging in Europe. The cognitive process of "thinking in action" postulates that every action is finalized and situated because it depends strongly on a particular context and its *reconstruction* by the subject (Suchman, 1987; Mc Bride, 1991; Kirshner & Whitson, 1997). This model assumes that a researcher studies student activity in an authentic learning setting. The student-centered model is concerned with reflective practice about action (Ansubel, 1968; Vygotski, 2000; Schön, 1983).

It is interested in reflection of learner strategies. The purpose is for the learner to deconstruct and reconstruct a sense of action (Piaget, 1934), and to produce knowledge within and about the action (Gobbo & Chi, 1986; Chi, Glaser & Farr, 1988; Chi, Bassrock, Lewis, Reimann & Blaser, 1989).

In fact, the student-centered point of view considers the learner as an autonomous actor responsible for his own behavior: it redefines teachers' tasks on learning. Learning, referred to systemic and constructivist theories, is no more considered as a knowledge-acquisition process by piling up and passing on, where modeling and memorization take an essential role. Learning consists of reorganizing, during interaction with context, the representation systems determining action. The semioconstructivist approach is useful for explaining the way students construct knowledge (Alibali, Kita & Young, 2000). Yet constructing a meaningful activity relies on interpreting the setting context from the acting subject's point of view (Greimas, 1983, 1986; Courtès, 1976a, 1976b).

The emerging research in French PETE programs attempts to comprehend the learning setting complexity viewed by student, taking into account the diversity of the context variables (Barbier, 2000; Nachon, Mahut, Mahut & Gréhaigne, 2001). This paper is based on the two concepts of "situated action" (ecological model) and of "reflective attitude" (semioconstructivist approach). The activity of constructing meaning depends on interpreting the context of the setting from the subject's point of view (Jaeglé & Roubaud, 1990). Three assertions can be formulated:

1. According to the constructivist approach, it is within the confrontation with problem-solving that a student elaborates his strategies (Piaget, 1930).
2. The Parisian Semiotic School (Greimas, 1983; Courtès, 1976a) considers that "What we call reality, is interpreted by the one who gives it meaning. Our perception of reality is constructed within a constant interaction of subjective and objective facts from real objects" (Jaeglé & Roubaud, 1990, p.10).
3. Linguistic productions about action can be defined as "behavior in acts" (Masselot, 1999, 2000). Reflective thinking emerges from the interpretation of situations and from the formalization of action (Bernicot, Caron-Pargue & Trognon, 1997). Language allows information to be obtained about a part of the subject's reality. Generated as a representation system, this language acts as a mediator of the expression of symbolic register: it reflects a reality (Jaeglé & Roubaud, 1990). That is the reason reflective thinking (Schön, 1990) emerges from the interpretation of situations and from the formalization of action (Brien, 1990). For studying these phenomena, one can use two theoretical frameworks named "Situated Action Model" (Doyle, 1986; Clancey, 1997) and "Reflective Practice Model" (Schön, 1990). The *Situated Action Model* considers that it is within subject and environment interactions that knowledge in action is elaborated. This ecological model supposes researchers study student activity in authentic learning settings. More, Clancey (1997, p. 263) assumes that "An affordance is not merely a physical state of affairs. People are interacting with their own constructions, not merely with the ambient light array." That means that the ecological model shifts from a precious information-processing conception to a conceptual and semiotic-processing conception. The second model concerns *reflective practice* about action. It consists of generating reflection about learner strategies, making him *deconstruct and reconstruct sense* of action and produce

knowledge "in" and "on" action (Schön, 1990). Reflection about action is a moment where students verbally encode the sense in which they attribute the meaning that they are the only ones able to give to the opposition relationship. Only the pertinent characteristics of the setting contribute to the knowledge-in-act building.

Making explicit a part of that semiotic activity by verbalization represents our subject matter. The purpose of this study was to study how pictures of reality were constructed and perceived by students. We postulate the existence of a complementary nature between the meaning construction during action and the semiotic activity within the rapport of strength in badminton.

Badminton is a physical activity that has the advantage of needing a construction of tactical knowledge within the action (Mc Pherson & French, 1991; Mc Pherson, 1993, 1994, 1999). The purpose is to analyze the way students interpret the opposition relationship in badminton, and re-elaborate their strategy based on action rules. This reading and interpretative attitude of the adversary's action decoding leads to a particular opposition relationship: it is favourable to student verbal productions. The player would have to decode the adversary game according to his or her own expectations (Bouthier, Pastré & Samurçay, 1995). If information is not pre-existent in the didactic learning settings (Viviani & Stucchi, 1992), the participant attributes a relative importance to the context according to his motor skills level and his producing sense ability (Fortin & Rousseau, 1989; Delignières, 1994). In return, this interpretative activity founds new motor acquisitions.

Three questions emerge: 1. How does the student interpret the power play during a badminton game? 2. What knowledge-in-action emerges from action rules during verbalization? 3. At least, is it possible to formalize the interpretation of the game play during a course? We postulate that language is an act, so student verbal reports represent a way to reach thinking in action. In this perspective, do verbal reports about action ("talking about doing") allow student learning strategies to come out (Vermersch, 1995)? Have these verbal reports an impact on action efficiency?

The aim of this study is to build up foundations of a new theory based on a semioconstructivist approach, in order to describe and to model praxis. After describing the frame of references, one can see the method and the results, before defining epistemological limits and perspectives.

Theoretical Framework

The constructivist approach of learning considers that it is the participants, within interaction with environment, that elaborate their adaptation strategies from their representation system (Abernethy, 1988; Griffin, Mitchell & Oslin 1997; Blomqvist, 2001). The underlying assumption is that active problem-solving attitudes allow students to transform themselves. One of the conditions to learn is the confrontation to problem-solving settings, and active search for adaptation solutions (Mc Pherson & French, 1991; Mc Pherson, 1993, 1994, 1999). It means that an intense reflective activity mobilizes critical thinking and subject's interpretative faculties. Knowledge is built/deconstructed/reconstructed *on the basis of a confrontation* between *reached* observed results and *expected* results of action (Bouthier, 1993; Gréhaigne

& Godbout, 1995, 1998; Gréhaigne, Godbout & Bouthier, 1999, 2001). In this context, intention within action is a determinant component of the strategies building (Mosston & Ashworth, 1986). If learning processes are partially implicit, studies on verbal productions about action try to access thinking from the one who produces action. This metacognitive approach postulates that a reflective practice exists, which serves as foundation to context interpretation and to decision-making (Sève, Durand, Saury & Avanzini, 2000). Three concepts are useful in this domain:

The Concept of "Expectation Horizon"

Action signification network is included within an "expectation horizon" (which allows the subject to give sense to action according to his representations, his experience, his knowledge, his interpretative ability (Barbier, 2000). The concept of "expectation horizon," developed through the German Constanz School of "Esthetics of reception" (Gilly, 1992), is based on the following fact: every interpretative act consists of actively *anticipating* the sequence of events and planning plausible ins and outs of the coming action. Verbal information about a part of the subject reality can be obtained from this expectation horizon. Used language allows formalizing thinking in action in relation to motor productions.

The Concept of "Semic Load"

The expectation horizon is not limited to selecting and treating information: the informative "semic load" must be taken into account. Action comprehension supposes the construction of a semic model. Only the subject is able to attribute *significant weight* to contextual elements with regard to his project. Critical attitude is constructed from what is felt, known, and interpreted about action. The immediate return to intended action allows the present situation to be improved and regulates the next action. As there remains a relative autonomy between the representational system (language), its form, and the expression of the content, the reflective process in action can be defined as a semiotic activity of representational reworking. To "give meaning" to the problem, a player has to interpret significant elements within game configuration. These pertinent-for-him elements, which semiotics names "semic treats," are the basis on which he interprets, gets in touch, and understands (carries with him, *incorporates*) the problem. Doing this way, he uses an intense describing, comparative, classifying, memorizing activity in order to decode necessary elements to solve the problem. At the time of this activity, action main dimensions are questioned and interpreted with regard to personal characteristics, so a higher level of signification network is constructed.

The Concept of "Debate of Ideas"

One of the possible ways of accessing the transformational operation of a subject is to analyze verbalizations about physical action (Schunk, 1986). We propose a specific modality of verbalization about action, which involves the "debate of ideas" (Gréhaigne & Godbout, 1998; Gréhaigne, Godbout & Bouthier, 2001). This pedagogical setting consists of bringing a student face-to-face with a problem to solve; then, after action, he is told to produce verbal commentaries while watching the videotape of his immediate past-motor production. He exchanges verbal feedback with his opponent in badminton. This verbalization constitutes a reflective act about action, and allows action determinants to make the subject's point of view explicit. Then, a return to action allows the validation, or not, of the action rules formulated during the debate of ideas. The goal is to confront action representations with those present within the observed effective action. The definition of the "debate of ideas" is: "Situations in which students express themselves (overt verbalization) and exchange facts and ideas, based on observation or on personal activity experienced. The debate may concern the results obtained during the action situation, the process involved, and so on" (Gréhaigne & Godbout, 1998, p. 114).

So this debate of ideas is crossing thinking and action: it allows critical feedback on action and helps provide a distanced attitude by movement analysis. This "critical attitude" spreads on what is felt, known and interpreted about action. The comeback to directing action intentions allows exceeding the present setting, and regulating coming action. At term, one can model student signification registers, which characterize a certain interpretative degree about learning problem solving.

Method

The purpose is to study student verbal reports about action in authentic learning settings.

Hypotheses

There are three hypotheses:

1) The debate of ideas helps learning motor skills in badminton. One has to verify whether this constructivist approach has a favourable impact on student learning.
2) The way situations are interpreted allow identifying and modeling the player's expectation horizon. This model helps explain the player's functioning while constructing knowledge.
3) There is a relationship between the way a player formulates the action rules and his/her skill level. In fact, intended actions must be related with actual motor possibilities and this management of resources illustrates a certain level of strategy.

The used method consists of a longitudinal study comparing the student's language productions in authentic conditions. During a course of eight lessons of one and a half hours (n = 12), a sample of badminton beginner students (n = 21, age: 12-13 years old) was asked to debate about action after a 10-minute game play. A constructivist approach of the oppositional relationship in badminton was used. The settings and the students' debate of ideas were videotaped. Then, they returned to action. Each playing phase had a 21-point set duration (with 2 points difference to win). We used an interpretative map to link the verbal reports and the motor-skill level.

Population

Student motor-skill level during opponent relationship was balanced, and they were already familiarized with the debate of ideas setting in a precedent-learning scenario. The experienced teacher (more than 15 years) specialist of this activity volunteered for this experience.

Debate of Ideas Setting

The debate of ideas setting (about three minutes duration) (Deriaz, Poussin & Gréhaigne, 1998; Gréhaigne & Godbout, 1998) called for students to comment on videotaped sequences produced just before. Students were invited to describe, discuss, and propose activity ameliorations about motor productions. Efficient action rules emerging from the debate were verbally formulated and then immediately tested with return to action. In this nondirective setting, the teacher's role was to incite openings and ideas making: he let students explore the problem areas during verbal exchange.

Significance of this Study

The interest of such an approach is to propose, immediately after acting, a recorded but reproducible reading of concrete produced actions. It allows describing the recorded images linked with felt sensations. The participants identify and make explicit the action determinants, then they validate them, or not, within action. Action representations are so confronted with existing ones in effective observed actions: a "critical attitude" is developed, which turns on what students see, feel, and know about action.

Data Collection and Treatment

The debating setting was videotaped. Verbal reports were fully transcribed and coded by two independent coders (Ripoll, 1988). A verbal report interpretative map (Bardin, 1975; Chi, 1997) allowed describing and extracting formulated action rules, and identifying knowledge emerging within action (Ericsson & Simon, 1993). A behavior observational motor-skill grid, constructed by badminton specialists, tracked students before and after the debate of ideas (Dodge, 1993), and measured possible behaviour transformations (Bouthier, David & Eloi, 1994).

Instrumentation

The data treatment is mainly qualitative. It consists, on one hand, in extracting action rules formulated by students, and, on the other hand, identifying the player's expectation horizon about opposition relationship all along the lessons. The efficient action rules are supports, extracted from action, which present an identity, a necessity, and a foreseeable nature of action. They present a corrective and a standardizing dimension of action (Quéré, 2001, p. 148), and constitute for action resources to better understand the problem areas. "Action rules define conditions to be enforced and elements to be taken into account if one wants to ensure efficient action. Such rules are basic to tactical knowledge about the game, and they are used—whether isolated or in connection to other rules—to provide an answer to a given problem." (Gréhaigne & Godbout, 1995, p. 95; Vergnaud, Halbvacks & Rouchier, 1978). The purpose is to model, from these formulated invariants, the expectation horizon within the reading/interpreting process of adversary tactical intentions, and of the personal strategy of the learning player.

Results

First of all, the purpose of the study was to examine the impact of the debate of ideas on the performance. It has already been shown in similar conditions in table tennis: learning by repetition is neutralized by the importance of the verbal report stimulation framework about action (Nachon, Mahut, Mahut & Gréhaigne, 2001). But knowing the briefness of the debate of ideas setting (no more than 10 minutes), one postulates that without risks, it has no negative effect on learning, if effective time practice remains consequent.

Result 1: The Debate of Ideas, a Verbalized Changing of Nature

There is an evolution over eight lessons. The more students improved their badminton games, the more they were able to verbalize their actions. During the students' language production about action, they used nonverbal means when they did not have the words to describe their actions. The role of gestures/nonverbal productions changed over the eight lessons of the course. Initially, gestures took the place of verbalization. Then, they were used to emphasize and illustrate verbalization. Verbalization became dominant towards the end of the badminton course.

Result 2: Action Rules, a Quantitative and a Qualitative Evolution

As beginners felt it hard to verbalize action, and did not initially produce much with the frequent stimulation of the teacher, one could see at the end of the course a quantitative change and a fluency in commenting on action. The terms chosen to designate an action were more precise and pertinent, the range of vocabulary was wider, using action verbs, with reference to time and space. The production of action rules increased throughout the course; the more a student increased his/her motor experiments, the more he/she was able to extract action rules from practice (for instance, about talking hitting the shuttlecock: "He hits the shuttlecock like that...It would be better to hit it from down below"...To "In fact, I am shuttlecock-centered, and I do not take the opponent's location into account.")

Action rules became more precise, in terms of tactical knowledge, as the course progressed. In fact, whereas verbalizations produced during the first lessons where randomly focused, in the last lessons one or two domains were explored systematically. Everything happens as if the expectation horizon was closing in around one or two of the player's major preoccupations, in relation to the oppositional relationship.

Result 3: A Sense Shift of the Player Expectation Horizon

Action rules, referring to the situation that produced them, showed an evolution within the player's expectation horizon. The shift in the player's concern allowed us to understand how he/she structured his/her expectation horizon, and the different stages of that construction. There were three characteristics of a beginner's expectation horizon:

1. A shuttlecock-centered attitude: preoccupations related to trajectories, racket holding...and so on.
2. The constraint of the court, and the corresponding position/re-positioning of the player.
3. The opponent (later in the course). One could see at once that this expectation horizon was incomplete compared with that of a top player: regulation constraints and adversarial strategies constraints were almost nonexistent.

These characteristics did not emerge at the same time, or in the same ways, depending upon the player. In fact, the evolution of the player strategies showed us that they shifted the interpretation of a game and during the evolution within the relationship to the opponent.

Result 4: An Emerging Model of Expectation Horizon

Stage 1: A self-centered reflection. The first stage showed a player's expectation horizon which was relating linearly external information about the physical environment (i.e., shuttlecock, net, racket...) to personal reactions. This stage can be defined as a "self-centered reflection." The student's attention was essentially preoccupied by the shuttlecock he had to send back, and to the center of the opponent's court. This discourse produced the presentation of three characteristics:

1. The player had an attitude of cooperative exchange in order to maintain the shuttlecock in the air: therefore, upper trajectories were produced.
2. The entire opposite court was considered as a target.
3. The player's position under the coming shuttlecock made him move within a tube: hits were from top to bottom and from bottom to top, in a frontal plane.

During this first stage, which lasted about two lessons, the debates of ideas were descriptive and centered on failures. One heard verbal reports like "I do not replace quickly enough, I can not catch the flying shuttlecock, and my backhand stroke is not precise..."

Stage 1: A Self-centered Reflection

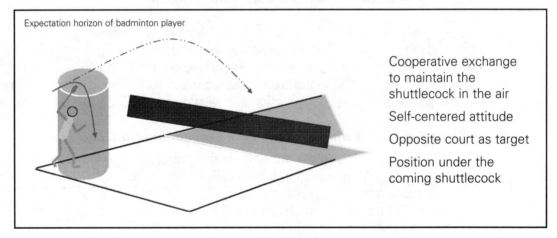

Expectation horizon of badminton player

Cooperative exchange to maintain the shuttlecock in the air

Self-centered attitude

Opposite court as target

Position under the coming shuttlecock

Figure I.

Stage 2: A lateralized view. During this stage the player showed the ability to take into account the opponent's behavior. Thus, critical thinking by induction/deduction emerged, linked to the opponent's strategy. This hypothetic-deductive attitude was a factor in the elaboration of a strategy constructed before acting, and verified during action. For instance, a verbal report might say: "If I try to put the shuttlecock on the right court, then the opponent has to move on the other side. So, I cross the next stroke to the left side." One could see an emerging lateralized view: the purpose was to make the opponent move left and right. The shuttlecock target was an alley situated laterally on both sides of the opponent's court. Trajectories alternated from right to left, and the hits were produced in a sagittal plane.

Stage 2: A Lateralized View

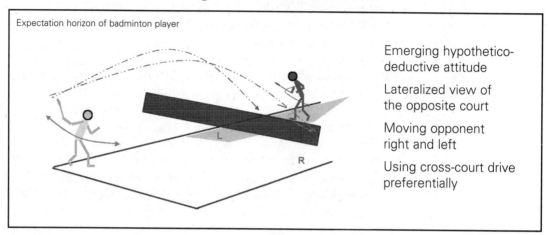

Expectation horizon of badminton player

Emerging hypothetico-deductive attitude

Lateralized view of the opposite court

Moving opponent right and left

Using cross-court drive preferentially

Figure II.

Stage 3: A new rapport to time. The third stage emerging was the ability of the player to take advantage of the opponent. The problem was to put the opponent under pressure in terms of time. This new relationship to time was expressed by the intention of varying the shuttlecock's speed. The new target was an alley situated near the net and front court. The problem was to alternate smashes and drop shots, in order to outstrip the opponent. Shuttlecock trajectories were straight. The player's position was within a circular area where he went forward to the moving target. Verbal data included: "*I try to alternate backhand drop and fast drop, so that the opponent has always to move frontcourt and backcourt, and has no time to catch the shuttlecock.*"

Stage 3: A New Rapport to Time

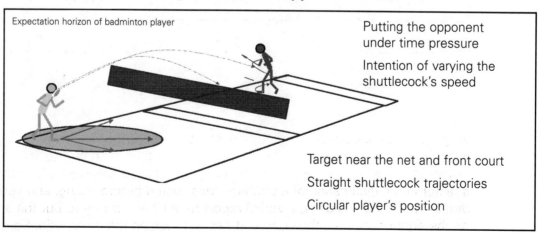

Expectation horizon of badminton player

Putting the opponent under time pressure

Intention of varying the shuttlecock's speed

Target near the net and front court

Straight shuttlecock trajectories

Circular player's position

Figure III.

Stage 4: Moving and replacing on the court. In this stage, the characteristic of the debate of ideas was to force the opponent to react to actions, which could be considered as attacks. This strategy of a superior offensive level indicated an interpretative attitude of the opponent's action. Further, this attitude took into account more pertinent informational elements, and a real internal dialogue emerged. The strategy consisted of "pushing to fail" by placing the shuttlecock and re-positioning oneself after acting on it. After eight badminton lessons, the expectation horizon was broadened, and a complex interactive system of an oppositional relationship was constructed.

The critical attitude was expressed through verbalization, and one saw the construction of tactical knowledge emerging within action. When one considered the construction of a player's space he acted on, one could see an evolution in the way the player represented his playing area. First, the player was front-oriented, and only the opponent's court was taken into account. Then, as already established, the lateral parts and the depth of the court was represented in his verbal reports. Action rules about the player's foot-position orientation emerged. Finally, positioning and re-positioning took on an interactive dynamic: the player considered a central area out from which he radiated. The evolution of the player's preoccupations showed a moving area structured through action; this area evolved according to the rapport of strength experienced with the opponent.

Stage 4: Moving and Replacing on the Court

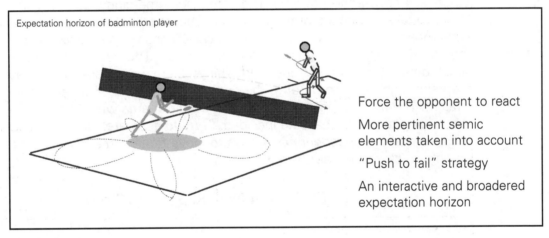

Expectation horizon of badminton player

Force the opponent to react

More pertinent semic elements taken into account

"Push to fail" strategy

An interactive and broadered expectation horizon

Figure IV.

Result 5: The Player's Construction of Space

When one considered the construction space players acted on, one could see an evolution in the way he/she represented his/her playing area. First, he/she was front-oriented, and only the opponent's court was taken into account (Figure V). Then, as already seen, the lateral parts and the depth of the court was represented in his/her verbal reports (Figure VI). Action rules about his foot positions orientation emerged (Figure VII). Finally, position/re-positioning took on an interactive dynamic: he/she considered a central area out from which he/she radiated (Figure VIII). The evolution of the player's intentions showed in a moving area structured through action.

The Player's Construction of Space
(Stage 1)

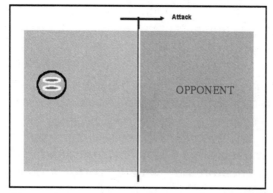

Figure V

The Player's Construction of Space
(Stage 2)

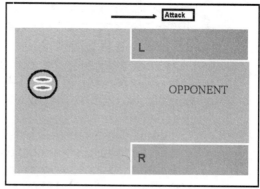

Figure VI

The Player's Construction of Space
(Stage 3)

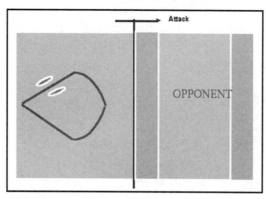

Figure VII

The Player's Construction of Space
(Stage 4)

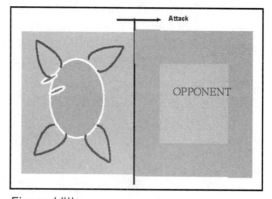

Figure VIII

Discussion

Two key conclusions can be observed. First, students can verbally describe an action as long as they recognize meaningful order in their badminton games. In fact, to score or win, they must extract a significant configuration from the succession of actions produced: action produced results and events to interpret. Secondly, this interactive and continual process of expectation horizon construction allows the player to interpret past and future actions with regard to problem solving. After stabilization, these actions become the basis of interpretation of future actions. The student interprets the following actions, and gets out their interpretation in reality. By a process of reciprocal exchange, the badminton player becomes an "interpreter" who constructs strategies while reading the characteristics of the playing area. This meaning construction emerges in action by the meaning of a complex hypothetic-deductive activity, and serves as a basis for learning. Interaction produces regularities and expresses the identity of the one who produces it.

In this study, one has not verified directly the relation between the debate-of-ideas impact and student motor-skill performances. The purpose was to model the different stages of the strategy knowledge construction. This effect had been previously shown in table tennis, in similar conditions (Nachon, Mahut, Mahut & Gréhaigne, 2001). That is, this study was not designed to be a comparative study.

Students can express actions that they recognize in a sense order within badminton-game action links. In fact, they must extract a significant configuration of the contingent succession to produce gestures to win the score. Produced action generates results and events to interpret. Learning by repetition is neutralized by the importance of the stimulating test of verbal productions about action. Meanwhile, because of the briefness of the debate of ideas setting, one can postulate that without any risks it had no negative effect on learning, in relation with the same time allowed to action.

Between "saying" and "doing," student verbal reports inform partially about elements of the setting he designates himself as pertinent, the ones he takes into account to interpret and to act on. So he makes explicit the way he links certain events together to facts and to tactical intentions.

These pre-reflexive phenomena find their natural extension within transition to action. This process allows validating, or not, emerging action rules from subsequent actions. At their turn, these emerging action rules lay the foundation for interpretation of coming action.

This interactive and continual process of expectation horizon construction allows the actor interpreting past and future actions with regard to the problem-solving area. After stabilization, these actions become the interpretation basis of future actions. A student interprets actions, and becomes what his/her interpreted acting reality was. By this way, knowledge-in-action is incorporated within language as symbolic structure, as basis for reflective thinking, and as an explaining tool.

Conclusion

This study's aim is clearly not to generalize and prescribe a model for teaching. But it looks at the student's dynamic confrontation with problem-solving. This study revives the didactic perspectives of the debate of ideas within a confrontation of badminton. The student elaborates tactical knowledge in accordance with his/her interpretation of the situation. The network of significations he/she uses to solve the problem produces different expectation horizons, as revealed in this study concerning verbalization of action. These results question physical education teacher training, directing physical education teachers to an interpretative attitude concerning a student's semiotic activity.

Emerging efficient action rules enables an understanding of the way students learn. Students elaborate action strategies in accordance with the setting interpretation. The critical thinking development about action is enriched with this reflection in, and on, action. In return, these results question PET Training, directing teachers to an interpretative attitude about the student's semiotic activity. Perspectives of this research are oriented to a longitudinal study in order to model the student expectation horizons all along the secondary school training. Is the debate of ideas between students 12 to 18 years old comparable? A comparison on a longer training course, with control group learning, and a teacher-centred approach would give some complementary knowledge.

The reflections emerging at the end of this study propose a translation of the researcher point of view from the "Teaching Games for Understanding" to the "Learning Games for Understanding."

References:

Abernethy, B. B. (1988). The effects of age and expertise upon perceptual skill development in a racquet sport. *Research Quarterly for Exercise and Sport, 59,* 210-211.

Alibali, M. W., Kita, S., & Young, A .J. (2000). Gesture and the process of speech production: We think, therefore we gesture. Language and cognitive processes, 15 (6), 593-613. Psychology Press Ltd.

Ansubel, D. P. (1968). *Educational psychology: A cognitive view.* New York: Holt, Rinehart, and Winston.

Astolfi, J. F., & Develay, M. (1989). *La didactique des sciences.* Paris: PUF.

Barbier, J. M., (2000). *L'analyse de la singularité de l'action.* Paris: PUF.

Bardin, L. (1975). *L'analyse de contenu.* Paris: P.U.F.

Bernicot, J., Caron-Pargue, J., & Trognon, A. (1997). *Conversation, interaction et fonctionnement cognitif.* Nancy: PUN.

Blomqvist, M., Häyrinen, M., Selänne, H., & Luthanen, P. (2001). *Volleyball skill, game understanding and perceptual abilities in secondary school children.* Proceedings of TGFU Congress, 2-4 August. Plymouth, NH.

Bouthier, D. (1993). *L'approche technologique en STAPS: Représentations et actions en didactique des APS.* Orsay: University Press.

Bouthier, D., David, B., & Eloi, S. (1994). Analysis of representations and patterns of tactical decisions in team games: A methodological approach. In J. Nistch & R. Seiler (Eds.), *Motor control and motor learning.* Sankt Augustin: Academic Verlag, 126-134.

Bouthier, D., Pastré, P., & Samurçay, R. (1995). Le développement des compétences. Analyse du travail et didactique professionnelle. *Education Permanente,* 123.

Brien, R. (1990). *Science cognitive et formation.* Québec: Presses de l'université du Québec.

Brousseau, G. (1998). *Théorie des situations didactiques.* Paris: La pensée sauvage.

Chi, M. T. H. (1997). Quantifying qualitative analyses of verbal data: A practical guide. *The Journal of Learning Sciences, 6,* 271-315.

Chi, M. T. H., Bassrock, M., Lewis, M. W., Reimann, P., & Blaser, R. (1989). Self-explanations: how students study and use examples in learning to solve problems. *Cognitive Science, 13,* 145-182.

Chi, M. T. H., Glaser, R., & Farr, M. J. (1988). *The nature of expertise.* Hillsdale, NJ : Lawrence Erlbaum.

Clancey, W. J. (1997). *Situated cognition: On human knowledge and computer representations.* Cambridge, UK: Cambridge University Press.

Courtès, J. C. (1976a). *Introduction à la sémiotique narrative et discursive.* Paris: Hachette.

Courtès, J. C. (1976b). *Sémiotique, dictionnaire raisonné de la théorie du langage, I.* Paris: Hachette.

Cowley, S. J. (1997). Of representations and language. *Language and communication, 17*(4), 279-300. Pergamon Press.

Delignières, D. (1994). Apprentissages moteurs et verbalisation. *Echanges et controverses, 4,* 29-41.

Deriaz, D. Poussin, B., & Gréhaigne, J. F. (1998). Le débat d'idées. *Éducation physique et Sport, 273,* 80-82.

Dodge, Y. (1993). *Statistique, dictionnaire encyclopédique.* Paris: Dunod.

Doyle, W. (1986). Classroom organization and management. In M.C. Wittrock (Ed.) *Handbook of research on teaching.* New York: McMillan.

Ericsson, K. A. & Simon, H. A. (1993). *Protocol analysis: Verbal reports as data.* Cambridge, MA: MIT Press.

Fortin, C. & Rousseau, R. (1989). *Psychologie cognitive: Une approche de traitement de l'information.* Québec: Presses de l'université du Québec.

Fayol, M. (1997). *Des idées au texte. Psychologie cognitive de la production verbale, orale et écrite.* Paris: PUF.

Gilly, Y. (1992). Signifiant, Référent, Réel et texte littéraire. In Annales Littéraires de l'Université de Besançon (Eds.). *Signifiant, Référent, Réel.* Paris : Les Belles Lettres.

Gobbo, C. & Chi, M. T. H. (1986). How knowledge is structured and used by expert and novice children. *Cognitive development, 1,* 221-237.

Gréhaigne, J. F., & Godbout, P. (1995). Tactical knowledge in team sports from a constructivist and cognitivist perspective. *Quest, 47,* 490-505.

Gréhaigne, J. G., & Godbout, P. (1998). Observation, critical thinking and transformation: Three key elements for a constructivist perspective of the learning process in team sport. In R. Feingold, C. Roger Rees, G. T. Barette, L. Fiorentino, S. Virgilio, & E. Kowalski (Eds.). Education for life. *Proceedings of the AIESEP World Sport Science. Congress.* New York: Adelphi University Press.

Gréhaigne, J. F., Godbout, P., & Bouthier, D. (1999). The foundations of tactics and strategy in team sports. *Quest, 18,* 159-174.

Gréhaigne, J. F., Godbout, P., & Bouthier, D. (2001). The teaching and learning of decision making in team sports. *Quest, 53,* 59-76.

Greimas, A. J. (1983). *Du sens II.* Paris: Seuil.

Greimas, A. J. & Courtès, J. C. (1986). *Sémiotique, dictionnaire raisonné de la théorie du langage, II.* Paris: Hachette.

Griffin, L. L., Mitchell, S. A., & Oslin, J. L. (1997). *Teaching sports concepts and skills: A tactical games approach.* Champaign, IL: Human Kinetics.

Jaeglé, P. & Roubaud, P. (1990). *La notion de réalité.* Paris: Messidor, Ed. Sociales.

Kirshner, A. C., & Whitson, D. H. (1997). *Situated cognition. Social, semiotic, and psychological perspectives.* Mahwah: Erlbaum Associates.

Masselot, M. (1999). *Image, langages. Recherche et pratiques enseignantes.* Paris: INRP.

Masselot, M. (2000). *Multimedia et construction des savoirs.* Besançon: PUFC.

McBride, R. E. (1991). Critical thinking. An overview with implications for physical education. *Journal of Teaching in Physical Education, 11,* 112-125.

McPherson, S. (1993). Knowledge representation and decision making in sport. In J. L. Starkes & F. Allard (Eds.). *Cognitive issues in motor expertise.* Amsterdam: North-Holland Ed.

McPherson, S. (1994). The development of sport expertise: Mapping the tactical domain. *Quest, 46,* 211-223.

McPherson, S. (1999). Expert-novice differences in performance skills as problem representations of youth and adults during tennis competition. *Research Quarterly for Exercise and Sport, 70*, 233-251.

McPherson, S. L. & French, K. E. (1991). Changes in cognitive strategy and motor skill in tennis. *Journal of Sport and Exercise Psychology, 13*, 26-41.

Mosston, M. & Ashworth, S. (1986). *Physical education: From intent to action*. Colombus, OH: Merrill.

Nachon, M., Mahut, N., Mahut, B. & Gréhaigne, J. F. (2001). Student's construction of strategies in table tennis: Design of the expectation horizon within debate of ideas. *AIESEP Proceedings. Taipei (TW), June*.

Piaget, J. (1930). *Le langage et la pensée chez l'enfant*. Neuchâtel: Delachaux et Niestlé (2d Ed.).

Quéré, L. (2001). Les savoirs professionnels. In J. M. Barbier (Ed.). *Savoir pratiques, savoirs d'action*. Paris: PUF.

Rink, J. E., French, K. E., & Tjeerdsma, B. L. (1996). Foundations for the learning and instruction of sport and games. Journal of Teaching in Physical Education, 15, 399-417.

Ripoll, H. (1988). Utilisation d'un dispositif video—oculographique d'enregistrement de la direction du regard en situation sportive. *Sciences et motricité, 4*, 26-31

Rumelhart, D. E., & Ortony, A. (1977). *The representation of knowledge in memory, schooling and the acquisition of knowledge*. Hillsdale, NJ: Erlbaum Associates.

Schön, D. A. (1983). *The reflexive practitioner*. US: Basic books.

Schön, D. A. (1990). *Educating the reflective practitioner: Toward a new design for teaching and learning in the professions*. San Francisco: Jossey-Bass.

Schunk, D. H. (1986). Verbalization and children's self-regulated learning. *Contemporary Educational Psychologie, 11*, 347.

Seve, C., Durand, M., Saury, J., & Avanzini, G. (2000). L'analyse de l'activité de pongiste de haut niveau en compétition: Perpective pour l'entrainement. *Science et motricité, 38*, 26-31

Suchman, L. (1987). *Plans and situated actions: The problem of human-machine communication*. Cambridge UK: University Press.

Tardif, J. (1998). *Pour un enseignement stratégique*. Montréal: les éditions logiques.

Theureau, J. (1992). Le *cours d'action: Analyse sémio-logique. Essai d'une anthropologie cognitive située*. Berne: Peter Lang.

Vergnaud, G., Halbvacks, F., & Rouchier, A. (1978). Structure de la matière enseignée, histoire des sciences et développement conceptuel chez l'enfant. *Revue Française de Pédagogie, 45*, 7-18.

Vermersch, P. (1978). Analyse de la tâche et fonctionnement cognitif dans la programmation de l'enseignement. *Bulletin de psychologie, 33*.

Vermersch, P. (1995). Du faire au dire (l'entretien d'explicitation). *Cahiers Pédagogiques, 336*, 27-32.

Viviani, P. & Stucchi, N. (1992). *Motor perceptual interactions*. In: E.G. Stelmach & J. Requin, *Tutorials in Motor Behavior*. Amsterdam: Elsevier Science Publishers.

Vygotski, L. (2000). *Pensée et langage*. Paris: La Dispute.

Authentic Assessment in Games Education: An Introduction to Team Sport Assessment Procedure and the Game Performance Assessment Instrument

Chapter 13

Jean-François Richard, Université de Moncton, Canada

Linda L. Griffin, University of Massachusetts at Amherst, United States

Introduction

This chapter addresses the role of assessment in teaching and learning of sport-related games. When implementing a TGfU model (i.e., tactical games, games-sense, and concept-centered games), teachers' goals for students focus on successful game play, which means that assessment should focus on game play (Veal, 1992). In other words, if the goal of games teaching is to improve game performance, then it is essential that assessment measures take into consideration two critical components. First, assessment measures should consist of all aspects of performance. A player's game performance includes concepts related to tactical awareness or understanding (i.e., what to do?) and skill execution (how to do it?). Second, assessment needs to measure game play (i.e., performance) in context (e.g., actual games or game forms).

Currently, when physical education teachers do assessments they have relied on skill testing to assess student performance. Using skill tests to assess game performance is problematic for several reasons (a) skill tests do not predict playing performance, (b) skill tests do not take into account the social dimensions of sport-related games, (c) skill tests are out of context, in situations not related to game play, and (d) skills tests do not reflect a broader view of game performance (Griffin, Mitchell, & Oslin, 1997; Oslin, Mitchell, & Griffin, 1998). Two assessment instruments, the Team Sport Assessment Procedure (TSAP) and the Game Performance Assessment Instrument (GPAI), have been designed and validated to assess students' performance in real-life learning scenarios—the game. The purpose of this chapter is twofold. First, we will introduce the major features of the TSAP and the GPAI. Second, we will provide pedagogical and practical implications for using the instruments in sport-related teaching and learning.

The Team Sport Assessment Procedure (TSAP)

The TSAP was developed by Gréhaigne, Godbout, and Bouthier (1997). The TSAP provides information that quantifies an individual's overall offensive performance in selected invasion (basketball, soccer, etc.) and net (volleyball) team sports, reflecting both technical and tactical aspects of game play (see Gréhaigne et al., 1997). The information provided by the individual variables, performance indexes, and performance scores are all macro-indicators of both technical and tactical performance (See Table I). These indicators are all related to successful game play (Gréhaigne et al., 1997).

Table I

The Relationships Between Observation Items and Types of Information Collected (based on the original work of Gréhaigne, Godbout, and Bouthier [1997]).

Observation Items	Information Collected
Received balls (RB)	Involvement of the player in the team's play (availability, accessibility to receive a pass)
Conquered balls (CB)	Information related to the player's defensive capacities
Offensive balls (OB)	Player's capacity to make significant passes to his/her partners (offensive capacities)
Successful shots (SS)	Information related to the player's offensive capacities
Volume of play (PB= RB+CB)	General involvement of the player in the game
Lost balls (LB)	A small number reflects a good adaptation to the game

---

The TSAP is based on two basic notions: (a) "How a player gains possession of the ball" (two variables) and (b) "How a player disposes of the ball" (four variables). According to these notions, a player's specific behaviors are observed and coded during game play on an observation grid such as the one presented in Figure 1.

Team Sport Assessment Procedure for Invasion Games

Name _____   Class _____

Observer _____   Date _____

Directions: Observe student's game play and place a tally mark in the appropriate box.

Gaining possession of the ball   **Played Balls (PB)**

Conquered Ball (CB)	Received Ball (RB)

Disposing of the ball

Lost Ball (LB)	Neutral Ball (NB)	Pass (P)	Successful Shot (SS)

Figure 1. Observation grid for the TSAP—Invasion games.

Two performance indexes and a performance score are then computed from the collected data (See Table II).

Table II
Observational Variables, Performance Indexes and Performance Score Computation Formula for the Team-Sport Assessment Procedure—Invasion Games (based on the original work of Gréhaigne, Godbout, and Bouthier [1997]).

Observational Variables: Operational Definition

A. Gaining possession of the ball

1) Conquered Ball (CB)
A player is considered having conquered the ball if he/she intercepted it, stole it from an opponent, or recaptured it after an unsuccessful shot on goal or after a near loss to the other team.

2) Received Ball (RB)
The player receives the ball from a partner and does not immediately lose control of it.

B. Disposing of the ball

1) Lost Ball (LB)
The player is considered having lost the ball when he/she loses control of it without having scored a goal.

2) Neutral Ball (NB)
A routine pass to a partner which does not truly put pressure on the other team.

3) Pass (P)
Pass to a partner which contributes to the displacement of the ball towards the opposing team's goal.

4) Successful Shot on Goal (SS)
A shot is considered successful when it scores or possession of the ball is retained by one's team.

The computation of performance indexes and performance score:

Volume of play index = CB + RB

Efficiency index = $\dfrac{CB + P + SS}{10 + LB}$

Performance score = (volume of play/2) + (efficiency index x 10)

A primary feature of the TSAP is that the data-collection process is accomplished by students. A recent study has demonstrated that students as young as 10 years old (grade 5) were capable of using the TSAP with a good deal of precision and reliability (Richard, Godbout, & Gréhaigne, 2000). The use of this assessment procedure combined with a TGfU model can offer an efficient means to develop students' learning of game concepts (Gréhaigne & Godbout, 1998).

Using the TSAP in Sport-Related Teaching and Learning

A major feature of the TSAP is its adaptability to different teaching scenarios. What has been explained up to this point is a procedure that possesses six different observational variables, which have been shown to reflect a student's global offensive performance in invasion games. When teaching more complex tactical problems at a higher grade level (i.e., high school), the integral version of the TSAP is recommended. A teacher might, however, not want to use the integral version of the TSAP as: (a) the learning outcomes s/he is pursuing might not require such a complex procedure (i.e., upper elementary and middle school programs); or (b) having not experimented with peer assessment very much, a teacher might feel that the students would need to be initiated with a simpler instrument. These are legitimate concerns as observational complexity and cognitive maturity are definitely factors that need to be considered when integrating students in the peer assessment process. With regard to the use of the TSAP, Richard, Godbout, and Picard (2000) have developed, experimented, and validated simpler versions of the TSAP in order to offer teachers alternatives for their assessment practices in relation to games education. The following pages offer a rationale for these modified versions in relation to their use in games education at lower grade levels (grades 5 to 8). For the purpose of this chapter, the TSAP will be presented pertaining to its use in relation to invasion games (for information on the TSAP-volleyball refer to Richard, Godbout, & Griffin, 2002).

Invasion Games (Basketball, Soccer, Handball, etc.): 1st Modified Version

Volume of Play (VP) = # of possessions (Conquered Ball (CB) + Received Ball (RB))

$$\text{Efficiency Index (EI)} = \frac{VP}{10 + \text{Lost Ball (LB)}}$$

Performance Score = (VP/2) + (EI x 10)

In this first modified version, the number of observational variables is reduced by half. With regard to the volume of play, no distinction is made between CB or RB. Only the total number of possessions is taken into consideration, along with the number of lost balls. The reasoning behind this decision is twofold. First, we have noticed through different experiments with the TSAP that younger observers have a tendency to indicate most ball possessions as received, even if they are conquered (i.e., intercepted). Secondly, the nuance between these two variables are not as important in relation to game concepts taught at the lower grade levels.

This version of the TSAP is simpler than the original version. The modifications permit teachers to progressively integrate students in the observation of game play behaviors, without having an overly complex instrument to use. Also, the variables that were retained for this first modified version allow teachers and students to still focus on the nuances of game-play concepts, such as getting away from a defender (represented by the volume of play) and ball circulation, which are mostly taught at the upper elementary level (grades 5 and 6) in most physical education programs. Through the efficiency index, we want students to realize that from their volume of play (number of possessions), the goal is to lose as few balls as possible which, in turn, reflects a good contribution to team success (i.e., student either passing or shooting on goal).

Invasion Games: 2nd Modified Version

Volume of Play (VP) = # of possessions (CB + RB)

$$\text{Efficiency Index (EI)} = \frac{\text{Pass + Successful Shot on Goal}}{10 + LB}$$

Performance Score = (VP/2) + (EI x 10)

Like the first modified version, this second version lets the teacher put a certain pedagogical emphasis in relation to his/her pursued objectives. In this case, the efficiency index's numerator is comprised of the number of passes and successful shots on goal. In this version, the pedagogical emphasis is on both gaining possession and disposing of the ball. The efficiency index helps the teacher guide the student to know what to do when s/he has possession of the ball (pass or shoot on goal). This second modified version of the TSAP increases the number of observational variables to four. Consequently, this second version could be considered an intermediate version to the original TSAP.

The Game Performance Assessment Instrument (GPAI)

The Game Performance Assessment Instrument was developed to be a comprehensive assessment tool for teachers to use and adapt in assessing a variety of games. Teachers can use the GPAI for different types of games across the classification system (e.g., invasion, net/wall) or within a particular classification (e.g., basketball, soccer). The different observational variables included in the GPAI permit the coding of behaviors that demonstrate the ability to solve tactical problems in games by making decisions, moving appropriately (off-the-ball movement), and executing skills (Griffin et al., 1997).

Seven observable game components have been identified and formulated in the initial development of the GPAI (see Table III) (Oslin et al., 1998). Game components can be coded on observation grids (see Figures 2 and 3). All components are related to game performance however, not all seven components are applicable to a particular game (Oslin et al., 1998). For example, all components except "guard" are important for field/run/score/ games such as softball. On the other hand, all components except "base" are important for successful soccer performance (Oslin et al., 1998).

Table III	
Components of game performance (Note: all table and figures are adapted from Griffin et al., 1997; Mitchell & Oslin, 1999; Oslin et al., 1998).	
Base	Appropriate return of performer to a recovery (base) position between skill attempts
Decision-Making	Makes appropriate decisions about what to do with the ball (or projectile) during a game
Skill Execution	Efficient execution of selected skills
Support	Provides appropriate support for a teammate with ball (or projectile) by being in position to receive a pass
Guard/Mark	Appropriate guarding/marking of an opponent who may or may not have the ball (or projectile)
Cover	Provides appropriate defensive cover, help, backup for a player making a challenge for the ball (or projectile)
Adjust	Movement of performer, either offensively or defensively, as necessitated by the flow of the game

Game Performance Assessment Instrument

Invasion Games

Class _____ Evaluator _____ Team _____ Game _____

Observation Dates (a) _____ (b) _____ (c) _____ (d) _____

Scoring Key: 5 = Very effective performance
4 = Effective performance
3 = Moderately effective performance
2 = Weak performance
1 = Very weak performance

Components/Criteria

1. Decision-Making—
   a. Student attempts to pass to an open teammate
   b. Student attempts to shoot when appropriate
2. Skill Execution—
   a. Reception-control pass
   b. Pass-ball reaches intended target
   c. Dribble-control and adjust and moves position
3. Support—
   a. Students attempt to move into position to receive a pass from teammates (i.e., forward toward goal)

Name	Decision-Making	Skill Execution	Support

Figure 2. GPAI for Invasion Games

Game Performance Assessment Instrument

Net/Wall Games

Class: _____ Evaluator: _____ Team: _____ Game: _____

Observation Dates: (a) _____ (b) _____ (c) _____ (d) _____

Components/Criteria

1. **Skill Execution**—Students perform underhand ground strokes into opponent's court.
2. **Decision-Making**—Students make appropriate choices when to place a long (deep) or short shot.
3. **Base**—Students returns to recovery position between skill attempts.

Recording Procedures: Use a tally to mark the observed category. Mark each player's responses during the game. If the student you are evaluating strikes the ball long or short, be sure to mark whether or not she/he made an appropriate (A) or inappropriate (I) decision and whether the underhand ground strokes were executed efficiently (E) or inefficiently (I).

Name	Skill Execution		Decision-Making		Base	
	E	**IE**	**A**	**IA**	**A**	**IA**

Figure 3. GPAI for a net/wall games unit

The GPAI was designed to be a flexible observation instrument that can be used to assess students' performance either in a live setting or from videotapes. Teachers can choose to observe any or all components related to a particular game depending on the context of the instructional environment (grade level, unit objectives, etc.) (Oslin et al., 1998). Simplification of the GPAI (number and particular components to be observed) is especially useful when students are involved in peer assessment.

The GPAI has shown to be a valid assessment instrument. Content, construct, ecological validity have all been established during its preliminary development (Oslin et al., 1998). Furthermore, instrument and observer reliability have also been established (Oslin et al., 1998).

Using the GPAI in Sport-Related Teaching and Learning

The appeal of the GPAI is that teachers can adapt the instrument for use based on the aspects of the game taught and the type of game being played in a lesson. There are two basic scoring methods for using the GPAI (a) the 1-5 scoring system (see Figure 2) and (b) a tally scoring system (see Figure 3).

Mitchell and Oslin (1999) pointed out that the 1-5 scoring system is efficient for two reasons. First, observers who are primarily teachers do not have to record each time a player is involved in the game. In invasion games and some net/wall games, it is impossible to keep track of players' complete involvement because of the tempo, flow, and unpredictability of those games, especially with players that have a wide range of skill levels. Second, the 1-5 scoring system makes consistency of scoring possible. Teachers need to create criteria for the 5 indicators (i.e., very effective performance to very weak performance) and the indicators should be based on lesson, unit, and curriculum objectives, as well as student abilities.

The tally system can be used with fielding (e.g., softball) and some net/wall games because they are played at a slower pace, which gives the observer an opportunity to score (tally) every event. The tally scoring system provides a more explicit game performance measure. As you can see in the net/wall GPAI form (see Figure 3), components are scored as either "appropriate" or "inappropriate" or "efficient" or "inefficient." Teachers can then develop percentage scores made from the total scores (Mitchell & Oslin, 1999). For example, a decision-making percentage would be calculated by dividing the number of appropriate decisions made by the total decisions made (see Table IV).

Table IV
Sample GPAI Performance Measures

Performance Measure	Calculation
Decision-Making Index (DMI)	Appropriate Decisions Made/Appropriate Decisions Made + Inappropriate Decisions Made x 100
Skill-Execution Index (SEI)	Efficient Skill Executions/Efficient Skill Executions + Inefficient Skill Executions x 100
Support Index (SI)	Appropriate Support/Appropriate Support + Inappropriate Support x 100
Game Performance	$\dfrac{DMI + SEI + SI}{3}$ x 100
Game Involvement	Appropriate Decisions + Inappropriate Decisions + Efficient Skill Execution + Inefficient Skill Execution + Number of Appropriate Support Movements

can also provide students with a view of the bigger picture of their game ... alculating "game involvement" and "game performance." Game involvement ... measured by adding together all responses that indicate involvement in the ... including inappropriate decisions made and inefficient skill execution (see ... et al., 1997). Do not, however, include inappropriate guard/mark, support, ... and cover because an inappropriate response in these components indicates ... yers were not involved in the game. Game performance is a more precise measure and is calculated by adding scores from all components assessed and dividing by the number of components assessed.

Both teachers and students (i.e., peer assessment) who have used a version of the GPAI in live settings to assess game performance have been considered reliable (i.e., they have been consistent with a fellow observer in their assessment of performance approximately 80% of the time) (Oslin et al., 1998; Griffin, Dodds, & James, 1999). The key to establishing reliability is in the quality of the criteria stated for observation (i.e., they should be specific and observable) (Mitchell & Oslin, 1999).

Pedagogical Implications

As assessment should be an integral part of the teaching-learning process, there are certain considerations and implications that should be addressed in order to help teachers systematically implement the proposed instruments into planning sport-related games instruction. Both instruments provide information that can help and guide teachers toward effective sport-related games instruction. Pedagogical implications focus on two primary considerations (a) the process for planning (yearly, unit, and lesson) and (b) the construction of knowledge and skills.

First, teachers need to consider the notion of planning and, in particular, the notion of *alignment* between *learning outcomes*, *teaching strategies*, and *assessment* (Cohen, 1987). Teachers need to understand that *planning what to teach is the same as planning what to assess* and that there needs to be a strong link between these two facets of the teaching-learning process. The TSAP and GPAI can help teachers organize a *planning cycle* within and across lessons in order to help in making the teaching-learning process more *congruent*. This cycle has three phases:

◆ first, students are confronted with a situation or problem to solve;
◆ second, students are in action (i.e., practice or game); and
◆ the final phase involves student reflection on their actions (i.e., critical thinking and problem solving).

For example, in a soccer lesson, students are presented with solving the tactical problem of creating space during attack. Students are placed in an initial game with the goal of solving the tactical problem. After the initial game, students are asked to reflect on questions about their success in reaching the goal. Students are then placed in a situated practice that helps them practice creating space during attack. Finally, students play another game similar to the initial game in order to modify and improve their game performance. Using a version of the TSAP or the GPAI can help teachers and students reflect on students' abilities related to an isolated objective, such as the one described above, or toward a more global performance that essentially reflects the sequence of a series of games' objectives.

The second pedagogical implication builds on the first and involves the construction of knowledge and skills. *Constructivism* is a theory about learning that describes learning as a building process by active learners interacting with their environment (physical and social) (Fosnot, 1996). A principle derived from constructivism that can and should guide games instruction is *reflective thinking*. By using either instrument, students are given time to reflect on such aspects of game play as choice of motor skill, decisions made (individual and team), and team strengths, which help them make meaning and connections across their experiences (Gréhaigne & Godbout, 1995). As mentioned earlier, in order to get the most out of the teaching-learning process, these instruments must be used appropriately. To this end, participating teachers who have used either instrument cannot stress enough the importance of using appropriate variables reflecting pursued objectives, instead of always using the integral form of the instrument (Griffin et al., 1997; Richard, Godbout, Tousignant, & Gréhaigne, 1999).

Conclusion

Assessment can, and should, be a part everyday teaching. The information that different assessment strategies can provide students and teachers is critical to the regulation of the teaching-learning process. As authentic assessment instruments, the TSAP and the GPAI offer teachers the opportunity to promote the construction of game knowledge and skills. Authentic assessment procedures can help teachers teach and students learn about how to make connections within and among games (i.e., intra- and inter-transfer). Students clearly articulate that playing the game is a meaningful activity to pursue in physical education. Why? Playing a game provides structure and outcomes that give meaning to performance. Students want to play games well.

The TSAP and the GPAI provide students with the opportunity to reflect and learn (i.e., formative assessment) about themselves as games players. Both instruments provide students with both means (process) and ends (products) that are interrelated. Through game performance assessment, students will learn that each small element has a value in itself but is part of a coherent whole. Authentic assessment instruments, such as the TSAP and GPAI, can help teachers plan developmentally sound game experiences that can lead to more *sport literate* learners and essentially help students better appreciate the playing of games.

Acknowledgements

Parts of this paper are the end products (practical applications) from different research projects funded by the Social Sciences and Humanities Research Council of Canada (410-99-1263). The first author would like to thank this granting agency for its ongoing support.

References

Cohen, S. A. (1987). Instructional Alignment: Searching for a Magic Bullet. *Educational Researcher, 16*(8), 16-20.

Fosnot, C. (1996). *Constructivism: theory, perspectives, and practice.* NY: Teachers College Press.

Gréhaigne, J. F. & Godbout, P., (1995). Tactical knowledge in team sports from a constructivist and cognitivist perspective. *Quest, 47*, 490-505.

Gréhaigne, J. F. & Godbout, P., (1998). Formative assessment in team sports in a tactical approach context. *Journal of Physical Education, Recreation, and Dance, 69*(1), 46-51.

Gréhaigne, J. F., Godbout, P., & Bouthier, D. (1997). Performance assessment in team sports. *Journal of Teaching in Physical Education, 16*, 500-516.

Griffin, L. L., Mitchell, S. A., & Oslin, J. L. (1997). *Teaching Sport Concepts and Skills: A Tactical Games Approach.* Champaign, IL: Human Kinetics.

Griffin, L. L., Dodds, P., & James, A. (1999). *Game performance assessment in a 5th/6th grade tactical badminton curriculum unit.* Paper presented at the annual Association Internationale des Ecoles Superieuruesd d'Education Physique World Sport Science Congress, Besancon, France.

Mitchell, S. A. & Oslin, J. L. (1999). *Assessment series K-12 physical education series: Assessment in games teaching.* Reston, VA: National Association of Sport and Physical Education.

Oslin, J. L., Mitchell, S. A., & Griffin, L. L. (1998). The Game Performance Assessment Instrument (GPAI): Development and preliminary validation. *Journal of Teaching in Physical Education, 17*, 231-243.

Richard, J. F., Godbout, P. & Gréhaigne, J. F. (2000). Students precision and reliability of team sport performance. *Research Quarterly for Exercise and Sport, 71*(1), 85-91.

Richard, J. F., Godbout, P. & Griffin, L. (2002). Assessing game performance: An introduction to the Team-Sport Assessment Procedure. *Health and Physical Education Journal, 68*(1), 12-18.

Richard, J. F., Godbout, P., & Picard, Y. (2000). La validation d'une procédure d'évaluation en sports collectifs. *Mesure et évaluation en éducation, 23*(1), 43-67.

Richard, J. F., Godbout, P, Tousignant, M., & Gréhaigne, J. F. (1999). The try-out of a team-sport assessment procedure in elementary and junior high school PE classes. *Journal of Teaching in Physical Education, 18*(3), 336-356.

Veal, M. L. (1992). The role of assessment in secondary physical education—A pedagogical view. *Journal of Physical Education, Recreation, and Dance, 63*, (7), 88-92.

Evolution of the Model: Extending Our Debate

Introduction to Chapters 14-17

Proponents of the TGfU model (i.e., tactical games or game-sense model) have done much in the way of creating games teaching and learning debate. Debates of the ideas are a vital part of the educational process and provide us with time to reflect and change our thinking or even beliefs. Debates stimulate dialogue among professionals. Ultimately, debates can assist teachers, teacher educators, and researchers to design research-based practices that help students learn.

The sport-related teaching debate or the "games debate" started with researchers comparing a TGfU approach to the traditional skill-based approach. While asking these types of research questions have not provided conclusive evidence about which approach works best yet, they have stimulated debate related to the teaching and learning of games. We need to embrace this type of scholarly dialogue and keep pushing each other to reflect, explore, design, implement, and study our ideas to improve practice for teaching and learning.

The chapters in this section focus on extending our debate about games teaching and learning, specifically as it relates to the TGfU model. In Chapter 14, Tony Rossi explores the possible links between dynamical systems of motor control and learning and TGfU. Such scholars as Piggot (1983) have explored these links before however, new ways of thinking about motor-skill acquisition requires a reassessment of the relationship with games teaching. This chapter makes such a reassessment and makes a case for a broader research agenda to fully analyze how a TGfU approach might contribute to skill acquisition and at the same time preserve the radical agenda within the model.

In Chapter 15, William Strean challenges the dichotomy of the skill-based and tactical approach debate and highlights two aspects that need attention, so that we can further understand the methods that motivate students. First, he proposes that we might revisit the four fundamental pedagogical principles (sampling, modification-representation, modification-exaggeration, and tactical complexity) used to guide the practice of planning a games curriculum. Second, he explores the learner-centered feature of the model and suggests future possibilities with regard to the cognitive, affective, and behavioral domains.

In Chapter 16, Wendy Piltz describes and analyzes "Play Practice," which is a games approach to teaching sport-related games. The play-practice approach is positioned within a constructivist learning theory framework and evolved through reflective practice in professional preparation programs in physical education at the University of South Australia.

In the final chapter in this section, Chapter 17, Enrique Bengoechea and William Strean examine the possibility of using TGfU in coaching youth sport. The authors employ a semi-structured interview process to analyze the instructional approach of youth sport coaches. Specifically, they examined the contributions of coaches' perceptions of both technical and tactical approaches as well as the coaches' use of direct and indirect coaching methods. Several issues were identified that primarily related to the teaching of the technical components of the game. These issues should enrich the discussion regarding our instructional endeavors related to sport-related games.

The authors of these four chapters provide us with a starting point for furthering our professional discourse regarding teaching and learning sport-related games. As we continue to explore the potential that a TGfU model has to offer teachers, coaches, students, and players, we wish to encourage you to continue to push the "games debate" forward.

Linking Games for Understanding with Dynamic Systems of Skill Acquisition: Old Milk in New Bottles or Have We Really Got a New Research Agenda in Physical Education and Sport?

Chapter 14

Tony Rossi, University of Southern Queensland, Australia

Introduction

Making connections between Teaching Games for Understanding (TGfU) and the field of motor-skill acquisition has been attempted before, but within the limits of the information-processing model. This chapter attempts a new connection, drawing from the advances in the dynamical model. In 1983, shortly after the Bunker and Thorpe (1982) model appeared in the literature, Piggot (1983) attempted to make links between Schmidt's (1975) Schema Theory and TGfU. The rationale for this link was based on the notion of variability of practice, which is the basic premise of schema theory, which provided a theoretical frame for thinking about TGfU. Moreover, Schmidt's Schema Theory was only about eight years old and was being explored by researchers. Basically, the key conceptual structure in the Information Processing Model (IPM) is that variable practice allows for the expansion of the motor program. The basic premise is that with constant reappraisal and reapplication, the motor program adapts to ever-changing contexts. Drawing from this, Piggot made the connection to TGfU since variable practice is inherently linked to the changing nature of game environments. This theory however, has not been empirically examined in real-world settings.

The notion of variable practice is still attractive—it perhaps appeals to physical educators and coaches intuitively because there is possibly no greater form of variability than a game itself. The links made by Piggott (1983) seemed plausible in spite of the insistence of motor behaviorists to use small, isolated tapping-style tasks upon which to both build their theories and later test them.

The current debate surrounding the IPM versus dynamics is persistent and will be resolved neither easily nor in the near future. This chapter however, is an attempt to take the theoretical position of dynamical systems, and some of the research studies within this model, and show how the model can offer support for an understanding approach to teaching games.

Starting From a Different Point

There is value in theorizing the pedagogy of games and possible links to skill-acquisition models from a different starting point. A useful point of embarkation is a coalescence of work by Rovengo and Kirk (1995), Kirk and Macdonald (1998), Kirk and McPhail (2000), and the work of Langley (1995, 1997). The development of this type of discourse is that it links a number of seemingly disparate areas such as sociology, psychology, pedagogy, and motor behavior, and at the same time provides an intricate case for the reappraisal of motor-skill acquisition approaches to teaching (TGfU) and theories of learning

The challenge of this collection of work is that pedagogical practice in physical education becomes linked again to the idea of skill acquisition. Skill acquisition has been traditionally viewed as the physical educators "core business" though, in teacher education programs, the link between pedagogy and skill-acquisition courses have become tenuous at best. This might, on the surface at least, seem even more tenuous with courses in motor-skill acquisition having taken such convoluted theoretical turns in the developing research field of ecological/dynamical systems of motor control. However, what perhaps is of particular interest to the teacher of games or coach is that the theory has, at its heart, an interaction and interrelationship between the individual, the task, and the context/environment. These are known as the "constraints" to performance. Even Schmidt (see Schmidt & Wrisberg, 2000), perhaps the most well-known motor-behavior researcher, has incorporated what he calls a "problem-based approach to motor performance and learning" into his ideas. One of the unexpected outcomes of this is that it has provided an opportunity for other researchers, among these is Langley, to theorize about skill acquisition in a qualitative, individual and human sense rather than a predictive-behavioral-cybernetic sense.

Taking Skill Acquisition Further—The Work of David Langley

Langley (1997) argues that researchers in motor behavior have not paid sufficient heed to the subjective nature of learning. In other words, Langley suggests it is important to give attention to how learners actually experience the teaching and learning context. Langley referred to Locke (1990), who suggests teachers need to have a deep understanding of how learners actually encounter the subject matter (subject-content knowledge) in schools.

Langley made a case therefore, that along with conventional research in skill learning, interpretive research developed through narrative provides a far more developed picture of this process than currently exists. Reading Laws and Fisher's (1999) work brings this notion to life. Their account of how a young schoolboy in a British study said he preferred rugby to soccer because it was on the lower field and therefore out of the biting wind, shows something of how children experience curriculum activity. The important point here is that firstly, we can hardly expect

children to "understand" games, much less acquire the com...
techniques, and concepts needed to play them, if their experi...
negative. Secondly, that narrative can address some of these ...
narrative can be seen as the storied nature of human experienc...
represents a form of knowing in humans. Finally, and not unreas...
is a form of human knowing, then it follows that it can contribute...
learning and as teachers, our *understanding* of motor-skill learning...
Elsewhere, Langley (1995) stresses that skill learning is not depend...
on the error-detection mechanisms within the motor system. Rather, ...learning
is a holistic process and narrative can help organize the multiple realities of learning
in a coherent way, especially as these constructed realities may well be different
for each learner. Langley argues then, that motor-skill learning is situated within an
individual's historical context.

Langley's ideas then, would be regarded as constructivist, since they place the
learner at the center of the learning enterprise. As he argues, this facilitates the
construction of personal responses to set motor tasks. In the dynamical/ecological
approach to learning skills, two of the constraints, the environment and the individual,
emphasize that there is a "constructedness" about skill learning. This is supported
by Rovegno and Kirk (1995), who describe the notion of learning in physical activity
as a situated phenomenon (see also the more recent work of Kirk & Macdonald,
1998; and Kirk & McPhail, 2000, based on Lave and Wenger's, 1991, ideas).

personal response

In a similar way to Langley (1995, 1997), Rovegno and Kirk (1995) explored the
potential of the ecological/dynamical approach to motor learning as it is an
interactionist theory of motor development and abandons the behaviorists' model,
which suggests that motor competency develops solely through an error-detection
model. An interactionist model places the individual at the center of the activity in an
exploratory context. A behaviorist model suggests that there are "given" processes
in motor control that "become available" as we learn to detect and correct motor
error. Rovegno and Kirk suggest that an ecological approach fits well with a socially
critical agenda, particularly with the learning of games, which have tended to be
exclusionary and isolationist.

New Motor Learning Theory

It is important to ask "why has a dynamical theory of motor control/learning emerged?"
Dynamical systems theory stems from the difficulty some motor behavior
researchers have with feedback loops and the idea of a comparator i.e., that thing
that allegedly lies somewhere in the central nervous system, which acts as an
assessment mechanism for motor output and goal achievement (see Ingvaldsen &
Whiting, 1997). For example, Ingvaldsen and Whiting ask where comparator is to
be found and how is the "ideal" motor output stored (presumably as some kind of
image) so that it can be effectively used for feedback loops? Researchers who support
such a view are much more attracted to the idea that movement responses emerge
through the interaction of the three "constraints" which were alluded to earlier (the
individual, the task, and the context). This eliminates the need for a comparator,
since as a context changes (for example in game play), then so the need for an
alternative response emerges.

If the human being is perceived as a collection of adaptive systems, it suggests that crucial time-honored assumptions about movement acquisition appear to be misplaced. Primarily, this is because feedback loops, as we have come to accept them in the information processing model, are simply not sophisticated enough to overcome the apparent anatomical limitation of the degrees of freedom case put forward by Bernstein (1967).

Bernstein's idea is that movement is a complex arrangement of coordinated actions that somehow are brought together so that the moving organism moves "as one." To use the language of Bernstein, bringing about coordinated, controlled movement that has purpose and meaning (i.e., a goal) is about controlling (or at least reducing) the degrees of freedom within a motor system. The notion of the motor system is also an issue both in the experimental research and for us in the teaching of physical education, but specifically games. The information-processing approach has tended to treat the "motor system" as entirely a human phenomenon. However, Turvey, Fitch, and Tuller, nearly 20 years ago (1982a & b), argued that not to consider the environmental factors a part of the motor system is tantamount to removing the very purpose of movement itself. Since most movement environments change constantly, particularly in the medium of games, it is crucial that this becomes part of the system of control.

Bernstein's ideas have been foundational in the intellectual thrust of the dynamical systems argument. Turvey, Fitch, and Tuller (1982a & b), in trying to capture the essence of Bernstein's ideas, suggested that the totality of forces within a "system" must be considered for other forces to act as constraints for movement outcomes. Hence the notion of an executor simply running a motor pattern is, for these researchers, a limited view of movement control. This is because it assumes great memory capability which seemingly allows the storage of an infinite number of movement patterns under the guise of a generalized motor program which can then be "executed" at will in constantly changing environments.

In an almost sarcastic tone, the authors describe the degrees of freedom required to bring about coordinated movement in the arm, based on planes of movement, muscular action, and motor units of the central nervous system to this particular limb. The authors estimate (conservatively) that there are in excess of 2,600 degrees of freedom to control in order to bring about coordinated movement that is goal directed. This also assumes, of course, that the movement environment does not change too dramatically. In simple terms, the authors are trying to express how the variability in the subsystems' muscular, mechanical, and neuro-physiological must be controlled to bring about skilled movement, "...acquiring a skill is essentially trying to find ways of controlling the degrees of freedom and of exploiting the forces made available by the context" (p. 261).

This suggests that degrees of freedom within a motor system can be reduced because muscles work together over many joints to form a coordinative structure. In 1990, Turvey came to describe this as parts of the system cooperating though "some kind of mutual understanding in achieving a common goal" (p. 939). The development of a skill then, comes when the learner finds a way to make these coordinations.

Newell's work (1985) on constraint theory has been of significant influence in this research agenda. The key argument in his proposed model of skill acquisition is that there are three stages: coordination, control, and skill. Significant to his argument is that the body's coordinative structures make adaptations to the nature of the task and that as humans we use a "search a select" mechanism to try to solve the motor task or problem. Williams, Davids, and Williams (1999) argue that the performer or learner "explores" what they call the "perceptuo-motor workspace" (p. 319). The learner, they suggest, is in search of a "landscape of possibilities" (p. 319) in order to address the task within the environmental constraints. The predictive notion of task performance that might emerge for example in a *drill* where movement reproduction is taking place (or not, as the case may be) is removed, since the learner is trying to "discover" a solution to the movement problem.

Williams et al. (1999) also suggests that as teachers we are intuitively aware, however we have not been equipped to articulate. They make the point that, though the nature of constraints are inherently interactive, teachers or coaches need to be mindful that developmental progress in movement production and movement problem solving are more likely to depend on social and other environmental factors, rather than anatomical constraints. The authors acknowledge however, that early in the learner's life, movement problems present a significant challenge from an anatomical point of view. Their point is that the anatomical "limiter" will be different for each learner; therefore the responses to the movement task will be individualized. The idea of there being a right and wrong response then seems to be quite untenable.

The most impressive part of Williams et al.'s work is their reference to the learner as a *novelist*. Essentially, the authors argue that learners should be free to explore the dynamics of the perceptuo-motor workspace. Learners should be able to explore movement environments rather than be artificially restricted by narrowly imposed constraints set by a teacher or a coach. The role of teachers and coaches is to manipulate the constraints such that the adaptive systems within learners are constantly challenged (Williams et al., 1999). Games, a dominant component of most physical education curricula, are consistent with the constantly changing environments described by Williams et al. (1999). Games are highly volatile environments that lack stability. The idea of learning a range of movements that will not correspond to the reality of constantly changing contexts can be seen for the folly that it is.

To return to Williams et al. (1999), they describe the individual as having a unique story line in terms of motor-problem response. The important thing for teachers and coaches, they suggest, is to provide localized pressures by way of manipulating the environmental constraints so that the possible solutions emerge as new environmental challenges unfold. In defense of discovery approaches, Williams et al. claim that highly directed teaching and coaching "does not allow learners how to learn how to search" (the perceptuo-workspace) (p.320).

Understandably, these researchers are cautious in their claims. For instance, they indicate that a complete random searching of the "workspace" may be very time consuming and at times potentially dangerous. What they do suggest, though, is that while more research is desirable in the area of ecological psychology and dynamical models of skill acquisition, they are providing ways for teachers to reappraise discovery forms of learning and therefore the teaching and coaching styles that might bring this about.

Vereijken and Whiting (1988), also raise the notion of discovery learning to a higher profile in a paper that reports on a set of sophisticated experiments using a slalom-ski simulator. Whilst this is removed from the games context, the message is much the same as Williams et al.'s (1999) work. Vereijken and Whiting believe that learners who were not restricted by a set of parameters imposed by a feedback system explored the movement context to a far greater extent. On the transfer trials, it was found that these subjects performed no worse than any other participants did and a great deal better than many others. In additional work included in the same paper, the authors found that control groups who had no training time also performed no worse. The authors speculated that the necessity to explore a range of possible outcomes from their movement output allowed for a deep level of learning, which resulted in high levels of subsequent performance.

In a further twist, Ingvaldsen and Whiting (1997) agree that the cybernetic model is of limited use. They prefer to make alliances between Skinner's Stimulus—Response (S-R) psychology and newer work in ecological psychology since they suggest, that this approach addresses not only the "how" of movement (ecological/dynamical systems) but the "why" (S-R). An important reason for such a rapprochement, they suggest, lies in the complementarity not only in intellectual discourse, but in methods also. The scientific study of motor behavior, they suggest, must give way to what they call single-case studies and serial designs. It seems such ideas are not too far removed philosophically from Langley's (1995, 1997) ideas.

Whatever position is taken, what seems to be inescapable is that skilled movement behavior is only really acquired in the context in which such behavior belongs. As Gibson (1986), one of the significant and oft-cited authors in this emerging field, argues, behaviorist approaches to psychology are too narrowly framed and fail to explain the interdependence of an organism in situ. His concern is with the co-evolution of organisms and their environments. As he says:

> Moving from place to place is supposed to be "physical" whereas perceiving is supposed to be "mental," but this dichotomy is misleading. Locomotion is guided by visual perception. Not only does it depend on perception but also perception depends on locomotion insomuch as a moving point of observation is necessary for any adequate acquaintance with the environment. So we must perceive in order to move, but we must also move in order to perceive. (p. 223)

Relating Dynamics to Teaching Games and Using an Understanding Approach

TGfU is built on the notion that the development of games sense should come before a strict regime of "skills and drills." Skills and drills de-contextualize games, which means they lead to movement behaviors that are of limited value. The thrust of Bunker and Thorpe's work, since 1982 to more recent work (Thorpe & Bunker, 1997), is that an understanding of the games environment is important for skills to develop.

Kirk and his colleagues in Australia (Kirk & Macdonald, 1998) and the UK (Kirk & McPhail, 2000) prefer to describe the understanding approach to teaching games as a response to the situated learning opportunities in the changing contexts of games. Drawing on the work of Lave and Wenger (1991), they argue that the "situatedness" of games requires learning that has meaning to each participant in the "situation." In the teaching of games then, it is important to ensure that the abstract nature of games does not render the learning as pointless and unconnected. This, though, is the whole point of a dynamical approach to skill learning. As the protagonists would argue, the ecology of the environment, the game situation (even in its modified form as called for by Bunker & Thorpe, 1982) is a dynamic of the learning and shifts in the situation demand ecologically suitable responses. Such responses from learners then have meaning, they are not isolated responses entirely de-contextualized from the "real" games situation as happens in a "drills approach." Hence the performance of "technique" can manifest to become a skill in the genuine sense, because it is performed in a context in which it belongs. In games, the context constantly changes and so does the nature of the required response. A TGfU approach therefore fits neatly with the notion of constraint, which lies at the heart of dynamical theory.

But Is It Old Milk in New Bottles?

There is a range of literature that might offer some clues to this challenge. I have decided to draw on just one example simply for reasons of space. Many physical education teachers particularly those "trained" in the British traditions of the late 1960s through to 1980 would be familiar with the work of Mauldon (1981) in educational gymnastics and her work with Redfern on games teaching. The essence of this work was to place the child at the center of the activity. For him or her to come up with movement solutions to the problems posed by the teacher, or more importantly the context itself. Their description of the complexity of games emphasizes the necessity for learners to be creative problem solvers to deal with the constantly changing environment:

> General body agility has therefore to be combined with manipulative dexterity in relation to *an object in motion*...Moreover, in a game not only is the player on the move himself, but often he also has to adapt to others, whether members of his own side or opponents, who themselves are on the move. Spaces frequently alter in shape and size, and timing is all-important; a burst of speed, a momentary hesitation or an abrupt halt may be called for; sudden swerves, about-turns and rapid changes in direction are often required...(p. 18)

Mauldon and Redfern (1981) go on to suggest that the developmental requirements for such movement are seldom in place—it is the adaptation to rapid change that creates the complexity in so many movement problems. Mauldon and Redfern do not so much argue against direct forms of pedagogy. Rather, they suggest drills (usually of adult invention) are of limited purpose, as they provide a very narrow experience of movement requirements—*particularly* (but not exclusively) in games. Mauldon and Redfern's views can be found elsewhere in the literature including the work of North (1973), Bilborough and Jones (1963, 1970), and in official documents, for example *Movement* published in the UK by the Department of

Education and Science in 1972. Even Whiting, in his classic 1969 text, indicated that to teach an activity, which clearly sits so far outside the so-called "real situation" must surely be of limited value, since how is the learner to make sense of where the "learned" movement behavior actually fits in.

Challenges to the Teaching Games for Understanding Approach

There is no empirical research within the TGfU approach that makes links to dynamical systems of motor behavior. As a result, only philosophical challenges can be made in these terms. This does suggest a viable research agenda exists to explore the links which intellectually, at least, seem to be likely. Most challenges to TGfU come from pedagogical research. Hence any advocacy for TGfU must be tempered by these challenges.

In many respects, it is easy to be reminded of Locke's now classic piece in 1977 in which he looked for hope in research on teaching physical education, to which he referred as a "dismal science." His charge at the time "Aside from data-free excursions into the realm of instructional models..." (p. 2) could be levelled at TGfU today and this is in spite of the project having a 20-year lineage. Turner and Martinek (1995) make such a claim, though Kirk and McPhail (2000) argue that there is a research literature related to this approach to games. However, both the research questions and the methods of inquiry are diverse and it would be difficult to establish any real patterns from the available studies. It is probably not unreasonable to say that for many, TGfU appeals both philosophically and intuitively but it may well be that the research in dynamical models of skill acquisition represents its closest ally in research terms.

There is some research on the TGfU approach, but little of it so far relates to competency levels of participants and the relationship of this to the model itself. This might be because the "measurement" of games sense, decision-making, skilled action in context is somewhat difficult and to be fair was not necessarily the only major objective of TGfU. Indeed, Kirk and McPhail (2000) allude to this very point.

It is worthwhile though to reflect on some of the research that questions the TGfU approach. First Laws (1994) wondered whether it was little more than a rhetorical justification for the purposes of school documentation. In a three-year case study at a British school, Laws considered many aspects of school physical education. He found that while mission statements and programs of work alluded glowingly to an "understanding" approach to games teaching, the actual practice of teachers differed little from time-honored procedures of drills and skills.

Rink, French, and Tjeerdsma (1996), while indicating many positive outcomes for students from a TGfU approach, were unable to say with any certainty (within the research paradigm used) that TGfU was any better than other methods for developing games techniques. Turner and Martinek (1992, 1995) have also challenged whether a TGfU approach actually develops superior decision-making and tactical skills. Again, it might be that the research approaches were at fault rather than the thing being researched.

Finally, in a philosophical challenge, Fleming (1994) argues that the term "understanding" is not particularly helpful for practitioners trying to shape their pedagogical practice, or to theorists trying to make sense of this approach. He argues that the use of the preposition "for" is arbitrary and it could just as easily be replaced with "by," "through," "to," "with," etc., suggesting that all of these are important in the games-learning experiences. Moreover, he suggests that the use of the word "games" also focuses the agenda on "content" lines rather than "process."

A Final Comment

The intellectual and philosophical links between TGfU and dynamical systems of motor behavior seem to offer viable research possibilities to determine the efficacy of TGfU as a problem-solving approach to acquiring both games skills and games sense. In addition, the work of Langley (1995) also suggests that motor-behavior research should be extended to include the learner's subjective analysis of their own learning. A research program into TGfU, which draws upon a combination of paradigms, may well provide new insights into games teaching. Such insights are long overdue.

References

Bilborough, A. & Jones, P. (1970). *Physical education in the primary school.* (3rd ed) London: London University Press.

Bernstein, N. (1967). *The coordination and regulation of movements.* Oxford: Pergamon Press.

Bunker, D. & Thorpe, R. (1982). A model for the teaching of games in secondary schools. *Bulletin of Physical Education, 18*(1), 5-8.

Department of Education and Science. (1972). *Movement.* London: HMSO.

Fleming, S. (1994). Understanding "understanding": making sense of the cognitive approach to the teaching of games. *Physical Education Review, 17*(2), 90-96.

Gibson, J. J. (1986). *The ecological approach to visual perception.* Hillsdale, NJ: Lawrence Erlbaum.

Ingvaldsen, R. P. & Whiting, H. T. A. (1997). Modern views on motor skill learning are not representative! *Human Movement Science, 16*, 705-732.

Kirk, D. & Macdonald, D. (1998). Situated learning in physical education. *Journal of Teaching in Physical Education. 17*(3), 376-387.

Kirk, D. & Macphail, A. (2000). Teaching games for understanding and situated learning: Rethinking the model. A paper presented to the Pre-Olympic Congress Symposium on Student Learning in Physical Education. Brisbane, September 7-13.

Langley, D. (1995). Examining the personal experience of student skill learning: A narrative perspective. *Research Quarterly for Exercise and Sport. 66*, 116-128.

Langley, D. (1997). Exploring student skill learning: A case for investigating subjective experience. *Quest, 49*(2), 142-160.

Lave, J. & Wenger, E. (1991). *Situated learning: Legitimate peripheral participation.* Cambridge, UK: Cambridge University Press.

Laws, C. (1994). *Rhetorical justification for new approaches to teaching games—Are teachers deluding themselves.* Proceedings of the 10th Commonwealth and Scientific Congress. Victoria, Canada; University of Victoria.

Laws, C. & Fisher, R. (1999). Pupils interpretations of physical education. In C. Hardy & M. Mawer (Eds.), *Learning and teaching in physical education.* London: Falmer Press.

Locke, L. (1977). Research on teaching physical education: New hope for a dismal science. *Quest, 28*, 2-16.

Locke, L. (1990). Why motor learning is ignored. A case of ducks, naughty theories and unrequited love. *Quest, 42*, 134-142.

Mauldon, E. & Redfern H. B. (1981). *Games Teaching* (2nd ed). Plymouth, UK: Macdonald and Evans.

Newell, K. (1985). Coordination, control and skill. In D. Goodman, R. B. Wilberg, & I. M Franks (Eds.), *Differing perspectives in motor learning and control.* Amsterdam: Elsevier Science.

North, M. (1973). *Movement Education: A guide for primary and middle school teachers.* London: Temple Smith.

Piggot, B. (1983). A psychological basis for new trends in games teaching. In L. Spackman (Ed.), *Teaching games for understanding.* St. Paul's & St. Mary's College, Cheltenham, UK.

Rink, J., French, K., & Tjeerdsma, B. (1996). Foundations for the learning and instruction of sport and games. *Journal of Teaching in Physical Education, 15*(4), 399-417.

Rovegno, I. & Kirk, D. (1995). Articulations and silences in socially critical work on physical education : Toward a broader agenda. *Quest, 47*(4), 447-474.

Schmidt, R. A. (1975). A schema theory of discrete motor skill learning. *Psychological Review, 82*, 225-260.

Schmidt, R. & Wrisberg, C. (2000). *Motor Learning and Performance.* (2nd ed). Champaign: Human Kinetics.

Thorpe, R. & Bunker, D. (1997). A changing focus in games teaching. In, L. Almond (Ed.), *Physical education in schools* (2nd ed). London: Kogan Page.

Turner, A. & Martinek, T. J. (1992). A comparative analysis of two models for teaching games (technique approach and game-centered (tactical focus) approach). *International Journal of Physical Education, 29*(4), 15-31.

Turner, A. & Martinek, T. J. (1995). Teaching for understanding: A model for improving decisions making during game play. *Quest, 47*(1) 44-63.

Turvey, M. T. (1990). Coordination. *American Psychologist, 45*, 938-953.

Turvey, M. T., Fitch, H. L. & Tuller, B. (1982a). The Bernstein Perspective. The problems of degrees of freedom and context-conditioned variability. In S. Kelso (Ed.), *Human Motor Behavior: An Introduction.* Hillsdale, NJ: Lawrence Erlbaum.

Turvey, M. T., Fitch, H. L., & Tuller, B. (1982b). The Bernstein Perspective: II. The concept of muscle linkage or coordinative structure. In S. Kelso (Ed.), *Human Motor Behavior: An Introduction.* Hillsdale, NJ: Lawrence Erlbaum.

Vereijken, B. & Whiting, H. T. A. (1988). In defence of discovery learning. *Canadian Journal of Sports Science*, 15(20) 99-106.

Whiting, H. T. A. (1969). *Acquiring ball skill.* London: Bell.

Williams, A. M., Davids, K., & Williams, J. G. (1999). *Visual perception and action in sport.* London: E & FN Spoon.

Beyond Technical vs. Tactical: Extending the Games-Teaching Debate

Chapter 15

William B. Strean, University of Alberta, Canada

Enrique García Bengoechea, University of Alberta, Canada

Introduction

Games have been a primary part of the majority of physical education curricula. Fittingly, there has been recent debate regarding the delivery and learning outcomes of games experiences (e.g., Fleming, 1994). The introduction of the Teaching Games for Understanding (TGfU), (Bunker & Thorpe, 1982) approach has been the catalyst for discussions of theoretical and pedagogical aspects of games teaching. The purpose of this paper is to examine relevant research and theoretical perspectives, drawing together the diverse issues related to TGfU, to sharpen the focus of pedagogical research in this area. (see Holt, Strean, & García Bengoechea, 2002). The focus here is on the learner and the affective domain.

As the interest in the TGfU approach grew, a strong debate developed to respond to the challenge TGfU presented to traditional "skill-drill" pedagogical approaches. The central tenet of the debate focused on the relative merits of the TGfU approach over a traditional technical (i.e., skill-drill) approach. Although theoretical and pedagogical aspects of TGfU have been discussed in a research (Kirk, 1983; Rink, 1996; Thorpe, 1992) and professional context, there has been limited empirical research considering the *range of outcomes* that may arise from tactical approaches to teaching games.

Research comparing technical and tactical approaches to games teaching has tended to concentrate on cognitive and psychomotor learning outcomes (e.g., Allison & Thorpe, 1997; Rink, 1996; Turner & Martinek, 1992, 1999). Despite the appeal for discussion regarding tactical-versus-technical approaches in terms of skillful performance outcomes, the TGfU debate is multifaceted (Gréhaigne, Godbout, & Bouthier, 1999). The analysis of performance outcomes is part of the TGfU debate; however performance may not be the central feature. It appears that an edifice of research has been built on the foundation of a false dichotomy, or perhaps, investigators have set up extreme ends of a technical-tactical continuum as a false dichotomy. Further, the pitting of technical-against-tactical approaches, purely in terms of the performance outcomes they produce, was not the apparent purpose of the original TGfU model. In fact, one of the reasons the TGfU model was originally introduced was due to British children leaving school having experienced little success in games because of the emphasis on performance (Werner, Bunker, & Thorpe, 1996), where "performance" is understood in terms of observable outcomes.

TGfU's proponents (Booth, 1983; Burrows, 1986; Werner & Almond, 1990) have provided some anecdotal evidence for the benefits of a tactical over a technical approach. Empirically, Turner and Martinek (1999) noted that researchers have considered the effects of technical and tactical approaches to games teaching on both cognitive outcomes (decision-making, declarative, and procedural knowledge) and performance (behavioral observations), but preliminary findings have been somewhat equivocal.

French, Werner, Rink, Taylor, and Hussey (1996) failed to show the superiority of a tactical over a technical approach for student decision-making in high school, and similar results have been found with middle school students (Mitchell, Griffin, & Oslin, 1995; Turner & Martinek, 1992). Mitchell et al., (1995), however demonstrated that off-the-ball movement was enhanced for students taught with a tactical approach. In a long-term study (conducted over 15 lessons), students learning field hockey through a TGfU approach made better decisions during games than those taught with a technique approach. In another study, a TGfU group of middle school children displayed better control and passing execution in field hockey than their technique counterparts, though a number of other outcome measures (e.g., tackling, dribbling, shooting) showed limited improvement (Turner & Martinek, 1999). There may be a number of reasons underlying the equivocal nature of these findings, as Turner and Martinek (1999) noted, the correct decision does not necessarily correspond with the correct action-reflecting the difficulty of interpreting cognitive activity from behavioral responses (cf. Rink, 2001).

The introduction of TGfU as a reaction to the traditional skill-drill model may well have contributed to the direct comparison of the approaches from an empirical perspective. Researchers have struggled to provide evidence for which approach is "better." As Rink (2001) argued, "when you spend all of your effort proving that a particular kind of teaching is better than another kind of teaching, you limit what you can learn about the very complex teaching/learning process" (p. 123).

Our perspective is that skill *and* tactical instruction, as well as a combination of both, promote student learning in areas of skill and cognitive knowledge development (also see Lawton, 1989; Turner & Martinek, 1992). Skill development is explicitly included in tactical approaches, just as games play is a part of technical approaches. The crucial point is *when* to introduce tactical or technical skills. TGfU suggests that tactical game understanding should be introduced first, then, when students have discovered when and why skills are needed in the game context, the technical execution of skills are introduced.

As the TGfU model evolved, and the debate concerning technical-versus-tactical approaches to games instruction gathered momentum, two vital components of the debate may have been overlooked by the interested parties (i.e., teachers and researchers). First, Thorpe, Bunker, and Almond (1984) presented the idea that a games curriculum can be developed based on the TGfU model *coupled* with four fundamental pedagogical principles. Beyond the six-component curriculum model (Bunker & Thorpe, 1982), the four fundamental pedagogical principles of sampling, modification-representation, modification-exaggeration, and tactical complexity have not been widely considered from a research perspective. Consequently, we presented an expanded TGfU model that incorporates the curriculum model, pedagogical principles, and a more holistic view of the learner. (Holt, Strean, & García Bengoechea, 2002).

Second, the learner is at the center of the TGfU model, but the experience of the learner has not been central to the academic debate. In particular, whereas cognitive and psychomotor domains have been more the focus of research and discussion in the literature, the affective domain has not been extensively examined. As the scope of literature surrounding tactical and technical issues in the teaching of games expands, researchers investigating the pedagogy of games teaching would do well to consider who the learner is, how the learner is motivated to continue to participate, and the importance of affective outcomes. This opportunity is important because affective outcomes resulting from the TGfU approach may have implications for children's physical activity experiences, future motivation to participate, and, in turn, psychological and physical health.

Extending The TGfU Debate: Considering Learners' Affective Experience

The learner is at the center of the TGfU model, but the experience of learners has not been central to the TGfU debate in the academic literature. Rink (2001) urged researchers to consider the learning processes experienced by the learner. The teacher must consider the relationship between behavioral, cognitive, and affective domains when selecting the instructional environment. Likewise, researchers should consider implications of games pedagogy for each of these domains, and how each domain may influence the other. We recommend considering the TGfU learner from the whole-child perspective (Wall & Murray, 1990). Being able to accommodate for individual differences in cognitive, affective, and behavioral domains is a crucial challenge for educators. Instruction must be understood in terms of the learning theories upon which teaching methodologies are founded, and the influence these methodologies, like TGfU, have on the learner (Rink, 2001).

There has been wider consideration of cognitive and behavioral outcomes of TGfU instructional approaches. For example, cognitive outcomes have been examined in high school and middle school settings (Mitchell et al., 1995; French et al., 1996; Turner & Martinek, 1992). Behavioral measures to assess game involvement and effectiveness have been developed to assist with measurement of performance (Gréhaigne, Godbout, & Bouthier, 1997; Oslin, Mitchell, & Griffin, 1998), and skill outcomes have been assessed in conjunction with cognitive outcomes (Turner & Martinek, 1999). Nevertheless the affective domain has received little attention from researchers to date.

Work on the affect and enjoyment in sport (e.g., Boyd & Yin, 1996; Kimiecik & Harris, 1996; Scanlan & Simons, 1992; Strean & Holt, 2000; Wankel, 1997) may offer some direction for bringing greater consideration of the affective domain into games teaching. For example, children, coaches, and parents all acknowledged that games and game-like situations were more fun than technically oriented drills (Strean & Holt, 2000).

Many of the processes involved in the affective domain (e. g., having fun) are primary motivators for children's involvement in sport and games (Ewing & Seefeldt, 1990; Scanlan & Simons, 1992; Wankel & Kreisel, 1985). However, the majority of research associated with TGfU focuses on outcomes in terms of performance or learning. Skill development is another important reason why children participate (Chalip, Csikszentmihalyi, Kleiber, & Larson, 1984), but, as Werner et al. (1996) suggested, the primary purposes of teaching any game should be not only to "improve student's game performance [but also] to improve their enjoyment and participation in games, which might lead to a more healthy lifestyle" (p. 32). Affective outcomes, such as fun and enjoyment, may be enhanced through TGfU.

In one of the few articles that discuss the learner from a psychological perspective, Thorpe (1992) analyzed the psychological underpinnings of TGfU using the incentives framework (Alderman & Wood, 1976). Because TGfU stresses the game and guides learners to discover the game, it capitalizes on affiliation (i.e., social interaction, social reassurance, and making friends) by encouraging children to develop rules, and challenging them to work out ways to arrive at appropriate tactics. Skill is practiced individually, or in small groups, anticipating children can work with others to foster affiliation. Thorpe (1992) argued achievement (in the sense of doing something well or better) is fostered by TGfU because it is possible to have a good game with poor techniques. That is, a learner can still be effective in a tactical sense, such as creating space, even if sometimes her skill execution, such as passing the object, is poor. Thorpe (1992) stressed the importance of creating a positive climate for learners, and not just judging their success on the basis of whether skills were performed well or not. Sensation may be facilitated by allowing children to keep score if they want, or still playing competitive games and not keep score if they prefer, so in this way more individuals can be accommodated (Thorpe, 1992). Finally, Thorpe pointed out that skill-based lessons may show the teacher some immediate effect of skill improvement, but the social and skill-related interactions over time may convince students of their lack of ability.

There are a number of interesting questions related to TGfU and motivation that have not been widely addressed. Thorpe's (1992) article stands in isolation in the application of a theoretical motivation framework to the TGfU model. Some preliminary attempts have been made to assess the motivational implications of tactical approaches to teaching games. In a comparison of technical and tactical approaches to invasion games, with respect to enhancing intrinsic motivation, no statistically significant differences from either instructional approach were reported (Mitchell et al., 1995). Although the findings may be counterintuitive (and perhaps disheartening for those favoring a TGfU approach), the nonsignificance may possibly be a result of the nature of the design, measurement, or sample size.

There is some emergent research to show that children report games as being more fun than drills in organized sport practice environments (Strean & Holt, 2000). If this finding is robust, then the adoption of modified games that characterize TGfU may have numerous benefits for children's affective experiences. Facilitating more enjoyable experiences may, in turn, have implications for motivation and continued participation, even after schooling has been completed. There is also considerable opportunity for research here in relation to the health benefits of continued participation arising from fun and enjoyable games experiences. Rather than consider the benefits of a variety of tactical approaches in isolation, the affective benefits of teaching common principles across a category of games must be considered. That is, future research may consider the affective, motivational, and health benefits for children in schools that have a TGfU games curriculum. Ultimately, considering the affective implications of TGfU for learner motivation, and subsequent possible future involvement in physical activity, is significant for both psychological and physical health outcomes.

Conclusion: Future Research

By presenting the learner from a whole-child perspective in the TGfU model, it becomes easier to understand the possibilities that the model can offer for games pedagogy. Taking a holistic view of the child is also congruent with the reasons that underpin the introduction of the curriculum model in the first place. We believe that it is vital to assess children's "performance" in terms of criteria that move beyond the mere analysis of game performance. We assume that physical education is about more than the development of physical skills, and that cognitive and, in particular, affective implications of games teaching should be of paramount importance.

We suggest that the next phase of research into games pedagogy will be characterized by some divergence from the technical-tactical debate. Researchers interested in examining the whole TGfU model, considering outcomes in terms of learning, performance, and affective benefits for children will have the potential to make significant contributions to the debate. On the other hand, specific elements of the approach may be more closely scrutinized. For example, particular attention may be paid to the delivery of the four fundamental pedagogical principles across different games categories. Associated with understanding more about specific elements of the model, pedagogical questions about how to make abstract, dynamic concepts like space more concrete and accessible for younger learners may be addressed through close examination of modification and exaggeration principles. Progressions seem to be based on privileging of cognitive concerns, yet the affective implications (which we have argued need to be highlighted) may be important in designing instruction.

To understand student motivation, it is important to understand the methods that motivate students (Rink, 2001). Consider the following research question: "Do children taught invasion games through predominantly TGfU methods participate more frequently in other invasion games than children taught through a predominantly skill-based approach?" To move research beyond the comparison of the two approaches, the whole TGfU model may be incorporated in this question (curriculum model, four fundamental pedagogical principles, games classification, and keeping the learner at the center). Moving beyond the analysis of isolated aspects of the TGfU model, to consider curricular issues (e.g., teaching concepts across game categories), cognitive, affective, and performance outcomes may demonstrate more clearly the benefits of the approach. Questions surrounding affective influences of TGfU approaches for children's experiences have important implications for their future motivation.

From a developmental viewpoint, the structuring of lesson progressions has been emphasized for younger children, but there are still questions concerning when and how tactical structures should be introduced to students. The introduction of less-complex games first (e.g., target games first) makes theoretical sense, but (a) there is no clear evidence that this approach facilitates learners' experiences in more complex games and (b) often children want to play team invasion sports first. What are the tactical structures that should be first introduced that are most readily transferable across other games in a category?

An interesting spin-off from this pedagogical discourse in physical education is that individual sport governing bodies are turning toward more games-based instruction. For example, the Canadian Soccer Association has developed a new coaching scheme based on teaching in, and through, the game, rather than isolated skill-drills, encouraging inexperienced coaches to follow the maxim "let the game be the teacher." The development of more games-based approaches in specific sports should not be confused with TGfU, but there is ample scope for integration of such schemes into the TGfU research base.

Through this review, we hope to challenge researchers to move beyond the technical-versus-tactical impasse, and in particular consider the motivational and affective implications arising from the way in which teachers deliver games in physical education. Though there are certainly many questions related to the effectiveness of various strands of games pedagogy, we believe the continued participation of learners in games throughout their lives is of paramount importance. Therefore, we challenge teachers and researchers to consider the evolution of the TGfU model, and to participate in the journey forward, while considering learners from behavioral, cognitive, *and* affective perspectives.

References

Alderman, R. B. & Wood, N. L. (1976). An analysis of incentive motivation in Canadian athletics. *Canadian Journal of Applied Sports Sciences, 1*, 169-176.

Allison, S. & Thorpe, R. D. (1997). A comparison of the effectiveness of two approaches to teaching games within physical education: A skills approach versus a games for understanding approach. *British Journal of Physical Education, 28*(3), 17-21.

Berkowitz, R. J. (1996). A practitioner's journey: From skill to tactics. *Journal of Physical Education, Recreation and Dance, 67*(4), 44-45.

Booth, K. (1983). An introduction to netball: An alternative approach. *Bulletin of Physical Education, 19*(1), 27-31.

Boyd, M. P. & Yin, Z. (1996). Cognitive-affective sources of sport enjoyment in adolescent sport participants. *Adolescence, 31*, 383-395.

Bunker, D. J. & Thorpe, R. D. (1982). A model for the teaching of games in secondary schools. *Bulletin of Physical Education, 18*(1), 5-8.

Burrows, L. (1986). A teacher's reactions. In R. D. Thorpe, D. J. Bunker, & L. Almond (Eds.), *Rethinking games teaching* (pp. 45-52). Loughborough, UK: Loughborough University.

Chalip, L. M., Csikszentmihalyi, M., Kleiber, D., & Larson, R. (1984). Variations of experience in formal and informal sport. *Research Quarterly for Exercise and Sport, 55*, 109-116.

Ewing, M. E. & Seefeldt, V. (1990). *American youth and sport participation.* Study conducted for the Athletic Footwear Association.

Fleming, S. (1994). Understanding "understanding": Making sense of the cognitive approach to the teaching of games. *Physical Education Review, 17*(2), 90-96.

French, K. E., Werner, P. H., Rink, J. E., Taylor, K., & Hussey, K. (1996). The effects of a 6-week unit of tactical skill or combined tactical and skill instruction on badminton performance of ninth-grade students. *Journal of Teaching in Physical Education, 15*, 439-463

Gréhaigne, J. F., Godbout, P., & Bouthier, D. (1997). Performance assessment in team sports. *Journal of Teaching in Physical Education, 16*, 500-516.

Gréhaigne, J. F., Godbout, P., & Bouthier, D. (1999). The foundation of tactics and strategy in team sports. *Journal of Teaching in Physical Education, 18*, 159-174.

Holt, N. L., Strean, W. B., & García Bengoechea., E. (2002). Expanding the teaching games for understanding model: New avenues for future research and practice. *Journal of Teaching in Physical Education, 21*, 162-176.

Kimiecik, J. C. & Harris, A. T. (1996). What is enjoyment? A conceptual/definitional analysis with implications for sport and exercise psychology. *Journal of Sport and Exercise Psychology, 13*, 50-64.

Kirk, D. (1983). Theoretical guidelines for teaching games for understanding. *Bulletin of Physical Education, 19*(1), 41-45.

Lawton, J. (1989). Comparison of two teaching methods in games. *Bulletin of Physical Education, 25*(1), 35-38.

Mitchell, S. A., Griffin, L. L., & Oslin, J. L. (1995). The effects of two instructional approaches on game performance. *Pedagogy in Practice: Teaching and Coaching in Physical Education and Sports, 1*(1). 36-48.

Oslin, J. L., Mitchell, S. A., & Griffin, L. L. (1998). The game performance assessment instrument (GPAI): Development and preliminary validation. *Journal of Teaching in Physical Education, 17,* 231-243.

Rink, J. E. (1996). Tactical and skill approaches to teaching sport and games. *Journal of Teaching in Physical Education (monograph), 15,* 397-516.

Rink, J. E. (2001). Investigating the assumptions of pedagogy. *Journal of Teaching in Physical Education, 20,* 112-128.

Scanlan, T. K. & Simons, J. P. (1992). The construct of sport enjoyment. In G. C. Roberts (Ed.), *Motivation in sport and exercise* (pp. 199-215). Champaign, IL: Human Kinetics.

Strean, W. B. & Holt, N. L. (2000). Players', Coaches', and Parents' perceptions of fun in youth sport. *Avante, 6,* 84-98.

Thorpe, R. D. (1992). The psychological factors underpinning the "teaching for understanding games" movement. In T. Williams, L. Almond, & A. Sparkes (Eds.), *Sport and physical activity: Moving toward excellence (Proceedings of the AIESEP World Convention, Loughbough, UK)* (pp. 209-218). London: E & FN Spon.

Thorpe. R. D, Bunker, D. J., & Almond, L. (1984). A change in the focus of teaching games. In M. Piéron & G. Graham (Eds.), *Sport pedagogy: Olympic scientific congress proceedings, Vol. 6.*(pp. 163-169). Champaign, IL: Human Kinetics.

Turner, A. P. & Martinek, T. J. (1992). A comparative analysis of two models for teaching games (technique approach and game-centered (tactical focus) approach). *International Journal of Physical Education, 29*(4), 15-31.

Turner, A. P. & Martinek, T. J. (1999). An investigation into teaching games for understanding: Effects on skill, knowledge and game play. *Research Quarterly for Exercise and Sport, 70,* 286-296.

Wall, J. & Murray, N. (1990). *Children and movement.* Dubuque, IA: WMC Brown.

Wankel, L. M. (1997). "Strawpersons," selective reporting, and inconsistent logic: A response to Kimiecik and Harris's analysis of enjoyment. *Journal of Sport and Exercise Psychology, 19,* 1-12.

Wankel, L. M. & Kreisel, P. S. J. (1985). Factors underlying enjoyment of youth sports: Sport and age group comparisons. *Journal of Sport Psychology, 7,* 51-64.

Werner, P. & Almond, L. (1990). Models of games education. *Journal of Physical Education, Recreation, and Dance, 61*(4), 23-27.

Werner, P., Bunker, D., & Thorpe, R. (1996). Teaching games for understanding: Evolution of a model. *Journal of Physical Education, Recreation, and Dance, 67*(1), 28-3.

Teaching and Coaching Using a "Play-Practice" Approach

Chapter 16

Wendy Piltz, University of South Australia, Australia

Introduction

Teachers and coaches of games and sport are constantly seeking better ways to structure learning to develop competent game players, to encourage positive dispositions towards lifelong activity, and to attain a broader range of learning outcomes (Launder, 2001; Read, 1989; Siedentop, 1994; Werner, Thorpe, & Bunker, 1996). A key factor to moving in this direction is to ensure that a more comprehensive range of player competencies are developed in enjoyable or playful settings that exhibit quality teaching and learning practice (Launder, 2001; Rink, French, & Graham, 1996; Rink, French, & Tjeerdsma, 1996).

A variety of new approaches for teaching and coaching games have been advocated to counter an array of problems associated with traditional methods of games teaching. The traditional approaches that evidence poor quality of teaching and learning practice range from unstructured game play, where the ball is simply thrown out amongst the large group of players with minimal instruction, through to formally structured practices, which lack relevance to the real game demands or where drills and isolated technical practice dominate at the expense of the development of other critical elements of effective play, including tactics and decision-making. These practices not only result in a lack of player participation and active engagement in relevant game-like learning they also contribute to the lack of success in developing game players with a deeper level of understanding about the real nature of the game and how to operate skillfully in it. Additional issues have been raised concerning learning environments that overemphasize direct teaching approaches or feature excessive repetitive technical practice and mindless drills. An overemphasis on coach-dominated, direct instruction can disengage players from the learning process while mundane technical practice and tedious drills can produce boredom, stifle player enjoyment, and suppress creativity. An additional problem associated with some monotonous drills is that they teach stereotyped thinking and response patterns, which show little transfer of learning to the real game demands requiring rapid problem solving, flexible thinking, and dynamic responses (Launder, 2001; Griffin, Mitchell, & Oslin, 1997; Bunker & Thorpe, 1982).

The Teaching Games for Understanding (TGfU) approach developed by Almond, Thorpe, and Bunker at Loughborough University in England in the early 1980s, presented an alternative teaching approach to the traditional technique-focused method of games teaching that was so prevalent in English schools at that time. The authors proposed that games provide problem-solving challenges for participants and they identified a range of common tactical challenges presented by families of games. They suggested that by reducing the technical demands of the game

ropriate modifications, participants are able to firstly develop an
...g of the tactical aspects of the game and then build on this with
...ctical practice to progress towards the adult form of the game. The
... Approach (Griffin et al., 1997), derived from TGfU, advocates similar
...e authors proposed a variety of levels of tactical complexity and a
...ntic framework for assessing game performance. Games Sense was
...itle given for a series of coaching workshops presented by Thorpe in 1996 with
the Australian Sports Commission. While labeled differently, the workshops were
based on TGfU concepts. They challenged coaches to rethink traditional technical
coaching methods and encouraged them to consider strategies for developing
thinking capacities in players. The ideas surrounding this approach have been
collated and published as the Game Sense approach by Kirk & MacPhail, (1999).

The Sport Education Model (SEM) (Siedentop, 1994) has provided an alternate
curriculum framework for planning and instructing sport experiences in a variety of
physical education settings. The instructional approach proposed in Sport Education
focuses on collaborative learning to enhance individual and team leadership and the
development of competent, literate, and enthusiastic sports participants. The SEM
advocates active involvement in small-sided game play and a more holistic
understanding of the sport culture (Siedentop, 1994).

Charlesworth, the highly successful coach of the Australian Women's Hockey team,
coined the phrase "designer games" to describe a specific type of game practice
that he used extensively at training sessions to achieve game competency and
leadership outcomes for his players. By thoughtfully manipulating playing variables
such as space, numbers, and scoring, game scenarios were created that closely
replicated the complexity and pressure experienced in competition (Charlesworth, 1994).

Recent research on games teaching has focused on the merits and impact of
technical-versus-tactical focus to games instruction. This orientation has attempted
to compare the tactical game-first approach with the traditional technique-first
approach (Allison & Thorpe, 1997; Rink, 1996; Mitchell, Oslin, & Griffin 1995; Turner
& Martinek, 1992). While some of the findings indicate increased level of enjoyment,
motivation, and tactical understanding of players in the tactical-based environment,
the results have been generally inconclusive about the superiority of either teaching
approach. A major concern with this type of research is the claim that either a
tactical or a technical approach is better for developing competent game players.
This assumption indicates serious shortcomings in the level of understanding of the
complexity and diversity of the demands of major games and it highlights a
misunderstanding of the conceptual framework of TGfU in relation to the
importance of both technique and tactics in competent game play (Kirk & MacPhail,
2002; Rink, French, & Tjeerdsma, 1996). Despite the conceptual and research
developments associated with the TGfU model, there still remains a significant void
in the articulation of usable strategies that can guide and integrate theory with
professional practice (Chandler, 1996). What appears to be missing is a comprehensive
framework for analyzing elements of effective play and a structure with usable
strategies that can inform and guide professional practice in the teaching and
coaching of these games.

What personal & social aspects can be developed through the Sport Model?

The intent of this chapter is to describe and analyze the Play-Practice approach to teaching and coaching sport developed by Launder (2001). The chapter will include (a) an appraisal of the evolution of the Play-Practice approach, (b) a review of the key principles of the approach in relation to contemporary learning theory, (c) a description of the innovative features of the approach, and (d) an outline of the strategies advocated to guide professional practice. A variety of practical examples of play practices will be included through out the chapter to illustrate key concepts and elements of the approach.

Play Practice—Its History and Defining Influences

Play Practice is a practical, functional, eclectic approach to teaching and coaching sports developed by Launder, who has been deeply involved in sport over a lifetime as a participant, coach, physical education teacher, and a teacher/coach educator. The approach has evolved in parallel to TGfU and its derivative frameworks through the process described by Launder (2001) as "reflective tinkering," where ideas are created, implemented, evaluated, modified, discarded, and improved on in the form of an action-research cycle. The author's collective wisdom—generated from a wealth of professional experience in teaching and coaching in a variety of contexts in Great Britain, the United States, and Australia; an expertise in pedagogy; and a deep understanding of the nature of games and game theory—has culminated in the creation of the theory, principles, and strategies of the Play-Practice approach. It is interesting to note that the prime motivation in the development of this approach has been essentially pragmatic in nature. The intent has been driven by a desire to discover better ways of joyfully engaging participants of all levels in quality sport experiences. Consequently, the theoretical underpinnings of Play Practice have followed, not preceded, the successful practical application of many of the ideas that the approach provided (Launder, 2001).

A review of the history and major influences that have contributed to the evolution of the Play-Practice approach reveals a rich and lengthy history of continual development. Launder (2001) identifies the seminal work on games teaching by Almond, Bunker, and Thorpe at Loughborough University in the early 1980s, particularly their contribution to the development of understanding in games and the use of modified game forms to emphasize the importance of tactics in skilled play.

A second influence was the popular, informal pick-up games that are linked to major sports, such as 3-vs-3 basketball. These games typically feature joyful engagement in activity and a freedom to play to learn in an environment where mistakes are legitimized as a part of the process. In addition, pick-up games demonstrate high levels of participation due to the small-sided playing numbers, minimal equipment, efficient use of limited space, and a playful, fun atmosphere.

The third significant influence was the ideas and methods emerging in English soccer coaching in the 1950s under the leadership of Wade. Key features included the value of small-sided games and the importance of using the principles of play to teach important game tactics. The final influence was the responses of physical education students with whom the author worked at the University of South Australia from 1973-1994. During that period, the teaching methods courses and the school practicum experiences served as key learning laboratories for the implementation and refinement of play-practice ideas. The subsequent responses from students served to initially confirm the value of play-practice strategies and then extend aspects of the approach (Launder, 2001).

Theoretical Underpinnings of Play Practice

In order to improve the quality of the learning experiences presented in sport and physical education settings, professional practice must conform to quality teaching and learning practice and be positioned within a relevant theoretical base (Kirk & MacPhail, 2002; Launder, 2001; Rink, French, & Graham, 1996; Rink, French, & Tjeerdsma, 1996). The theory and principles of Play Practice are aligned with a range of contemporary theories that are briefly outlined in the following paragraphs. This includes theories on intrinsic motivation, enjoyment, play, and need fulfillment that inform many of the play-practice strategies for engaging and promoting participation and learning theory drawn from constructivist, neuroscience, and dynamic systems perspectives that inform the strategies advocated for teaching and learning.

Intrinsic Motivation and Play

The Play-Practice approach focuses on bringing joy back into sport education. It does this by advocating a framework for developing a vast array of practice scenarios that harness the immense power of play to motivate and enthuse participants. Games that are structured to produce challenges by matching task and player ability are advocated to stimulate player interest and promote positive and purposeful involvement (Launder, 2001). By focusing on task mastery and the development of game competence, players are able to experience and embody feelings of enjoyment. Educators are able to promote awareness of this feeling and add to it through the development of a positive and success-oriented learning atmosphere. The significance of enhancing intrinsic motivation through strategies such as optimum challenge, achievement, game play, and competence is recognized as a positive basis for learning (Chandler, 1996; Glasser, 1998; Mitchell & Chandler, 1992; Stork, 2001).

Engaging Emotions—Enjoyment

The work completed by Csikszentmihalyi (1990) on enjoyment and flow experiences suggest that novel, playful environments—where challenge is aligned to the performers abilities—generate a state of enjoyment or flow that provides a powerful internal motivator for human behavior. Recent advances in neuroscience indicate the positive effects and benefits of promoting intrinsic motivation over external reward systems and highlight the value of engaging appropriate emotions in learning (Jensen, 1998). Game play, drama, and the use of strategies such as celebration, rituals, personal reflection, and performance are suggested as key learning experiences for promoting an emotional context (Fogarty, 1997; Hannaford, 1995). These elements feature within Play-Practice action fantasy games where novel, fantasy sporting scenarios are created for participants to play out the game in a national league or as a sporting hero (Launder, 2001).

Fulfilling Needs—Belonging, Power, Freedom, and Fun

The Play-Practice approach applies Glasser's choice theory through many of the suggested strategies for enhancing motivation. Choice theory is an internal control psychology that suggests motivation for human behavior is based on individual attempts to satisfy four genetically determined needs for love and belonging, power, freedom, and fun (Glasser, 1998). The games structure and the focus on individual choice and responsibility advocated in the Play-Practice approach enables participants to fulfill each of these needs. Peer support and team collaboration that nurtures a helping attitude allows individuals to fulfill needs for love and belonging. Opportunities for students to take on roles in coaching, managing, officiating, and to demonstrate personal competence, cater to the fulfillment of power needs. Choices in the organization of the learning environment, in personal challenges, and in team goal setting accommodate the need for freedom. The need for fun is fulfilled through engagement in enjoyable game settings that promote individual success and learning.

Constructivist Approaches to Teaching and Learning

The Play-Practice approach engenders a learner-centered perspective on instruction and it advocates an eclectic array of teaching methods ranging from directed task to indirect pedagogies including problem-based learning. Sport educators are encouraged to thoughtfully consider the learners' needs and context as a basis for establishing connections with previous experiences and for scaffolding learning. Participants are encouraged to construct meaning and reflect on their learning as they engage in finding solutions to the diverse array of problems that are presented in games. They play to learn and, in the process, learn to play by building personal competence and confidence and an array of other essential learning including thinking skills, interdependence, and personal responsibility. These principles are consistent with constructivist perspectives on learning, which view the learner as active in the process of taking in information and building knowledge and understanding (Perkins, 1999). The key learning principles of maximum individual participation, alignment, and transfer are defined as explicit prerequisites in the construction of any Play Practices. These principles ensure that participants have adequate opportunity to engage in the learning setting and that the practice is relevant and contextual. Learning is further enhanced by the provision of feedback from a variety of sources including self, peers, the instructor, the task, video, and through quality time for reflection.

Complexity of Teaching and Learning—Dynamical Systems Perspective

Three theoretical strands of knowledge are identified as key considerations that underpin the process of constructing play practices that enhance individual learning. The first strand includes a sensitive consideration of the nature of the learners and what they desire from a sport experience. Launder (2001) proposes a range of key precepts including the learner's preference for playing the game rather than practicing, a desire to be competent and not embarrassed whilst playing, a preference for participating with friends, an interest in participating in even, fair competition, and in receiving acknowledgement from significant others. The second strand relates to learning and particularly the conditions that promote learning. Launder (2001) suggests that learning is enhanced when learners really want to learn, have a clear model of the learning task, feel that the task is challenging but attainable, have many opportunities to practice in a positive environment, clearly understand the relationship between the practice and the real activity, receive feedback about the quality of their performance, are not threatened by immediate or continuing failure, are recognized by significant others for their efforts, improvement, successes, and are able to quickly apply what they have learned in what they see as real situations. The third strand is the nature of the activity and the competencies needed to participate effectively and enjoyably in the activity. Launder (2001) highlights the need for educators to have a thorough understanding of the nature of the activity and to recognize the social and cultural context of the sport. By identifying these three strands of knowledge, Launder (2001) recognizes the complexity of the teaching and learning process. This perspective is aligned with the dynamical systems theory of motor learning that views the process of motor learning as a part of a dynamic system where constraints imposed by the organism, the environment, and the task at hand serve to shape the learning in a dynamic interplay (Clark, 1995; Abernathy, 1986).

Innovative Features of Play Practice

In order to determine the competencies required to play a sport effectively and subsequently construct relevant learning experiences, sport educators must thoroughly understand the nature of the activity. It is within the realm of game theory and games teaching that Launder (2001) makes a significant contribution for sport educators. He does this by clarifying the characteristics of effective play; defining terms such as technique, game sense, skill; and then presenting a framework for designing relevant learning experiences. A reason why traditional approaches to games teaching have prevailed is because of the confusion in terminology associated with games and a lack of understanding of the complexity of effective sport performance. The term *technique* is used in place of the word skill to describe the actions that players use in games to control and redirect the object. This includes actions like kicking and trapping in soccer, the drop shot in badminton, or batting in softball as examples. The concept of *game sense* is introduced and defined as

> ...the ability to use an understanding of the rules; of strategy; of tactics and most importantly of oneself to solve the problems posed by the game or by one's opponents. Defined in this way, game sense bridges the gap between understanding and action and incorporates the process of decision making (Launder, 2001, p. 36).

By clarifying these key constructs, it is then possible to understand skillful play as the combination of games sense and technical ability. When viewed in this way, it is possible to acknowledge the contextual nature of skilled play and how the relative importance of technical ability and good decision-making, as displayed through game sense, can vary from one sport to another, from one player role in a game to another, and from one game moment to another. Sports educators can apply this understanding to analyze the development needs of their players. Their players may require a better understanding of the rules, of tactics, of individual or team strategy, or it may be some aspects of technique that needs attention. To further clarify the range of competencies required to be an effective player, Launder (2001) proposes a series of elements that can be applied to better understand the nature of games. Each component contributes to effective play in various ways. *Athleticism* is needed to get quickly into the right spaces in games; a *knowledge of rules* is required, as it determines what can be done in the game;

knowledge of *tactics* permits good positioning and intelligent movement into space; *communication* ensures teamwork; *fitness* enables players to continue to get into the right places and maintain good positioning throughout the game; *technique* allows the player to control and redirect the object effectively; *mental toughness* and *resilience* enable the player to keep on keeping on, particularly in the tough phases of play. Being able to *read the play* and anticipate enables the player to have more time to make good decisions and react in game play. This framework, when applied to various games, provides practitioners with a clearer and more detailed appreciation of the nature of the sport and identifies the array of competencies needed to be addressed in order to produce competent performers.

Games as Key Learning Experiences

Play Practice advocates the use of games as the key learning experience and sport educators are able to create a variety of games to improve different aspects of player or team performance. Modified, mini-games and *conditioned* games—created by the thoughtful manipulation of variables from the real game, such as playing numbers, space, equipment, rules, and scoring—are ideal for the development of game sense. For example, four-goal soccer is a conditioned game that is designed to teach the importance of switching play from heavily defended areas using cross-field passes. Four-goal soccer uses a large soccer goal in each corner of the field, which encourages the attackers to switch play across the field to create a more open shot on goal.

Cooperative *build-up games* and *target games* are recommended for use in situations that require repetitive technical practice. An example of a build-up game from table tennis is when two players working on a technique such as the backhand push, cooperate to try and build up as many consecutive shots as possible. When a mistake breaks the sequence, they go back to the beginning and start again. This practice assists players to stabilize their technique by encouraging control and consistency. Target games are particularly suited for use in racket sports such as table tennis, tennis, and badminton that require controlled practice to develop effective technique. In table tennis, a target such as a wooden block is placed on each side of the table. Points can only be achieved by hitting the target, they cannot be lost even if the ball is hit into the net or off the table. This game reduces perceptual and movement demands of the task, allowing players to concentrate on developing perfect technique whilst still trying to win the game.

Sector games promote the development of technical and tactical awareness in games such as cricket or softball. In these games, a section of the field is represented in a defined playing space and a game is constructed around play into that space. Constructing an array of novel game contexts and scenarios to capture participant interest and motivate purposeful practice creates *action fantasy games*. An example of this type of experience is the creation of a setting such as the Australian "down-under" tournament. Team names, uniforms, and songs are designed to represent the Australian culture. The tournament games begin midway through a game at a prescribed setting, presented on a special game card. Action fantasy games are a valuable tool for developing technique or game sense when thoughtfully combined with previously mentioned games (Launder, 2001).

Games as a Context for Learning

A guiding principle advocated in the Play-Practice approach is to begin the session by playing a relevant game (where possible), and to continue to do so as often as possible throughout the session and subsequent sessions. For some activities, it may be possible to begin with a game that is very similar to the real game. For example, a small-sided 5-vs-5 soccer game can be played immediately following the clarification of primary rules pertaining to handball and safety. For other activities, it may be necessary to modify the type of equipment, the rules, or the playing space in order to present a game that promotes positive participation as well as an aligned game context. Grip-ball lacrosse is an example of modifying equipment in which grip-ball pads and balls replace lacrosse sticks to enable play in a mini-game of endzone lacrosse that uses the primary rules and game context of noncontact lacrosse. Starting the learning session with a relevant game allows players to develop an understanding of all the elements that constitute effective play and to place their learning in context. The game provides them with a framework for personal and/or team performance analysis that provides a meaningful benchmark for measuring future improvement, and it provides a foundation upon which new learning is introduced and practiced in a meaningful way. Players are more motivated to learn if they are able to see the connections between what is being learned and the overall picture of effective performance in the sport. These principles reflect a constructivist tenant to teaching and learning that indicates the importance of building on learners' prior knowledge and experience and engaging them in purposeful, contextual, and inherently interesting learning activities (Perkins, 1999).

The Processes of Play Practice

The Play-Practice approach provides a framework for the development of enjoyable, challenging practices that can be constructed to meet the needs of a diverse range of learners. Once the entry level of participants has been determined, the processes of *shaping play, focusing play,* and *enhancing play* are applied to create a vast range of realistic practice scenarios or play practices.

Shaping Play

The process of shaping play is about teaching *through* the game; it involves manipulating one or more of the variables that form the game, in order to create a variety of learning situations that emphasize particular aspects of effective play. Isolated technical practices can be converted into challenging and enjoyable play practices by designing sector or target games that promote the development of technique in relevant contexts. In the same manner, repetitious and isolated drills can be replaced by mini- and conditioned games to improve tactical awareness, reading the play, or applying game sense.

Shaping game rules. The game rules are a key variable that can be adjusted when shaping the play to emphasize specific aspects of skilled play. For example, if maintaining possession has been a focus for game play in soccer, then a condition such as five possessions before attempting to score can be included to promote this aspect of play. Another example of rule adjustment is to implement a rule that limits the attackers to two touches when controlling the ball in a mini-game of soccer, in order to develop passing and support-positioning skills. Other conditions—such as pass to every player before scoring, a scoring restriction, or a maximum time limit on possession of the ball in team games—can be instigated to ensure more equitable and inclusive play. Differentiated scoring is another form of rule adjustment that can be applied in many games to encourage players to include specific aspects in game play. Five points for a goal scored off a pass delivered from behind the goal in lacrosse is an example of how differentiated scoring can be used to promote the use of this space in attack.

Shaping player numbers. The number of players can be adjusted to increase player participation and to promote specific learning outcomes. Small-sided games such as 3-vs-3 basketball or 5-vs-5 soccer are ideal for increasing the opportunity to learn techniques and acquire game sense in a microcosm of the full game. Player numbers can be manipulated to create imbalances between the number of offensive and defensive players to simulate certain game situations or to provide progression in learning of tactics and game sense. For example, a 4-vs-1, to a 3-vs-1, and then a 5-vs-2 progression of play practices in games such as lacrosse, soccer, or hockey provides a numerical advantage to the attack that promotes learning to pass and to maintain possession of the ball. Defense numbers can be weighted (5 defenders vs 4 attackers) to place additional pressure on attack as they attempt to maintain possession of the ball for a prescribed number of passes or time. The size of the playing area, the scoring, and goal dimensions can be manipulated to create specific learning conditions.

Shaping playing space. Playing space is a significant variable to manipulate when constructing play practices because of its influence on the time available for players to demonstrate their skills. The available space impacts on the time that players have to make good decisions and to demonstrate good techniques. Playing space is also important in some games, as it influences the potential balance of the contest. For example, softball mini-games can be played successfully with 5 per side, by reducing the width of the diamond, including a back-fielding boundary, and a short area to delineate fair territory. These modifications ensure that the fielding team can cover the playing space fairly with reduced playing numbers.

Shaping the equipment. The equipment can be modified or adapted to enable players to enjoy the game experience and gain a real sense of playing the game. There are many examples of modified and user-friendly equipment, such as shortened rackets in badminton and tennis, slow-bounce tennis balls, and soft-skinned balls that create an easier entrance for novices into game play.

Focusing Play

The process of focusing play is about teaching *in* the game. Sport educators focus the play by emphasizing the important concepts or cues that assist with the development of specific learning outcomes in the play practice. They can do this by communicating direct information, such as "racket back early," to assist novice tennis players to prepare early for a groundstroke, or "brushing the ear," to assist cricket players to acquire a sound technique for bowling. Alternatively, they can focus the play using indirect methods by posing appropriate questions at various times during the play practice. The freeze replay is an important tool for focusing the play and increasing player understanding and learning. An example of this concept can be illustrated in a 3-vs-1 go-for-goal play practice that focuses on developing tactical awareness in basketball. Play continues until the coach observes a particular aspect of game play, such as support positioning in attack. Play is then stopped, using a predetermined signal, and the coach then questions the players about their positioning in relation to the ball carrier. This technique engages the players in solving the game problem, builds in time for reflection, and promotes learning during game play.

Enhancing Play

The process of enhancing the play is associated with player motivation and commitment to purposeful play. Enhancing play involves creating a range of novel ideas that serve to stimulate player interest and promote persistent practice. Action fantasy games are an innovative strategy for enhancing play, based on the creation of a range of game scenarios and cameo roles for players to participate in (Launder, 2001). The following scenario demonstrates this concept applied in tennis. It is the Australian Open and it is two sets-all in the final round. Hewitt, down 3 games to 4 against Aggasi in the final set, is serving at 15-30. Players choose who they wish to be and then play the match out. A series of action fantasy games can be created and compiled on separate cards for use with a class. Game cards can be selected from a box at the beginning of a session to quickly engage participants in purposeful activity. The scenarios can be developed further to include practice guidelines to be undertaken prior to playing out the game. The concept of action fantasy games can be combined with other strategies to enhance play, including restricting the playing time to short bursts to capture the exciting final moments of game play, applying certain conditions to maintain close and uncertain game results, and celebrating achievements.

Conclusion

The Play-Practice approach to teaching and coaching sport provides a comprehensive and coherent framework that can be applied to improve professional practice in sport education. Of particular significance is the contribution that this model makes to game theory through the clarification of terms and the deeper analysis of the competencies of effective sport performance. The approach provides new insights into the process of teaching and learning and a clear direction of how to begin to shape more playful learning environments for all participants. It challenges sport educators to think critically about their current professional practice and encourages them to make their own contribution to this innovation.

References

Abernathy, B. (1986). Basic concepts of motor control: Psychological perspectives. In B. Abernathy, V. Kippers, L. Mackinnon, R. Neal, & S. Hanrahan (Eds.) *Biophysical Foundations of Human Movement* (pp. 295 -311), Melbourne: Macmillan.

Allison, S. & Thorpe, R. (1997). A comparison of the effectiveness of two approaches to teaching games within physical education. A skills approach versus a games for understanding approach. *British Journal of Physical Education*, 28(3), 9-13.

Bunker, D. & Thorpe, R. (1982). A model for the teaching of games in secondary schools. *Bulletin of Physical Education, 18*(1), 1-4.

Chandler, T. (1996). Teaching games for understanding: Reflections and further questions. *Journal of Physical Education, Recreation, and Dance, 67*(4), 49-51.

Charlesworth, R. (1994). Designer games. *Sports Coach, Oct-Dec*, 30.

Clarke, J. (1995). On becoming skillful: Patterns and constraints. *Research Quarterly for Exercise and Sport, 66*(3), 173-183.

Csikszentmihalyi, M. (1990). *Flow: The psychology of optimal experience.* New York: Harper & Row.

Fogarty, R.(1997). *Brain compatible classrooms.* Australia, Hawker Brownlow Education.

Glasser, W. (1998). *Choice theory. A new psychology of personal freedom.* New York: HarperCollins.

Griffin, L., Mitchell, S., & Oslin, J. (1997). *Teaching Sports Concepts and Skills: A tactical games approach*, Champaign, IL: Human Kinetics.

Hannaford, C. (1995). *Smart moves why learning is not all in your head.* Arlington, Virginia: Great Ocean Publishers.

Jensen, E. (1998). *Teaching with the brain in mind, Alexandria, VA*: Association for Supervision and Curriculum Development.

Kirk, D. & MacPhail, A. (1999). The Games Sense Approach: Rationale, description and brief overview of research. Loughborough: IYS/ Human Kinetics.

Kirk, D. & MacPhail, A. (2002). Teaching games for understanding and situated learning: Rethinking the Bunker-Thorpe model. *Journal of Teaching in Physical Education, 21*(2), 177-192.

Launder, A. G. (2001). *Play practice. The games approach to teaching and coaching sports.* Champaign, IL: Human Kinetics.

Mitchell, S. & Chandler, T. (1992). Motivating students for learning in the gymnasium: The role of perception and meaning. *The Physical Educator, 50*(3), 120-125.

Mitchell, S., Oslin, J., & Griffin, L. (1995). The effects of two instructional approaches on game performance. *Pedagogy in Practice: Teaching and Coaching in Physical Education and Sports, 1*(1), 36-48.

Perkins, D. (1999). The many faces of constructivism. *Educational Leadership, 57*(3), 6-11.

Read, B. (1989). Artisans, players and gods: a reflection on the teaching of games. *Physical Education Review, 12*(2), 134-137.

Rink, J. (1996). Tactical and skill approaches to teaching sport & games: Introduction *Journal of Teaching in Physical Education, 15*, 397-398.

Rink, J., French, K., & Graham, K. (1996). Implications for practice and research. *Journal of Teaching in Physical Education, 15*, 490-502.

Rink, J., French, K., & Tjeerdsma, B. (1996). Foundations for the learning and instruction of sports and games. *Journal of Teaching in Physical Education, 15*, 397-398.

Siedentop, D. (1994). *Sport Education: Quality PE through positive sport experiences.* Champaign, IL: Human Kinetics.

Stork, S. (2001). When playing is learning. *Teaching Elementary Physical Education, Jan*, 30-31.

Turner, A. & Martinek, T. (1992). A comparative analysis of two models for teaching games: (Technique approach and game centred (tactic focus) approach). *International journal of physical education 29*(4), 4th Quarter 1992, 15-31

Werner, P., Thorpe, R., & Bunker, D. (1996). Teaching games for understanding: Evolution of a model. *Journal of Physical Education, Recreation, and Dance, 67*(1), 28-33.

Teaching Team Sports and Games: Extending the Debate to the Youth Sport Domain

Chapter 17

Enrique García Bengoechea, University of Alberta, Canada

William B. Strean, University of Alberta, Canada

Introduction

The introduction of the Teaching Games for Understanding (TGfU) framework (Bunker & Thorpe, 1982) has been considered as the catalyst for the emergence of a debate on theoretical and practical aspects of games teaching (e.g., Gréhaigne, Godbout, & Bouthier, 1999; Holt, Strean, & García Bengoechea, 2002). According to Gréhaigne et al. (1999), the most prominent facet of the debate has to do with the respective contributions of technical and tactical approaches to teaching games. Other aspects of the debate identified by these authors include the use of direct or indirect teaching strategies, the transformation of the subject matter into pedagogical content knowledge, and conceptual issues regarding the notions of tactics and strategy. An interesting development of the pedagogical debate in physical education is that some sport governing bodies are turning toward more games-based models of instruction. For example, the Alberta Soccer Association has designed a new coaching format (see Walker, 2002) based on teaching in and through the game, encouraging novice coaches to follow the maxim: "let the game be the teacher." Youth sport coaches' deeply held beliefs and conceptions about teaching games, however, may represent difficult obstacles for sport governing bodies and coach educators alike to experience success in their attempts to implement change (Ennis, 1994). The present study attempts to gain a better understanding of youth sport coaches' beliefs and conceptions about teaching games in light of the four facets of the current debate on teaching games outlined by Gréhaigne et al. Results are discussed in terms of the potential of such beliefs and conceptions to become barriers for change in the way games are traditionally taught in the youth sport domain.

Method

In light of the purposes of this study, a qualitative approach that provided enough depth and flexibility of analysis was adopted. This approach is explained in more detail in this section.

Participants

The participants were 14 coaches (4 female, 10 male) and were all currently involved with or had recent coaching/teaching experience in a youth sport program. Following standard ethical procedures, participants provided informed consent for participation in this study. On average, participants were in their late 20s (M = 28, R = 24-40). Their average coaching experience was 7 years (R = 4-12). Participants represented a variety of sports and games (e.g., tennis, badminton, golf, volleyball, soccer, basketball, water polo, rugby, ice hockey). Their level of involvement ranged from noncompetitive programs for beginner children to highly competitive programs for adolescent athletes (ages 9-17). Three coaches had completed Level I, five coaches Level II, and three coaches Level III, of the National Coaching Certification Program (NCCP). The NCCP is Canada's five-level coach education program designed to train coaches in over 60 sports (Gowan, 1992). Three coaches did not have formal coaching qualifications, but two of them had obtained a university master's degree in sport science and the remaining one a bachelor's degree in physical education. Overall, the participants represented a fairly experienced and educated coaching sample.

Data Collection and Analysis

Semi-structured interviewing (Seidman, 1998; Smith, 1995) was used as the data collection technique in this study. Smith (1995) noted that semi-structured interviews are particularly useful to gain a detailed picture of a participant's beliefs about, or perceptions or accounts of, a particular topic. The advantages of the semi-structured interview are that it (a) facilitates rapport and empathy, (b) allows a greater flexibility of coverage, (c) enables the interview to enter novel areas, and (d) tends to produce richer data (Smith, 1995).

Participants in this study took part in one semi-structured interview in which several aspects of their teaching and coaching approaches were addressed. All interviews were conducted by the first author and lasted one hour on average. The first part of the interview focused specifically on the participants' instructional approach to teaching team sports and games. As the interview progressed, the link between the participants' instructional approach and their conceptions of fun in youth sport was also explored. Rather than stemming from a rigid interview guide, follow-up questions were asked as needed, based on the responses of the participant. The purpose of these follow-up questions was to ask for clarification, seek concrete details, and request more information related to what the participant stated (Seidman, 1998).

The interviews were audio recorded, transcribed, and analyzed using an inductive-deductive procedure (Patton, 1990). An attempt was made initially to capture the richness of the themes emerging from the participants' responses. As a first step in analyzing the data, comprehensive profiles (Seidman, 1998) were developed that contained the most relevant topics and ideas discussed in each interview. This follows an idiographic approach to analysis, beginning with particulars and only slowly moving up to generalizations (Smith, 1995). Once the profiles were completed, participants were invited to comment on the appropriateness of the researchers' interpretations about what was most important and interesting in each interview. Coaches' profiles made it easier for the investigators to retrieve and compare meaningful data from different participants at different stages of the analysis. In this way, the profiles became a basis for reflection and discussion between the two investigators in their collaborative effort. This collaborative effort further contributed to enhance the credibility of our interpretations. Once the thematic analysis had been completed through the use of inductive techniques, a deductive procedure was applied. The goal of such procedure was to see how the themes fit into a preconceived framework, that is, the framework of Gréhaigne et al. (1999) for research and discussion on the analysis and teaching of team sports and games.

Results

In this section, results are presented in light of the four facets of the debate concerning the teaching of team sports and games proposed by Gréhaigne et al. (1999). These are (a) technical versus tactical focus, (b) the use of direct or indirect teaching strategies, (c) the transformation of the content knowledge, and (d) conceptual issues regarding the notions of tactics and strategy. Additional issues identified in the coaches' accounts that may be relevant to the debate are also outlined.

Technical-Versus-Tactical Focus

Gréhaigne and colleagues (1999) suggested that the most prominent facet of the debate regarding the teaching of team sports and games concerns the respective contribution of the tactical and technical approaches to teaching games and sports. As these authors indicated, a traditional view of teaching games and sports has been to promote, first, in drill situations, a mastery of techniques considered as fundamental for the practice of the activity, and second, a progressive introduction of tactical elements in game contexts. On the other hand, the tactical approach puts the priority on understanding and learning tactical concepts related to a game or sport, and proposes that techniques should be introduced when the need is perceived by the learners (Gréhaigne et al., 1999; Griffin, Mitchell, & Oslin, 1997).

The majority of coaches in the present study endorsed primarily a technical approach in which technical skills were viewed as *requisites* to play the game and as a *necessary base* from which "more advanced aspects" (i.e., tactics, strategy) build. The following quotations, from Rachel[1], a badminton coach, and Tom, a soccer coach, are illustrative of an emphasis on the technical aspects of the game:

> *The major focus is on learning basic skills that best prepare them for game situations, and even though they may not do well in [badminton] games, it's possible to do well at the skills, so they may have a correct stroke which has not enough power. So from the little kids down to the university the main focus is on learning the skills and learning the techniques (Rachel).*

> *Most of the stuff that I do revolves around fundamental skills...What I do is if I first take over a [soccer] team, for example, we spend quite a bit of work on fundamental skills. Things like passing and ball control are usually the first two that we go through because if you can't pass and control the ball any sort of practical training or counter training for other team tactics is really monotonous and useless... The other skills tend to build upon that...(Tom)*

[1] All coaches' names are pseudonyms

Two coaches in this study, however, endorsed views about teaching team sports that were more consistent with a tactical approach. Of most interest, were the challenges and obstacles that the two of them faced when trying to implement a primarily tactical approach. As Harold, a soccer coach, recalled:

> I can think of my experience when I coached an under-15 team here in [name of city], an indoor team, using tactical approaches, and I was working with another coach, and the coach had no idea what the type of approach was...So over time that barrier was difficult and overcoming the barrier of the athletes who had been used to a skill-drill approach was also very, very tough, very difficult.

The Use of Direct or Indirect Teaching Strategies

According to Gréhaigne and associates (1999), the second facet of the debate regarding the teaching of team sports and games concerns the use of indirect or direct teaching strategies. As these authors explained, coaches can choose to propose to learners the reproduction of ready-made solutions. Such an option, referred to as *direct teaching* (Gréhaigne et al., 1999), would be typical of a subject matter-centered approach. Likewise coaches can choose to propose to learners the discovery and even construction of suitable responses. Such an option would correspond to an *indirect teaching* (Gréhaigne et al., 1999) approach, combining in varying degrees both a subject matter-centered and a learner-centered approach.

Most coaches in this study reported the use of a combination of direct and indirect teaching strategies. On the basis of their responses, however, these coaches could be broadly ranged on a continuum from those who emphasized the use of direct teaching strategies to those who emphasized the use of indirect teaching strategies. Coaches emphasizing direct teaching strategies adopted primarily a subject matter-centered approach. Typically, the teaching style of these coaches was characterized by the frequent use of explanations, demonstrations, and corrective feedback as needed by players in order to assimilate the targeted skills and concepts. For example, Andreas, another soccer coach, stated,

> Demonstration is the key and that is how they learn the best and there is no other way to be able to show them. The ability for them to learn depends a lot on how I show it and if I show it properly and what techniques I use in order to get the information across.

On the other end, coaches who put the emphasis on indirect teaching strategies leaned towards a learner-centered approach in which they tended to encourage players to discover and even develop their own responses and solutions to problems arising in the game. On the basis of their accounts, the style of these coaches was characterized by a more frequent use of discussions and feedback in the form of questions in order to elicit players' reflection. Although this was particularly true as it refers to the tactical and strategic aspects of the game, the use of indirect approaches was also mentioned by coaches when referring to the teaching of technical skills. Josh, a golf coach, stated,

*I would stand in front of the players and ask them to go through their
swing very slowly, show me their swing. I can pick out what they
are doing wrong. I know it myself. I always ask it in the form of a
question. I want to see if they know what they are doing wrong.*

Interestingly, some coaches reported using a primarily direct style when teaching
the fundamental technical skills but left the door open for a more indirect style
when working on tactical aspects of the game. The following excerpt, from Ruth,
a basketball coach, illustrates this circumstance,

*When I teach them the fundamentals, like this is how you do it, you
know what I mean? This is how you shoot the ball. This is the proper
way to shoot the ball. This is the proper way to play defense, this is
the proper way to dribble the ball. That kind of stuff. Like that set.
The other stuff [tactics/strategy] is a little more open ended and the
kids have more opportunity to contribute their ideas. Whereas with
the fundamentals it is pretty much, those are the fundamentals.*

Overall, the results in this section suggest that the coaches in this study could be
broadly placed on a continuum from those who emphasized the use of direct teaching
strategies to those who emphasized the use of indirect teaching approaches.
Likewise, these results indicate that the use of indirect teaching strategies was
more common in order to teach the tactical components of the game.

The Transformation of the Content Knowledge

From a teaching-learning perspective, content knowledge relative to any particular
sport must be transformed into teachable knowledge (i.e., "pedagogical content
knowledge," Shulman, 1987). In other words, what coaches know about the
techniques, tactics, and strategies of a given sport must be translated into actual
learning situations. Furthermore, as Gréhaigne and colleagues (1999) suggested,
the content and evolution of learning situations is, more often than not, the result
of a careful planning process by coaches. Most coaches in the present study typically
reported the adoption of a teaching progression in which a focus on technical skills
in drill situations preceded work on tactics and strategies in game or game-like
contexts. This was true both for the structure of a typical practice and for the
evolution of learning situations across practices. Tom, for example, described the
sequence of a typical practice for his advanced soccer players (15-17 years) as follows:

*My practices were typically structured around something along the
lines of the following: there was usually a technical component at
the start that we collectively as a group were particularly weak on...
From there we would move to a tactical type of session...usually
trying to incorporate the technical part as well but moving on to a
tactical area that we needed to work on for an upcoming game. And
then, at the very end, I would try to incorporate both the technical
and tactical components into some type of game.*

Robert, an ice hockey coach, synthesized his approach to teaching basic skills as follows:

> *You explain to them once and show them. Then have them do it*
> *once and progressively they do it slowly, then faster. And then you*
> *add a puck and a goalie; you put it in a game situation so they know*
> *that they're not just doing this to skate better, but to become a*
> *better hockey player.*

Furthermore, as suggested in the previous excerpt, the teaching progression of most coaches was, in general, characterized by a principle of progressive complexity. That is, both when working on tactical/strategic situations and, especially, on technical skills coaches tended to break down the content to its most simple elements and to add progressively new "pieces" until the desired form or situation was attained. The following quotations, from Donna, a volleyball coach, and Edward, a basketball coach, are representative of the use of this principle for the teaching of both technical and tactical/strategic skills.

> *I like to do a visual demonstration so they can see how the skill is*
> *executed and I break it down into parts so I say: "Okay, what are the*
> *legs doing? What is the torso doing? What are the arms doing?" And*
> *then I let them practice like really simplistic movements so that they*
> *learn how to develop the skill (Donna).*

> *It is sort of a slow process of breaking things down and giving*
> *structure and trying not to let them play too free-flowing at first...*
> *Then, try to break the skills or the complexity of the game down into*
> *smaller skills easy for players to focus on instead of focusing on the*
> *whole big picture...(Edward)*

Of most interest were the reasons that some of these coaches gave to justify the teaching progression they adopted. For example, Andreas explained that working in game situations after working on technically oriented drills helped his soccer players to understand how technical skills relate to the game. This same coach also emphasized the importance of adopting a progression from techniques to tactics/strategies in order to provide the necessary practice structure so that players have a clear idea of what they are doing and where they are going. In the context of golf, Josh explained that playing games after practicing technical skills motivates players to try the skills. Along the same lines, David, a tennis coach pointed to the advantages of mastering technical skills first, both in terms of learning and fun:

> *If someone's techniques are off, it can hold them back from getting*
> *as far as they want and also having fun on the court. It is not fun to*
> *play tennis when every time you hit and miss, so if you can foster*
> *a technique it will stop the mistakes and hopefully have fun playing*
> *the game.*

Nevertheless, a few coaches also acknowledged that the teaching progression they endorsed created some learning problems. Specifically, Ruth, who coached basketball, talked about how her tendency to break down techniques to their most simple components sometimes made it difficult for her players to understand the skills being developed. Jeremy, another basketball coach, referred to the transfer problems that many of his players experienced because of an emphasis on working in drill situations first. As he put it:

> Lots of kids can't make the transition from the drill. They can do all the drills, but when they get in the game, they don't understand, you know, what exactly what it is the drill, how the stuff applies. So a lot of times, once we get through a lot of the drills, then we move to sort of a next station in practice or in development, where we get them to just basically break down the scenario as it happens in games...

In sum, the results in this section suggest that a majority of coaches in this study used a teaching progression or a sequence in the introduction of skills that is consistent with a traditional technical or skill-drill approach.

Conceptual Issues Regarding the Notions of Tactics and Strategy

According to Gréhaigne et al. (1999), the quality of the treatment of a subject matter in sport may be significantly affected by the development and precision of concepts relative to the subject matter itself. Despite the centrality of the terms *tactics* and *strategy* with respect to the nature and the teaching of games and sports, a review of literature (Gréhaigne et al., 1999) indicated that, in many cases, both terms appear to be appear to be used interchangeably without prior definition. Drawing on the tradition of the European school of team sports, Gréhaigne and Godbout (1995) introduced a distinction between the notions of tactics and strategy. Strategy refers to these elements discussed in advance in order for the team to organize itself. Thus, strategic decisions are made without significant time constraints. Tactics, for their part, are a timely adaptation to new configurations of play and to the circulation of the ball; they are therefore an adaptation to an opposition that operates under strong time constraints.

In the present study, coaches often talked about decisions made without significant time constraints (e.g., implementing a game plan, maintaining assigned field/court positions, running set plays) and decisions made under strong time constraints (e.g., efficient adaptations to and/or anticipations within the flow of the game). As an example of the former, Ruth, a basketball coach, said:

> I like to start off with basics. But of course, you always have to go through tactical stuff as far as when it comes to playing the games. I like to spend time with certain formations and certain plays that I would teach them so that they can use those in a game situation. Because I find without that kind of organization out on the court, it would be chaos.

As an example of the latter, Tom, who coached soccer, stated:

> If one of our players is making progress down the right flank and is getting ready to cross the ball in towards the goal area and you are in the middle of the field heading towards the goal area you've got some decisions to make...

Many of the coaches, however, did not articulate a clear distinction between the notions of strategy and tactics. That is, when referring to both types of decisions, some coaches used primarily the term "strategy," while others gave preference to the term "tactics," and others, finally, used both terms in a relatively undifferentiated way. The following quotations from Donna, a volleyball coach, and Edward, a basketball coach, illustrate the undifferentiated use of the terms tactics and strategy and even the relative confusion surrounding the use of both terms:

> Like tactics, I guess, are more like maybe like little specific details whereas strategies is more like an actual plan you can give your athletes. Like this is like your game plan that we are going to run, where tactics could be just like little points. I guess that is the only difference. I think they are pretty synonymous. [Donna]

> Yes, [tactics and strategy] I would say [are] probably basically the same...I think the strategies of our team were set out at the beginning of the year based on the players that we had and if we had a team that was really big. Then, you know, our sort of ideas, strategies, tactics would be to, you know, to work the ball to our big players and try to use them a lot. Now if we had a small team, fast team, we would try to run...[Edward]

In conclusion, results in this section highlight that coaches in this study were not always able to articulate a clear distinction between the concepts of tactics and strategy.

Adding Elements to the Debate

In addition to discussing topics that fall within the four facets of the debate proposed by Gréhaigne et al. (1999), coaches in this study also raised issues that may eventually contribute to enrich the debate concerning the teaching of team sports and games in the youth sport domain. These issues included (a) the sequence of skill introduction, (b) the degree of individual variation allowed in skill execution, (c) the relative importance of form versus outcome of technical-skill execution, and (d) different ways of structuring the practice in order to maximize performance. The first issue concerned the sequence of skill introduction, which deals with the order skills should be practiced over time so as to ensure an efficient learning progression. For example, Robert, who coached ice hockey, insisted on the importance of developing sound skating skills first, instead of giving priority from the beginning to puck skills, as other coaches do. The second issue concerned the degree of individual variation in technical skill execution that they should allow. For Jack, a volleyball coach, making such a decision became one of his biggest concerns when coaching his sport. He stated,

> That's probably the biggest decision you have to make: is this kid... does he have a bad habit or it's just because it is a little bit different but it's still getting the job done? That's sometimes I find the toughest thing. I don't want to have every kid be a robot, has to be exactly like this, but if it kind of strays too far away from that, and that's not a good thing either.

The third issue involved the relative importance that should be placed on the form versus the outcome of technical-skill execution. Thus, Josh explained that the "*outcome of the shot*," regardless of technical considerations, is the basic criteria he uses to determine whether a golf player is going to move on to the next level or not. On the other hand, David talked about the importance of "*not even worrying about where the ball is going*," but rather about always doing the "*right thing*" from a technical standpoint in order to ensure the progress of his tennis players.

Finally, the fourth issue concerned different ways of structuring practices in a way that maximizes both the players' and the team's performance. In this regard, Jack suggested that game-like situations in volleyball should always be introduced in the second half of the practice in order to ensure that players are tired enough and therefore will scrimmage/play in more realistic conditions. Vincent, a water polo coach, considered that practicing skills while being fatigued (e.g., after a hard swim set) leads to "*learning how to do things improperly*." Furthermore, this coach emphasized the importance of not always planning the same practice sequence/routine in order to foster players' capacity to learn and adapt to ever-changing competitive conditions.

The topics outlined in this section add to our knowledge of the specific teaching issues that youth sport coaches may face when designing practices in order to foster players' learning and improve the team's performance.

Discussion

The present study attempts to gain a better understanding of youth sport coaches' beliefs and conceptions about teaching games in order to determine potential barriers for change in the way games are traditionally taught in the youth sport domain. The four facets of the current debate on teaching games outlined by Gréhaigne et al. (1999) were used as an organizing framework to examine coaches' perceptions. Overall, each of the four facets of the debate proposed by Gréhaigne et al. (1999) was found meaningful in analyzing the coaches' responses and, therefore, relevant to the youth sport domain. In addition, several issues were identified that may potentially contribute to enrich the debate on teaching team sport and games. These issues, however, were mainly related to the teaching of the technical components of the game and to the concern with maximizing performance. This seems logical if we take into account that most coaches in the present study endorsed a primarily technical approach to teaching sports and games and that they worked in moderately to highly competitive youth sport contexts.

Specifically, the majority of coaches in the present study endorsed primarily a technical approach in which techniques were viewed as *requisites* to play the game and as "building blocks" for tactics and strategies. Such a view may be reflective of what Kirk and MacPhail (2002) referred to as the "traditional dualistic divide between cognition and physical performance" (p. 181). As these authors argued, this way of thinking appears to remain pervasive in physical education and sport in spite of growing evidence pointing to the fundamental interconnections between motor and cognitive aspects of the performance of sport skills (e.g., Abernethy, 1996; Thomas & Thomas, 1994).

Results from this study also revealed that youth sport coaches may face resistances from players and other coaches when attempting to move beyond traditional technical or skill-drill approach in order to adopt ways of teaching more consistent with the premises of a tactical approach. Typical youth sport practices do not take place in a social vacuum. Rather, they are embedded within "communities of practice" that generate and sustain knowledge (Kirk & MacPhail, 2002). In so doing, they shape young people—and coaches'—expectations of what it is to participate in youth sports and, specifically, of how sports are typically, and should be, taught in youth sport settings (Rovegno, 1999, cited in Kirk & MacPhail, 2002). As the stories of two coaches in this study illustrated, attempting to move beyond what is considered "normal" in a given community of practice, may be a source of problems and even conflicts for youth sport coaches. Faced with a way of teaching/learning a particular sport that challenges and, in some cases, threatens, fundamental beliefs and expectations developed over years, fellow coaches and players may react by being overly resistant to the proposed changes.

As many organized youth sport programs seem to follow a trend towards what has been called the "performance ethic" (Coakley, 2001, p. 114), the question remains of whether tactical approaches to teaching games can find their place within a structure that emphasizes short-term results (i.e., winning) over development and fun. At this juncture, it is important to remember that the TGfU model originated in England within a school physical education context in response to concerns including that children were leaving school with little success due to the emphasis on performance (Bunker & Thorpe, 1982). Nevertheless, proponents of the TGfU approach have also emphasized the importance of improving learners' performance along with their enjoyment as primary purposes of teaching games (Werner, Bunker, & Thorpe, 1996). Likewise, Griffin et al. stated that "the aim of a tactical approach is to improve students' game performance, which involves combining tactical awareness and skill execution" (1997, p. 8). It would seem, therefore, that tactical approaches—or at least some of their constituent elements—could be profitably put into use in the youth sport context as well, in order to promote both individual skill development and team performance, along with fun and enjoyment.

Of significance in the context of the current debate on teaching games was also the finding that many coaches did not articulate a clear distinction between the concepts of strategy and tactics while elaborating on their teaching approach. Further, although some of these coaches elaborated on tactical decisions and tactical knowledge underlying those decisions, other coaches did not seem to have developed a language to talk about tactical decisions and solutions to the same extent as to talk about techniques or strategies to be implemented. We believe, in line with Gréhaigne et al. (1999), that to the extent that coaches have not developed a language to talk about tactical decisions and underlying tactical knowledge to the same extent as to talk about techniques or strategies to be implemented, their use of tactical approaches may be compromised.

Bringing about change in the way games are traditionally taught in the youth sport domain may well require a paradigm shift in current conceptions of thinking about games teaching/coaching in sport. Such a shift is not likely to happen from one day to another. It may necessitate a concerted and sustained effort from all the agents involved in the transformation process (e.g., sport governing bodies, coach educators, program administrators). Failing to acknowledge that learning is socially organized within communities that tend to perpetuate existing conceptions and practices (Kirk & MacPhail, 2002) may compromise the success of any isolated attempts to implement change in the youth sport domain. Likewise, failing to acknowledge and accept the validity of coaches and players' negative emotional reactions to any changes that threaten their fundamental beliefs and to provide a sound rationale for the proposed changes may be as well a source of frustration and conflict. This can only slow down the change process.

References

Abernethy, B. (1996). Basic concepts of motor control: Psychological perspectives. In B. Abernethy, V. Kippers, L. T. Mackinnon, R. J. Neal, & S. Hanrahan (Eds.), *Biophysical foundations of human movement* (pp. 295-311). Melbourne: Macmillan.

Bunker, D. J. & Thorpe, R. D. (1982). A model for the teaching of games in secondary schools. *Bulletin of Physical Education, 18*(1), 5-8.

Coakley, J. (2001). *Sport in society: Issues and controversies* (7th ed.). Boston: McGraw-Hill.

Ennis, C. D. (1994). Knowledge and beliefs underlying curricular expertise. *Quest, 46*, 164-175.

Gowan, G. R. (1992). Canada's National Coaching Certification Program (NCCP): Past, present, & future. *Journal of Physical Education, Recreation, and Dance 63*(7), 50-54.

Gréhaigne, J. F. & Godbout, P. (1995). Tactical knowledge in team sports from a constructivist and cognitivist perspective. *Quest, 47*, 490-505.

Gréhaigne, J. F., Godbout, P., & Bouthier, D. (1999). The foundations of tactics and strategy in team sports. *Journal of Teaching in Physical Education, 18*, 159-174.

Griffin, L., Mitchell, S. A., & Oslin, J. L. (1997). *Teaching sports concepts and skills: A tactical games approach.* Champaign, IL: Human Kinetics.

Holt, N. L., Strean, W. B., & García Bengoechea, E. (2002). Expanding the teaching games for understanding model: New Avenues for future research and practice. *Journal of Teaching in Physical Education, 21*, 162-176.

Kirk, D. & MacPhail, A. (2002). Teaching games for understanding and situated learning: Rethinking the Bunker-Thorpe model. *Journal of Teaching in Physical Education, 21*, 177-192.

Patton, M. Q. (1990). *Qualitative evaluation and research methods* (2nd ed.). Newbury Park, CA: Sage.

Rovegno, I. (1999, April). *What is taught and learned in physical activity programs: The role of content.* Keynote presentation at the AIESEP Conference, Besancon, France.

Seidman, I.E., (1998). *Interviewing as qualitative research: A guide for researchers in education and the social sciences* (2nd ed.). New York: Teachers College Press.

Shulman. L. S. (1987). Knowledge and teaching: Foundations of the new reform. *Harvard Educational Review, 57*, 1-22.

Smith, J. A. (1995). Semi-structured interviewing and qualitative analysis. In J. A. Smith, R. Harré, & L. Van Langenhove (Eds.), *Rethinking methods in psychology* (pp. 9-26). London: Sage.

Thomas, K. T. & Thomas, R. R. (1994). Developing expertise in sport: The relation of knowledge and performance. *International Journal of Sport Psychology, 25*, 295-312.

Walker, J. (2002). *Small-sided developmental games for children under twelve.* Edmonton: Alberta Soccer Association.

Werner, P., Bunker, D., & Thorpe, R. (1996). Teaching games for understanding: Evolution of a model. *Journal of Physical Education, Recreation, and Dance, 67*(1), 28-33.

Acknowledgement

The preparation of this manuscript was supported by SSHRC grant #410-99-0351.

Reflections and Projections

Chapter 18

Joy Butler, Plymouth State College, United State

Linda Griffin, University of Massachusetts, United States

Ben Lombardo, Rhode Island College, United States

Richard Nastasi, Endicott College, United States

Claire Robson, Plymouth State College, United States

Reflections and Projections

The first chapter of this book traces the progress of TGfU from its conception at Loughborough University and on through its birth, growth, and adolescent struggle for acceptance in classrooms, colleges, and universities throughout the world. This chapter will attempt to assess the current position of TGfU at a time that can almost be described as its "coming of age." No longer the "newest kid on the block," TGfU is ready to assume its rightful place as a valid and useful educational model. The first international conference on TGfU held at Waterville Valley, NH, USA, in 2001, provided a timely opportunity to celebrate this debut.

With maturity comes responsibility. It is time for advocates to consolidate the TGfU initiative and move it forward. This chapter suggests ways in which the model can be effectively developed and promoted.

Tactical vs. Technical: Is It Time To Move On?

The disenchantment with the "technical approach" by the Loughborough researchers naturally led to comparisons between TGfU and the traditional games-content approach and also to attempts to prove the superiority of one versus the other in terms of student learning, performance, and engagement. There have been several recent calls from the research community for a laying down of arms in this "methodology war" (Rink, 2001; Holt, N.L., Strean, W.B., & Bengoechea, E.G., 2002). Pacifist banners tell us that "All War Is Bad," and it is true that, almost by definition, we can lose sight of the truth when we fight. As Rink (2001) argued, "When you spend all of your effort proving that a particular kind of teaching is better than another kind of teaching, you limit what you can learn about the very complex teaching/learning process" (p. 123). Rink hopes that TGfU research will move this pedagogical discussion (the best way to teach) beyond the "I believe" stage.

While Rink's call for peace is attractive, it is important to acknowledge that the intense ideological debate between the methodologies does serve a purpose, in that it helps us to examine and clarify our values, and can promote healthy change. In the same way that a worthy opponent helps us to elevate our game performance in the process of "striving together" (Nastasi, 1991), so a worthy opponent in debate forces us to abandon our complacency, and to reassess and refine our position.

Without a clear understanding of the central values of the different curriculum models and approaches, it is difficult, if not impossible, for educators to make intelligent choices about what to teach, how to teach it, and when it is developmentally appropriate to do so. The prevailing methodology in many schools has been, and continues to be, the traditional content approach, which is rarely questioned or examined. Its learning theories derive from the "central tenet that scientific laws can be uncovered through the objective measurement and systematic manipulation of variables. Its research, rooted in the traditions of behavioral psychology, dominated the first 25 years of education pedagogy" (Macdonald et al., 2002). Largely unchallenged, it continues to drive our physical education curriculum.

Teachers' beliefs about teaching, instructional strategies, and gender have all been shown to influence the way in which elementary students construct meaning in their physical education classes (Pissanos & Allison, 1993). If our beliefs about learning and teaching have such power to influence, it seems vital to make them conscious. There are various kinds of research that will help us in this endeavor. "Poststructuralist research makes visible what has been invisible; it provides new ways of seeing, and therefore acting, and thereby makes a difference...Socially critical researchers ask questions about other people's assumptions and purposes as well as their own" (Macdonald et al., 2002).

The restless buzzing of TGfU researchers stirs teachers into questioning "the way we do things." For instance, some populations are not well-served by the technical approach. These include the less-skilled, the differently able, and those with learning styles that are not compatible with the regimented approach. While interpretive research that focuses on the learning experience ("What is happening here, and for what purpose?") is vital, it is important that future research on TGfU employ multiple theoretical perspectives, that it is both theoretical and empirical, and that it continues to encourage discourse between all people involved, rather than limiting it to one group or one research perspective.

Unquestioning acceptance of any model, including TGfU, can be dangerous. Although comparing and evaluating alternative models can be uncomfortable and possibly conflictual, it is vital to our own growth as educators. Central to the health of our curriculum is the ability of both students and teachers to ask and answer challenging questions, which push us to better understand and trust our existing beliefs and/or to accept new ones. For example, the comparative debate has generated the following questions in the pedagogical arena.

Content of games education—What should children learn? What value do we place on skills, concepts, and strategies, or on student understanding? To what extent do we teach about democratic processes or what it means to be a concerned citizen?

Learning process—Do students understand better if they discover a concept and skill within the context of a game situation? What is the balance between cognition and physical engagement? How much information can students absorb at one time? In what order should this information be offered? How much is the effectiveness of learning dependent on factors such as imagination and discovery, and which lie within the affective domain?

Assessment—How do we know that learning has occurred? How do we measure different aspects of student learning such as acquisition, memory, and the ability to analyze and interpret?

Such questions may prove challenging and even threatening. Since they speak to underlying beliefs, they may move teachers out of their comfort zone and into the uncomfortable area of cognitive dissonance (Butler, 1999). This, in turn, may lead to defensiveness and ultimate retreat into the traditional model. The status quo is maintained simply because its basic assumptions are never questioned. Unless teachers make a paradigm shift in educational values and beliefs and examine their "*I believe basis,*" as Rink (2001) calls it, they have little incentive to change.

Once these questions are honestly considered, learning outcomes can be more easily determined. Teachers can consequently select a model, which is best suited to the desired outcomes. If the desired outcomes include students' ability to make reasoned and voluntary decisions, to be skillful in game play, to apply tactics and skills more effectively in game-like situations, to transfer game concepts to other games within the same classification and to be more motivated and enthusiastic, then TGfU would be an appropriate model.

At a time when teachers are looking for ways to make sense of a plethora of curricular innovations, the authors of this book have suggested ways to incorporate TGfU as a model in a curricular design where teachers have gone back to basics and built anew from there. Like Metzler (2000), we believe that teachers can best promote student learning by rethinking and restructuring teaching methodologies in a way that reflects clear and conscious choices. TGfU has great potential as a strong model in the context of a "models-based perspective for instructing physical education (Metzler, 2000)."

The model is built on the basic assumption that students learn best if they understand what to do before they understand how to do it. This is a predominantly cognitive focus. TGfU also shares the emphasis made by other models (such as Sport Education, Cooperative Learning, and Teaching Social Responsibility Model) upon the engagement of students through the affective domain.

Sport Education in particular (which has as its major goal the desire to develop competent, literate, and enthusiastic sportspersons [Siedentop, 1994]), can be seen as a model that is complementary to TGfU. Both models advocate a learning experience that is inclusive, developmentally sensitive, and focuses on balanced, whole-child development, with the ultimate aim of producing more knowledgeable games players who are also advocates for good sports practices. There is greater emphasis in the Sport Education Model, however, on the development of knowledge in other areas of sport, such as refereeing, score-keeping, and management and of social and personal growth through placement in positions of responsibility and leadership.

Defining the Elephant: What's in a Name?

Three blind men examined an elephant for the first time. The first man took hold of its trunk. "Why," he said, "an elephant is just like a snake!"

"Nonsense!" said the second man, who was feeling its massive leg, "an elephant is much more like a tree!"

"You are both wrong," said the third man, who had hold of the elephant's ear. "The elephant has large leaves, exactly like the mighty banyan tree."

An elephant is an elephant, whatever piece of it we have chosen to handle. One of the key concerns expressed at the 2001 TGfU Conference, Waterville Valley, was confusion with regard to the different terms used to describe what is, essentially, one model, rooted firmly in constructive philosophy. Macdonald et al. (2002) advise us to "avoid theoretical fads," and it is true that many teachers are wary of these, and reluctant to jump on the next new bandwagon with a snappy name. Instead of creating confusion and suspicion with different terms, is it possible to adopt one name, which could be universally recognized?

Since its inception, the TGfU model has been the product of collaboration and diverse influences. Mauldon & Redfern, (1981); Ellis, (1983); and Werner, (1990) each made their own unique contributions to the initiative, and Bunker, Thorpe, and Almond, who took it a step further, came from varied backgrounds, both as athletes and academics (Almond as a curriculum developer and Thorpe and Bunker as psychologists). TGfU has spread through curricula across the world and, naturally, it has evolved as it has adapted to new conditions and contexts. In England and Wales, it has informed the national curriculum and made its way into educational bureaucracy. In Australia, it became known as "Games Sense" in the 90s, when applied to the coaching environment, and is also known as "Play Practice," a model specifically aimed to encourage beginners (Launder, 2001). In the U.S., Griffin, Mitchell and Oslin (1997) renamed the model "The Tactical Approach," since they felt that this term would be better understood by teachers "since tactical is opposite to technical" (Oslin, 2002, email communication). Mitchell (2002, email communication) describes their "tactical games model" as no different from TGfU. "I look at the two as parallel paths up the same mountain. The goal is simply more-effective games-based teaching." Clearly, all curriculum models need to evolve in a process Kirk and Tinning (1992) describe as "praxis." Theory and practice cannot be separated, but will continue to refine and redefine each other in a continual process of organic change. Nonetheless, given the marginalization of TGfU in our schools and our teacher education departments, it may prove necessary for the movement to achieve greater clarity, in terms of identity, if it is to progress.

Arguably, the name "TGfU" carries the highest recognition, and, certainly, it has the right of seniority, but there are some problems. Even Almond, (Waring & Almond, 1995) one of the model's greatest influences, made an abortive attempt to rename it as "games-centered-games." In Chapter Two, Rossi draws our attention to Fleming's (1994) argument that "the term 'understanding' is not particularly helpful for teachers trying to shape their pedagogical practice, or to theorists trying to make sense of this approach." At the TGfU conference (2001), Kretchmar also suggested that we need to have a much clearer notion of what we mean by "understanding." Rossi goes on to cite Fleming's suggestion "...that the use of the preposition 'for' is arbitrary and it could just as easily be replaced with 'by,' 'through,' 'to,' 'with,' etc...that the use of the word 'games' also focuses the agenda on 'content' rather than 'process.'" He might also have added that the word "teaching" tends to place emphasis on the teacher, rather than the learner, indicating a teacher-directed, rather than child-centered, approach.

Although it may seem counterintuitive to add yet one more name to the existing pile, it is also true to say that the common denominator for all the current labels is the constructivist theory of knowledge and learning. If constructivism is the essence of the elephant, perhaps we should draw a name from that area. This would certainly identify us within the wider field of education, and allow us to form useful links with other subjects on the curriculum that share a constructivist approach. It might also be possible to retain the names of the current branches in the tree of TGfU evolution (e.g., Constructivism and Games Sense, The Constructivist/Tactical Approach).

Whatever we choose to call ourselves, the TGfU 2001 Conference, with its diverse range of issues and participants, proved that our intentions are not only to improve student learning, but to build democracy, to embrace ideals that are more important than winning—to pursue what Kretchmar (2001) calls "an ambitious affective end like delight." At the heart of the TGfU philosophy is a willingness to listen to every voice and to embrace a diversity that can only enhance our theoretical vitality. As Macdonald et al. (2002, p.150) point out, "If one voice or perspective dominates, there is a danger they may end up speaking to themselves." The trick will be to see if we can listen to as many people as possible, while moving our intentions forward in a cohesive movement with a coordinated, yet flexible, agenda for change.

Ideas for Future Research

In 1986, Thorpe and Bunker challenged researchers to answer the question, "Does TGfU work?" and urged us to undertake studies that involved questionnaire design, attitude measurement, and the collection of performance data. Today, this question remains largely unanswered. The following suggestions are offered in the context of multiple theoretical perspectives that will hopefully lead to broad and profound improvements in physical education and sport:

1) Look for strong empirical data that would support our intuitive sense that this approach works for students. Most TGfU scholars—including Kretchmar, Rink, Thorpe, and Bunker—have made this request.

2) Continue to explore and examine subjective outcomes (e.g., to play well and to enjoy playing) as well as objective outcomes (e.g., skill acquisition) and to value both, regardless of how difficult they are to assess and measure.

3) Focus on all aspects of the child—examine the outcomes of affective domain as well as the increasingly well-documented cognitive and psychomotor domains (see chapter 15).

4) Continue to emphasize and measure quality in all aspects of performance and all game play in context (see chapter 13).

5) Continue to consider the nature of understanding and consider its place in the learning environment (Rink, 2001; Kirk & MacPhail, 2000; Kretchmar, 2001).

6) Continue to ask good questions and to involve all major players in finding answers—teachers, curriculum designers, researchers, administrators, and students (Macdonald et al., 2002).

7) Fill the gap between theory and practice. This can be achieved by making the language in our research accessible to teachers, by including teachers in research projects (e.g., action research), and by testing theories by implementing them in the appropriate setting.

8) Examine the student-learning outcomes of different putative methodologies to determine if what we think we are teaching is actually what we teach.

9) Research the four fundamental pedagogical principles (1) sampling, (2) modification-representation, (3) modification-exaggeration, and (4) tactical complexity in order to guide the practice of planning the games curriculum (see chapter 15).

10) Build connections with the coaching community, such as between Australian "Games Sense" and TGfU.

11) Develop and validate authentic assessment instruments such as TSAP and GPAI (see chapter 13).

The Way Forward?

The TGfU conference at Waterville Valley initiated a new movement, or at least gave clearer direction and focus to the existing groundswell of advocates in this arena. TGfU needed a home, and found one October 2002, under the umbrella of the Association des Ecoles Superieures D'Education Physique (AIESEP) organization. The inaugural meeting of the TGfU International Task Force at the World Congress in La Coruna, Spain (22-25 October 2002) established a mission statement, together with short-term and long-term goals. The task force hopes to mobilize energy among TGfU advocates and promote the approach more effectively to teachers in the field and to students and professors involved in PETE programs.

Mission

The TGfU task force is a global representative group of institutions and individuals committed to the promotion and dissemination of scholarly inquiry and practical applications in teaching for understanding within sport coaching and physical education.

Short-Term Goals

1. Coordinate the worldwide initiatives that have clear and close connections with the TGfU movement.

2. Review the philosophy behind the original TGfU conception and its subsequent development to provide for an accurate representation of its purpose.

3. Promote discussion and dialogue among membership by establishing a forum on issues relating both to the TGfU theoretical and curriculum framework and to instructional practices.

4. Organize a conference for TGfU every two years. This will coincide with the AIESEP World Congress every four years, possibly as a pre-conference event.

5. Coordinate collaborative research efforts and publication of information after each workshop, meeting, or conference.
6. Create a clearinghouse for research.
7. Establish a website for TGfU. This will serve to offer a central site to host an email list, and also a place to collate publications and research and to provide information about conferences, workshops, and other initiatives.

Long-Term Goals

8. Disseminate scholarly information and teaching resources through a variety of media.
9. Establish teaching programs to assist institutions, schools, and individuals in the implementation of the TGfU approach.
10. Promote publications and research.
11. Secure funding for all these initiatives through appropriate grants.

Action Plan to Implement Objectives

◆ Establish a registry of interested members (list serve) with the physical education and sports coaching community to promote communication via the internet.
◆ Publish proceedings and resources materials to disseminate relevant information.
◆ Organize regular conferences to encourage scholars and practitioners to interact with others through personal dialogue and participation.

Conclusion

TGfU was initiated by a group of people who were dissatisfied with the kind of experiences students were being offered in games education. Their alternative model and framework gave many teachers pause for thought, and made us examine the way we were teaching, the way we thought about games education, and, by extension, the way we thought about physical education as a whole. The TGfU model is difficult to measure and assess because it is constantly evolving, and because it values learning experiences that may be difficult to assess in a culture that is more comfortable with a focus on the objective, the measurable, and the quantifiable. Perhaps unwittingly, TGfU has become embroiled in a "methodologies war" with the technical approach.

Though some have chosen to see this as a gladiatorial combat, in which one methodology will emerge victorious, TGfU proponents, or at least the majority of them, do not see it as desirable for any one model to achieve monolithic status in the curriculum. TGfU is not a cure-all. If used without real appreciation or understanding of its aims, it can be applied as blindly and unproductively as any other model (e.g., those classes in which teachers "roll out the ball" and "let the students play"). In any case, such a takeover is highly unlikely, since the struggle is less like that of evenly matched gladiators, and more like that between David and Goliath. The technical approach has the weight and strength of received wisdom, and the muscle that tends to be afforded to the status quo. Despite the unevenness of the match, the debate has been useful to all educators, since it has made us ask key questions, such as "What should be taught?" "Why should we teach it?" and "How do students learn?"

References

Butler, J. (1999). *Beyond the comfort zone: using cognitive dissonance to move from technique orientated teaching to a TGfU approach.* A paper presented at the AIESEP World Congress, Besancon, France.

Ellis, M. (1983). *Similarities and differences in games: A system for classification.* Paper presented at the AIESEP conference , Rome, Italy.

Fleming, S. (1994). Understanding "Understanding": Making sense of the cognitive approach to the teaching of games. *Physical Education Review, 17*(2): 90-6.

Griffin, L., Mitchell, S. & Oslin, J. (1997). Teaching sport concepts and skills. A tactical games approach. Champaign, IL. Human Kinetics.

Holt, N. L., Strean, W. B., & Bengoechea, E. G., (2002). Expanding the teaching games for understanding model: New avenues for future research and practice. *Journal of Teaching Physical Education, 21,* 162-176.

Kirk, D. & Macphail, A. (2000). Teaching games for understanding and situated learning: Rethinking the model. *Paper presented to the Pre-Olympic Congress Symposium on Student Learning in Physical Education.* Brisbane, September, 7-13.

Kirk, D. & Tinning, R. (1992). Physical education pedagogical work as praxis. *A paper presented at the annual meeting of the American Educational Research Association*, San Francisco, CA.

Kretchmar, S. (2001). *Understanding and the delights of human activity.* Paper presented at the TGfU International Conference on TGfU in Physical Education and Sport, Plymouth State College, NH.

Launder, A. L. (2001). *Play Practice. The games approach to teaching and coaching sports.* Champaign, IL: Human Kinetics.

Macdonald, D., Kirk, D., Metzler, M., Nilges, L., Schempp, P., & Wright, J. (2002). It's all very, in theory: Theoretical perspectives and their applications in contemporary pedagogical research. *Quest, 54,*133-156.

Mauldon, E. & Redfern, H. B. (1981). *Games teaching: An approach to the primary school.* London, MacDonald and Evans, Ltd.

Metzler, M. (2000). *Instructional models for physical education.* Boston, MA: Allyn and Bacon.

Nastasi, R. (1991). Model for conflict/competition in coaching and teaching athletics and physical education. *Educational Considerations.* Kansas State University.

Pissanos, B. W. & Allison, P. C. (1993). Students' constructs of elementary school physical education. *Research Quarterly for Exercise and Sport, 64,* 425-435.

Rink, J. E. (1996). Foundations for the learning and instruction of sport and games. *Journal of Teaching in Physical Education, 15,* 399-417.

Rink, J. E. (2001). Investigating the assumptions of pedagogy. *Journal of Teaching in Physical Education, 20,* 112-128.

Siedentop, D. (1994). *Sport Education.* Champaign, IL: Human Kinetics.

Thorpe, R. & Bunker, D. (1986). Is there a need to reflect on our games teaching? In R. Thorpe, D. Bunker, & L. Almond (Eds.). *Rethinking games teaching.* (pp. 25-34). England, University of Technology, Loughborough, Department of Physical Education and Sports Science.

Waring, M. & Almond, L. Games-centred-games. A revolutionary or evolutionary alternative for games teaching? *European physical Education Review*. Royaume UNI, 1(1): 55-66.

Werner, P. & Almond, L. (1990). Models of games education. *Journal of Teaching in Physical Education, 61*(4): 23-27.

Resources

Published by the National Association for Sport and Physical Education for Quality Physical Education Programs:

Moving Into the Future: National Standards for Physical Education, A Guide to Content and Assessment (1995), Stock No. 304-10083

Concepts and Principles of Physical Education: What Every Student Needs to Know (2003), Stock No. 304-10261

Beyond Activities: Elementary Volume (2003), Stock No. 304-10265

Beyond Activities: Secondary Volume (2003), Stock No. 304-10268

National Physical Education Standards in Action (2003), 304-10267

Active Start: A Statement of Physical Activity Guidelines for Children Birth to Five Years (2002), Stock No. 304-10254

Physical Activity for Children: A Statement of Guidelines (1998), Stock No. 304-10175

National Standards for Beginning Physical Education Teachers (1995), Stock No. 304-10085

Appropriate Practice Documents

Appropriate Practice in Movement Programs for Young Children, (2000), Stock No. 304-10232

Appropriate Practices for Elementary School Physical Education (2000), Stock No. 304-10230

Appropriate Practices for Middle School Physical Education (2001), Stock No. 304-10248

Appropriate Practices for High School Physical Education (1998), Stock No. 304-10129

Opportunity to Learn Documents

Opportunity to Learn Standards for Elementary Physical Education (2000), Stock No. 304-10242

Physical Education Program Improvement and Self-Study Guides (1998) *for Middle School,* Stock No. 304-10173, *for High School,* Stock No. 304-10174

Assessment Series

Assessment in Outdoor Adventure Physical Education (2003), Stock No. 304-10218

Assessing Student Outcomes in Sport Education (2003), Stock No. 304-10219

Video Tools for Teaching Motor Skill Assessment (2002), Stock No. 304-10217

Assessing Heart Rate in Physical Education (2002), Stock No. 304-10214

Authentic Assessment of Physical Activity for High School Students (2002), Stock No. 304-10216

Portfolio Assessment for K-12 Physical Education (2000), Stock No. 304-10213

Elementary Heart Health: Lessons and Assessment (2001), Stock No. 304-10215

Standards-Based Assessment of Student Learning: A Comprehensive Approach (1999), Stock No. 304-10206

Assessment in Games Teaching (1999), Stock No. 304-10212

Assessing Motor Skills in Elementary Physical Education (1999), Stock No. 304-10207

Assessing and Improving Fitness in Elementary Physical Education (1999), Stock No. 304-10208

Creating Rubrics for Physical Education (1999), Stock No. 304-10209

Assessing Student Responsibility and Teamwork (1999), Stock No. 304-10210

Preservice Professional Portfolio System (1999), Stock No. 304-10211

Order online at **www.aahperd.org/naspe** or call **1-800-321-0789**
Shipping and handling additional.

National Association for Sport and Physical Education

an association of the American Alliance for Health,
Physical Education,Recreation and Dance

1900 Association Drive
Reston, VA 20191
(703) 476-3410
www.aahperd.org/naspe